Thirty-five outstanding stories by men who are supporting other men to become the powerfully-enlightened, courageously-awakened, conscious role models they were born to be.

FOREWORD BY
Eric Edmeades
Founder of WildFit®

PRESENTED BY

AJ Maxwell, Alex Steffen, Andis Melngailis, Austin Wood, Bryce Malli, Cristian Agafi, Damian Culhane, David McDonnel, Benedicto, Faraaz Ãlì, Gavin Masumiya,James McMillen, Jimmy Naraine, Jon-Olaf Hendricks, Juan Pablo Barahona, Ketan Ladva, Kunal Jamsandekar, Marcus Young Kettles, Mark Eggimann, Martin Daniels, Martin Stork, Mike Shields, Nadim Jarjour, Øivind Grydeland, Oliver Mann, Parth Nilawar, Peter Giesin, Rawle James, Robert Vig, Santiago Rafael Pascual, Todd Murray, Vladimir Gontkovic, Warren Falkenstein, Yoram Baltinester, Zenas Chin

Published and printed by IGNITE Publishing a division of JBO Global Inc.

This book is dedicated to all men of every age, race, creed, and culture. It is for those who are brave enough to share their true self, and who trust so much in their own souls that they dare to stand confidently in their unique individuality. In doing so, they IGNITE the world and show up as the greatest version of themselves. - Peter Giesin Co-Founder of Ignite, father of four, husband, and modern-day superhero.

THE VOICE
Intuitive literation by Rawle James

It was a cold and snowy day. The kind of day were the weather reflected the unpredictability of what was. I was lost in the sea of my attention, surrounded by a fog that hosted the demons of torment. And out of nowhere, I heard the lighthouse of your voice which I could not see but I felt your space within.

For too long, I had been trapped as a victim in the echoes of my mind. Venom coursed through my veins as toxic words fumbled with each other impatiently waiting to be spewed. I was consumed by my victim's cry. My body slammed in anguish and battered from years of being lost and blinded by rage.

I straddled the thin (?line?) between here and there, as I swirled in my hangover of grief.

My arms acted like a cane that swayed side to side gingerly searching for a life line as I prayed that hope would shelter me from the turmoil of my memories. My mind was a distorted canvas of vibrant colours that housed the whirlwinds of chaos as I stood fully exposed at the crossroads of discomfort.

For a moment, my heart forgot its purpose and skipped beats as tears flooded its chambers with the waters of inevitability. In that moment, your voice was an invitation to the door of my rebirth. I was cocooned in the placenta of the unknown as dark clouds rained the numbness of sadness. And like a deer in the headlights I stood paralyzed unable to run from the fight.

My suffering had reached its boiling point from years of piling one sided perception beneath the canopy of my forest. Psychosis or the burning bush, either way, your voice echoed from the valley of my shadow as a lifeline to the madness of that moment.

a voice I knew...a voice I know

The tenor of your words was like a sunset backdrop in the eYe of my storm. A gift from the depths which provided a force-field protecting my battered soul as waves gently washed over me. Each serving as a reminder to the Spirit I am.

Caught in the intersectionality of the seconds, space was an illusion of linear time and I was an unbalanced hiccup of hindsight awaiting an audience. The gentleness of your voice revealed the wonders to my discomfort. I was still unsure of how or why, but unknowingly the process of shedding my old skin of suffering had begun.

There is a beginning—an end to all life. My dash is my vault of wisdom into which my experiences are deposited and insight awaits withdrawal. It also houses your voice as a reminder that the light cannot exist without the dark. I am but one drop in an ocean of drops. And I am here now to experience all otherwise this journey would be pointless and quite frankly boring. So, until further notice, I'm celebrating every damn thing.

Read Rawle James' full story on page: 206

Ignite Author's Testimonials

"Ignite is the perfect platform and collection of humans who provide an effortless structure and a strong container to support the writing experience and bring your message to life!" ~ AJ Maxwell

"As humans we are story consumers, but currently without a space to tell our own. Ignite opens a space for us to share, to explore and to speak up what we've held back. If one story can impact one life, it's already worth it." ~ Oliver Mann

"I'm very grateful for the opportunity to share my story in this tribe of inspiring, open and vulnerable men. It is my first time putting myself out there in my full vulnerability. But also very healing and empowering - there is a power, peace, and clarity in fully owning our stories. It was very meaningful, to fully aligned with my purpose of growing into the best version of myself and inspiring others to do the same to ultimately make this world a better place. Let's continue embracing our own stories written in our book of life and make it a masterpiece!" ~ Robert Vig

"Writing your first-ever chapter in a book is a scary process. The Ignite team has been extremely supportive in helping me find my story, defining it and, of course, writing it. Their team of editors were outstanding in terms of knowledge, professionalism and dedication to excellence. I am forever grateful to the Ignite team for the opportunity to share my story and hopefully help other men." ~ Cristian Agafi

"The IGNITE writing experience has been tremendously supportive in so many aspects! As a first-time writer whose first language is not English, I felt that the IGNITE team took extra effort to help me. My one-on-one interactions with the editors have not only helped me produce an engaging, well-polished, book-worthy quality story, but they have also helped me to become a better writer." ~ Yoram Baltinester

"My experience with the ignite team has been one that I am very grateful for. The knowledge acquired outweighs any resources committed. A wonderful learning and creative environment facilitated by a very supportive team." ~ Faraaz Ãli

Publisher's Note:

We are delighted to offer the forth compilation book in the IGNITE series. Our mission is to produce inspiring, motivational and authentic real-life stories that will Ignite You in your life. This book contains 35 unique stories told by 35 exceptional authors. They are of the highest caliber to offer engaging, profound and life-changing examples that will impact the reader. Our mandate is to build a conscious, positive and supportive community through our books, speaking events, writing workshops, ignite experiences, podcasts, immersions and a product marketplace. We welcome new authors onto our platform and new book ideas. Should you desire to be published and featured in an Ignite book. Please apply at www.igniteyou.life/apply or reach out to us at suppport@igniteyou.life.

Ignite Your Life For Men

Copyright © 2019 IGNITE PUBLISHING a division of JBO Global Inc.

First Edition August, 2019

Published by Ignite Publishing and printed by JBO Global INC.

5569-47th Street Red Deer, Alberta, Canada T4N 1S1 - 1 877-377-6115

ISBN# 978-1-7923-0667-9

Ordering Information: Quantity sales. Special discounts are available on quantity purchases by corporations, associations, and others. For details, contact the publisher at the address above. Programs, products or services provided by the authors are found by contacting them directly. Resources named in the book are found in the resources pages at the back of the book.

Printed in China.

Ignite
Your Life
for Men

JB Owen and Eric Edmeades

FOREWORD BY

ERIC EDMEADES

*International Motivational Speaker, Serial Entrepreneur
and founder of WildFit*

BE A MAN

What does it mean, today, to be a man? I suppose it means to show up as society wants men to show up. The challenge is that society is always asking us to show up in different ways. Each year, society redefines masculinity; what it takes to be a 'good man' is like a moving target.

That is why, when I was asked to write this foreword, I agreed without hesitation. This book is an example of precisely what I believe men, and men-to-be need to guide them through these ever-changing conditions.

Years ago, my wife and I led leadership programs that involved taking people to the summit of Kilimanjaro, the tallest free-standing mountain in the world. One year, our logistics partner, who had become interested in my work in nutritional anthropology, offered to take us to visit with some 'bushmen.' Of course, we agreed. Over the next few weeks we explored way off-road—often having to clear our way with machetes—looking for a rumored bushman tribe. Our explorations led us to the Lake Eyasi region of Tanzania and the first of many visits, over the next several years, with the Hadza people.

The Hadza tribe is one of the last genuinely nomadic hunter/gatherer cultures left on earth today. They number about 800, and only about 400 of them continue to live their traditional lives in the bush. Spending time with them has given me some fascinating insights into many areas of life: exercise; parenting; gender differences; and nutrition. The time we have spent with them has been invaluable to my research, work and purpose.

Stepping into a Hadza camp feels a bit like stepping out of a time machine, about 100,000 years ago. There is a lot to take in. Men working on their bows and arrows. Children playing and pretending to hunt. Women drying meat, breastfeeding, and looking after the smaller children. Most of this activity takes place around fires of which, every camp, has at least two. The men and older boys sit around one fire while the women and younger kids sit around another.

I can still remember sitting around the men's fire for the first time enjoying, if not understanding, their fascinating language. They speak with such passion; each sentence punctuated by a variety of percussive clicks. I turned to my guide, and now good friend, Gasper, and asked him about what they were saying.

"They are telling stories," he said.

"What about?" I was genuinely curious. I could tell from some of the gestures and sounds that they were talking about hunting and fighting, but I wanted to know more.

"The chief is the best story-teller. He is talking about a hunting trip they had last week," Gasper told me, and then he switched to direct narrative translation.

"We knew there were two of them [bushpigs] on the trail, and we followed them quietly. The tracks were very fresh, but they were moving quite quickly. My stomach was already getting excited as I sent two of the younger hunters up over the hill to trap the pigs on the other side. I warned them to be careful of the dangerous tusks..."

As he continued with the story, I reflected on how valuable this story might be to any of the younger, inexperienced hunters. Over the next few hours, the chief and other men told even more interesting stories: stories about great hunting trips, massive storms, bush fires, and a variety of valuable life experiences. As I sat there and listened, under a blanket of stars in the most vivid night-sky I had ever seen, I had a powerful realization. A young hunter has to be a relatively good hunter before he ever goes on his first hunting trip. How is that achieved? Through stories.

By the time a young Hadza hunter picks up a bow—at about age 10—and heads out for his first real hunting trip, he already knows a great deal about what to do and, of course, what not to do. Stories, like those shared by the chief, are educational and experiential. They are a powerful teaching tool and, the best way to pass knowledge on from one generation to another.

While the stories themselves will not make him a 'great' hunter, they will equip him with important information about hunting that will both keep him safe and increase his chances for success. Without those stories, what would his first hunting trip be like? Unsuccessful, at best, and quite possibly dangerous, at worst. Our ancestors learned powerful life lessons from stories told around the fire. Today, our children learn those lessons from cartoons, movies, and situational comedies filled with cynical, negative, and put-down humor. For our ancestors, their role-models were the most successful members of their family's tribe.

A young boy would, a few thousand years ago, look up to a great hunter. He would observe him, listen to his stories and begin the process of consciously imitating him and unconsciously adopting his behavior and beliefs. Both by observing him and listening to his stories. Today, our children look up to, model and learn from rap musicians, sports athletes, and action stars, many of whom seem hell-bent on glorifying violence, drug abuse, and antisocial behavior. Television, Netflix, and YouTube have replaced the vital tradition of fire-side and inter-generational story-telling; robbing new generations of essential personally-shared life lessons. Life lessons that may help them to live more productive and fulfilling lives, and inspire our boys, to be better men.

Once, as I faced one of the most difficult decisions I ever had to face as a father, I called my own father and asked him for advice. He listened carefully. He considered thoughtfully. And then he said, "What would you want Daniel (my son) to do if he were in the same situation?" In essence, my father was telling me something so simple but no less profound even in its simplicity: *Live the values you want your son to adopt.* First, his advice made my difficult decision unbelievably easy. Secondly, he gave me a great deal upon which to reflect. To raise a boy who would become a man who could be proud of himself, I would have to live a life of which I could be proud.

This book is a collection of modern fire-side stories; real stories told by real men. Stories with powerful lessons, examples, and inspirations that can serve to help each of us find our place in the world and step up as the kind of men, fathers, brothers, husbands, sons and role models, we truly want to be.

"Success in life is measured, most easily, by the number of days that a person is truly happy." - Eric Edmeades

The Power of a Men's Book
by JB Owen, Founder of Ignite

Ignite your Life for Men was created out of an important need to support men in becoming the powerfully-enlightened, courageously-awakened, conscious role models they were born to be. When my amazing husband Peter came to me and suggested we write a book specifically for men; inspiring other men, I was excited about the idea. I couldn't think of a book on the market that was designed to honor men overcoming the trials and tribulations they go through. Nor had I heard of a book filled with authentic and heartfelt accounts of monumental moments in a man's life, where he was allowed to show an even deeper expression of himself.

While enjoying the bliss of publishing Ignite Your Life for Women and Ignite Your Female Leadership, my husband often commented on how lucky I was to have a group of amazing women I could connect with. He voiced his slight jealousy over me being able to share, so joyously, with other ladies in an open and welcoming group space. He saw the close bonds we were creating by getting together weekly to talk about personal issues, parenting problems, financial goals, and even silly situations. Our calls were filled with a plethora of tears and laughter, sentiment and support.

As my husband witnessed, I was always enthusiastic and elevated after I finished a call. I continued many relationships outside the scheduled meetings and soon many of the authors were becoming good friends and daily contacts. Our women's network had flourished and I had more and more women to turn to for a multitude of things.

This bonding by women, in groups, gatherings and circles is a tradition that spans back to the dawn of time. As Eric shares how the men of the Hadza tribe gathered to tell stores, women convened throughout the entire day and connected with one another. Women are naturally drawn to this form of communicating and it is both accepted and welcomed by them. Men, it seems aren't this fortunate. The way of the warrior, the lone wolf, and the single-handed superhero is a common theme amongst men around the world today. Men have been taught to do it on their own, to not need anyone and to forge forward alone.

It was Peter who shared that this way can be quite lonely. Isolatory in fact. Why when the nature of the human is for connection have we plagued the man to go without? Why are men expected to be all alone, void of emotions, feelings or common doubts? Taking it even further, a man is expected to have no weakness, sadness, fear, confusion or sorrows. Additionally, he is expected to not yearn for socialization, authenticity, vulnerability or guidance. His role is to be stoic, strong, and solo.

I had to take a moment to think about where that mentality came from. Why have men been conditioned out of their feelings and ripped raw of their need to connect? Why are they expected to shut down that part of themselves that is fundamentally human? Emotions are human. Feelings are human. Communication, connection, caring separate us from the lower species and yet men are told to suppress and ignore those ingrained instances and face a lifetime of squelching a need we all have. It doesn't seem fair.

As a mother of an upcoming teenage boy, I saw these traits emerging. The days of cuddles and hugs, glee and joy had taken a back seat to toughness, roughness and needing to do it all alone. Touching on emotions seemed silly, asking probing questions became intrusive and crying about a loss our pain was utterly out of the question. By fourteen he was already reciting lines like "men don't cry", and "I'm supposed to be tough and not need anyone". As a mother raising a son, I don't see how these restrictions serve him. More shockingly, they are not opinions we have in our house, so where had he learned them? Somehow it was just a given he said. "Men simply do it on their own and don't show any emotions."

Possibly this was the crux of the issue in a very stunted relationship with my own father. I don't remember him showing a lot of emotion. Or recall a time when he was open or willing to share his inner feelings. He was the quintessential hard-working, driven provider. He did what he did and it didn't include emotionally connecting with me.

I followed that paradigm into my first marriage and produced a son that is now being shown that same inherent belief system. In my quest to enlighten myself, other women and society itself, I felt elated at the idea of pulling back the curtain on creating a platform for men to express their rawest emotions. Why should women be allowed to bond in intimate sharing circles and men be forced to forge on the Savanna alone? It was time for a change and a new dynamic to emerge. One supporting and enabling men of all walks of life and backgrounds to break from the confines of masculine suppression and speak freely....connect openly... and cry wildly if need be.

IGNITING MEN GLOBALLY

For every husband, son, and father, every male, man, and boy, this book is for you. These stories, each word, and every sentiment are for your heart to enjoy and absorb. They are for you to heed the triumphant call and grasp the painful whisper that another man longs to share. My wish is that when you read through these stories, you are deeply transformed by the courageous examples of stepping into manhood by first stepping into self. I hope that your heart opens, and your emotions awaken to how powerful you are in your own vulnerability and peace. That you see how strength comes from sharing and supportive grows through sentiment.

Each author in this book wrote his IGNITE moment to inspire you. Not to be tough and macho, but to be real and true. Not for accolades or recognition but to be free of the burden he may have been carrying and to heal his own battle wounds. These are a true account of his hero's journey, which may shine a bit of light on yours. Every story is crafted with the hopes of opening you up in your masculine discovery. Awakening the giant within. Written to encourage you to claim your Matterhorn, and live true to you.

We know it is one thing to act like a man out of necessity and responsibility, it is another to step forth with honor, compassion, and dignity. You will see throughout this book that authenticity is the common thread. Honesty, self-reflection, and truth are constantly present. Openness, patience, reflection, and purpose are the four pillars each one of these men have shared. Their masculinity is in honoring themselves first before they ever tried to prove anything to another. That is what makes this book so powerful and unprecedented. These men have not only embraced their truth, but they have walked over broken glass to get it. It isn't an idea, it is a new way of living.

As you turn the pages, you will find each story begins with a Power Quote. It is like a personal mantra or battle cry; a statement that inspires you to do even more and makes you think a little deeper. It is what your bumper sticker would say, or what you'd write on your office wall. Each Power Quote is designed to remind you of what you have inside – *MAGNIFICENCE*. Power quotes are statements you say when you need to muster the strength while bursting forward or pick yourself back up after letting the tears flow.

Next, is their *Intentions*. These are the author's hopes and wishes of what their story will do for you. It is a personal message, filled with meaning, and purpose. They want to Ignite YOU to begin living your most exceptional life and share it upfront. Their intentions set the tone for the story and are designed to both awaken and inspire you.

A powerful Ignite story follows. It is the truthful recollection of a time when being a man required colossal strength. When overcoming a hardship challenged the very core of their beliefs. We all have Ignite moments in our lives that define us, change us and set us on a new path or trajectory for life. These stories are those moments, told in the most authentic and genuine way.

They show that all of us have *those* moments and they not only define us but transform us.

Once you have finished their stories, you will find inspiring 'Ignite Action Steps'. These are the tangible things they did to support and expand themselves. Each author explains an easy-to-do, practical concept for you to close the book and try. They are the processes and practices that worked in their lives. Each one is different and unique and proven to yield magnificent results when done consistently.

FROM THE IGNITE COMMUNITY

We know that many people read compilation books to be inspired. If you feel that your personal story is still unfolding, or you're trying to figure it all out, we are with you. Many of us have been through hardships and go through them numerous times in our lives. Our stories may show our successes, but we still waffle, like everyone else. We support you full-out and will cheer you on as you find yourself. We all extend our hands should you need a bit of support, some advice or a shoulder to lean on. We offer ourselves should you ever want to reach out because something we said resonated or became exactly what you needed to hear. Please know we are all accessible and eager to connect so feel free to find us or seek the resources at the back.

The stories you are about to embark on are all our stories. They supersede race, culture, age and even gender. They are the human story, the experience of being a Being on this earth. They touch at the very heart of belonging, connecting and sharing. They are raw, real and unrestricted... that's what makes them so amazingly engaging. They shine a light directly on the heart of who we were born to be.

Ignite was created to ignite others and impact humanity. Our mandate is to do more, share more and spread a conscious, positive message to as many people as possible. We believe in the human connection, and that power comes from being heard, being seen and belonging to something greater than one's self. We invite you to Ignite others. To let your story be heard, share your experiences, find your voice. That is the mission and purpose behind IGNITE. There is power when one person touches the heart of another, and a spark begins. Be it inspiration, love others, support unwaveringly, encourage always, show compassion and stand in your beliefs.

May you have many Ignite moments that transform your life into the amazing person you were meant to be. – JB Owen, founder of IGNITE

PETER GIESIN

"Set no expectations and you won't be disappointed."

My intention is to show that we all have a choice in how we allow expectations to define our life. We each have ideas of how certain situations should unfold. Sometimes they are set by others and sometimes we set them ourselves. The ones others impose we have no control over and should therefore ignore them. The ones we set ourselves, however, can drive our lives in one of two directions: into the world of a victim or into the world of a hero. After reading my story I hope you choose the hero's path.

FALLING OFF THE PORCH

It was a bright summer morning and the sky was as blue as any ocean, as I walked out the door, ready for my first 'real' job. This was a big moment for me. I was 17, strong, youthful and totally excited to tackle life. I had just finished my junior year of high school and had landed a job at the local factory. I always had a job. Since the age of 11 I had worked alongside my father as we operated the family farm. When I wasn't busy taking care of the countless tasks, I worked for the town's youth employment center selling fruits and vegetables to the community. Work was just a way of life.

I couldn't really complain though. I enjoyed working with my father and the other local farmers learning new skills. It made me strong both physically and mentally as I had to problem-solve every day. The coolest thing was that I had money in my pocket, tons of it, at least for a young teenager.

As I left the house that summer morning, ready to embrace my new independence, I was walking tall. I was excited to begin a new job. One that would help me step into becoming a man. I was eager to show my dad I had learned everything that he had taught me. *I would make him proud.* My father and I shared breakfast after early morning chores. He was very quiet, not his normal jovial self. The conversation was very factual and to the point. I thought maybe he was just nervous about me taking my first step out into the real world. I didn't understand why he was being so cold towards me.

As the screen door closed behind me with a bang, I heard my father call out, "See you later faggot." Those four little words shattered my heart and shook the very foundation of how I believed my father saw me. He had never judged me this way before and suddenly I felt he no longer loved me or wanted me as his son.

Twelve hours previously, I sat alone in my room, a needle, an ice cube, a lighter and a diamond stud earring, on the bed in front of me. Like everything else in my life, I had spent countless hours debating the good and bad of making a bold decision. It was only an earring – what could be wrong with that?

I committed to the act. The pain was excruciating as I repeatedly held the ice cube on my ear lobe, numbing it, then slowly and methodically working the needle through the cartilage. After 10 minutes, I finally had the needle completely through. As the blood dripped off my ear, I proudly slid the stud through. I was ready to be one of the cool rocker-boys who didn't care what others thought. I knew the girls would love it, as well as my buddies. I felt on top of the world being this bold.

However, a mere twelve hours later, as I took that last step off the porch my knees buckled. My heart was pounding in my chest. I immediately knew why he had seemed so odd during breakfast. He did not approve of the '*sinful*' act, which I had committed the evening before. He didn't see this as me being edgy, instead it was something he passionately scorned and mocked me accordingly. I headed to work as if I hadn't heard him, yet, tears welled up in my eyes. This wasn't the response I was expecting. I wanted a more story-book father-son sendoff; an inquiry, admiration or even a humorous chuckle, something more accepting of what I had done.

I'll admit, I had an expectation of my father appreciating my nerve to stand out. I thought he would admire my tiny diamond earring, displaying the fact I was making my own courageous choices. Thinking back, these expectations, however irrational, were based on the numerous novels I read that allowed me to escape the doldrums of farm life. Many of these novels had the recurring theme describing the rite of passage between father and son; the boy had to break away from his father, to enter the world alone, naked and abandoned only to return transformed into a man.

As I read those stories I daydreamed of the moment when I would step into my own life with my father's blessing. He would embrace me, hold me close and say, "I love you. I believe in you, son." As in the novels, I would walk out the door and down the road with confidence, yet a bit afraid of the journey that lay ahead, knowing whatever happened, my father would be proud of me. I would leave with the feeling that he had taught me what it meant to be a man and I had embodied it.

Sadly, that was the exact opposite of what I received. I received no hugs, no loving words, no confidence to set me up for success. What I did get was mockery and criticism. In that moment I felt afraid that I was a failure in my father's heart. I was angry because he didn't believe in me enough to look past my decision to adorn my body and be different. My young mind couldn't understand why he would toss me out to the wolves in this manner, burdening me with self-doubt and ridicule. Why he would use such a slanderous word which was so condemning, so brutally prejudicial and hurtful to me. All I truly wanted was a father who had my back, regardless of what crazy decisions I made.

I didn't have a name for it then but that day, stepping off the porch, my shadow took over. I felt alone and unloved for the first time in my life. I felt like a blown egg, where nothing but the shell of a boy remained. The inner spark and passion slowly dripped out of me as I drove towards what was once my future and now felt like my grave.

I walked into the factory that morning head down, quiet and reserved, feeling disappointed, and dropped that diamond earring into the trash can, along with my creativity and zeal for my future. As I stood on the assembly line, I watched my self-worth transform into self-doubt. I no longer trusted myself to make a bold choice, to be different. I could only make my father proud by doing what he expected, not my whimsical desires.

I became the average American guy, graduated from university with not one but three different degrees, landed a high-paying job, owned a home, created a family including a dog. Everything I did was about making money, which my father appreciated. I was doing what he wanted, I was putting money in my pocket to prove my worth to him. Growing up, one of my father's favorite sayings was "Don't give me that damn good man shit, just put it in my pocket." He didn't want accolades, recognition or praise.

Instead he'd say to everyone, money in the pocket meant more than wasted words. Modeling my life after that notion, I went after success and gave up on making connecting important.

By many standards I had created a great outward life, however, it was missing one thing: friendships. I found myself stranded alone in a hotel room one evening while working out of town. It was the dead of winter, I was eating cardboard food and relying on the news for entertainment. I'd been away from my family for so many days, it had stretched into weeks. A massive blizzard had shut down the entire city. I was stuck in my room with nowhere to go and no one to talk to. My heart felt as frigid as the weather outside. My mind as barren, my ambition as cold.

For the second time in my life, my shadow side reared up and that lonely 17-year-old boy returned. I felt betrayed and broken...alone, naked and abandoned... not by another person but this time by myself. My shadow turned inward and simply shook its head asking, *"What the hell are you doing, Peter?"* My answer: "I'm making my father proud." I am doing all of this to make him respect me. I suddenly realized the young Peter was still doing everything possible to prove himself to his father. He was lost in a quagmire of seeking the acceptance which he never received. Yet, this time, the present-day Peter had a simple answer, *"He is proud of you. He always has been. The question is are you proud of yourself?"*

In that moment I knew something had to change. I was the loneliest I'd ever been. I had let my life drift and lead me to a place where I felt completely lost. In the years since I stumbled off the porch, I had done nothing but make acquaintances, no long-lasting friendships and lived a life of superficiality. I stopped letting people in, forming connections or doing anything that would equate to expecting love and support. I rejected all male companionship. I slipped in and out of social situations undetected and I never let anyone see the real me. That day, I felt in my bones that if I continued along this same trajectory, I was doomed to live a life of nonexistence. Even my wife and two children couldn't save me, as those relationships had withered away while I chased the dream of proving myself to my dad. Endless months of travel around the globe were spent in anguish wishing I was home, experiencing the joys of being a father. Instead I was chasing the dollar to earn some morsels of love from my own father.

My intellect has always allowed me to be successful, so I arrogantly assumed I could think my way out of my loneliness. Talking to myself (since I had no one else to talk to) I decided the solution was to find another career, better aligned with what Peter wanted, however – I didn't really know Peter

– so I made a choice blindly.

Stuck on my computer in that blizzard, I decided to give up the endless commuting and applied to yet another University for a secondary mathematics degree. Becoming a teacher would be my salvation I thought. I had always loved math and teaching would have me one-on-one with others. I'd be making a quarter of the pay, yet I'd be giving back to the community, and making friends I was so missing in my life. I knew my father wouldn't be happy, so this somehow felt like it had to be the answer.

I committed to this decision to recreate my life regardless of the financial impact, the rest didn't really matter. In less than a year, I was fully immersed in the education program. I'd quit my job, sold my house, moved my wife, two kids and the dog. Even the dog wasn't happy, but I was feeling great! I had finally made a decision of my own, one I thought would lead me to happiness and joy, strengthening my knees as I stepped into my life ahead. I dove into this new environment with vigor. I had new people around, I was eagerly connecting with the students and other teachers in the school. For the first time ever, I felt connected with others, and to Peter.

These feelings, however, didn't last long. I had made big changes on my own and only for me. I didn't take into consideration how this would impact my wife and children. In less than a year, my wife proclaimed, 'enough was enough', and decided our marriage was no longer something she wanted. I felt stabbed in the heart once again. I was so blinded by my drive to be the husband I thought I should be, that I didn't even see this coming. In fact, I thought I had the perfect marriage. Hell, I was doing all the perfect things I'd been taught, so why wouldn't my marriage be perfect? I was just so consumed with 'doing', I didn't notice that my marriage had been on the rocks for years.

I found myself feeling even more isolated than ever before. The friends I thought I had made at the University quickly disappeared. My demons and insecurities flared up. I had no idea how to be a father, especially a single dad to two young children, my wife had left me with. With my head hung low, I felt the shame that would come from the condemning comments of 'I told you so' from my father.

Despite his disapproval, I knew I had two children who needed me, a mortgage, a low paying job, and still no friends I could turn to. I also believed that I couldn't rely on my father. This was the moment of truth for me, my Ignite awakening. I knew I had to become the man who was ready to confidently tackle each step in life, not still be the boy who had fallen off the porch that day after my father's comment.

Trying hard to master it all on my own, I **panicked**! I hadn't done it before so what made me think I could do it now. Besides, a damn good man and father is defined by what is in his pockets, and my pockets felt empty on every level. In my brain, one option was clear, return to my old life. Fill my pockets again and we will be safe. I called an old manager, begging for a job. He had one; it started in two weeks. Phew... disaster averted, or almost!

As a single father I knew it was critical to focus on my kids, as well as myself. I knew I couldn't do this alone so felt forced to reach out for help for the first time in my life. This was a strange and uncomfortable feeling. I had never asked for help before as I believed it would be a sign of weakness ... my father would not approve.

I put my pride aside and realized I couldn't do it alone. I needed to ask for help. Stepping off the stairs this time, with my heart pounding again, I walked to the sweet lady who lived next door to see if she was available to babysit. I truly thought I was going to die. I didn't have the skills to connect with other people. I was weak. I saw mockery slide across her face as I started to speak. I wanted to run, however, my daughter stood there holding my hand like an anchor. I couldn't move. I stuttered, "Umm, would you, umm, be able to, maybe watch Jorja, after school, if it's not a bother? I am so sorry to ask." Her eyes shined and she smiled. "You know it takes a community to raise a child. I would love to help."

During the next few months, my life slowly shifted. I began connecting with other parents in my community, reciprocating and offering to help them as well. My life became more about being connected to the people around me and less about proving anything to anyone. Over time, I felt lighter and less burdened – like a real man in fact! I was proud, yet humble enough to ask for guidance and support. Not asking for help during those critical times left me lonely and insecure. The more I asked for help, the more people came into my life, building stronger and more meaningful bonds. I had found the support and love that I envisioned the day I stepped out the door those many years ago.

The compelling drive to make my father proud of me, began to dissipate. I was now proud of myself and the way that I was living my life. I thought back to that day with an earring in my ear and how *alive* I felt. I had these same feelings again. It was evident to me that my dad, in his own way, *had given me that loving embrace* I so desperately desired. It wasn't that he didn't like the earring. Instead, he was trying to tell me to be confident, bold with the choices I made in life. To go forward, be a man, live life to the fullest no matter what anyone says.

I never had the opportunity to share this story of the earring with my father. Sadly, he died just after I turned 50, just as I was becoming the man I had grown into. In our final few days together, I could feel his love and how proud he was of who I had become. I, myself, felt proud of me. My father fulfilled his responsibility of teaching me to be a MAN! He did it in his own way. As he passed, I simply embraced him and allowed him to take *his* next steps – that was a gift. We all need to step into our lives, our own way. The steps you need to take may not be easy, but they are yours to stumble over or leap two at a time. We all have a porch we need to step off of. Do it with confidence and no expectations. The only approval you will ever need is your own.

IGNITE ACTION STEPS

Do you sometimes feel like you don't love your life? Like, deep inside, something is missing? That's because you may be living someone else's life, allowing other people to influence your choices. To regain that passion for the life you want, you must recover ownership of your choices. No one knows yourself better than you. No one but yourself can choose how you live. Below are a few ideas for how to fall in love with your life.

*Love yourself first: The first step to getting rid of expectations is to treat yourself kindly. To take care of others, you have to put on your oxygen mask first—you can't truly love other people if you don't love yourself first.

*Adjust the way you think: You can not control what others think about you, but you can choose how you think about yourself. Pay attention to your self-talk. Are you being kind to yourself or adding pressure? Your expectations can box you in or set you free.

*Stop judging yourself: Expectations derive from being judgmental— when someone can't accept how you behave, they expect you to change. By learning to be more compassionate toward yourself, not only will you ease your own expectations, but you also won't feel the need to judge others.

Peter Giesin - Canada
CTO and Co-Founder of Ignite
https://www.igniteyou.life

OLIVER MANN

"If we can't face the shadow inside,
we can't face the light outside. "

My intention with sharing my story is simple. I want you to be able and willing to look deep inside yourself, and not fear what you see. Not fear what you carry with you all the time. I want for you to be able to look into the dark side, knowing it cannot hurt you, knowing that it will not hurt you. Because it is you.

WHEN THE WORST HAS ALREADY HAPPENED

I sat alone in my room. Sixteen. Music blaring out of the old speakers. My body ached. I was heavy. I didn't fit inside my skin. Something wanted out and I wanted it out. I just didn't know how.

I lashed out. I slashed posters on the wall, broke glasses, anything in my way was a target of destruction. Temporary relief. Until I sat down and formed a gun with my hand. I pointed my fingers to my head and wished two things: that I had a gun, and that I had balls enough to pull the trigger. I had neither.

This was one of many moments where I couldn't understand what was happening to me. I was carrying a monster inside. A darkness I couldn't look at. I couldn't even imagine looking at it. I knew it would consume me. It did consume me. Just not in the way I expected. It took two decades and more for me to look back. Now, at 41, I can see how this beast inside me was eating me up from the inside. The monster was stopping me from living. It made me hide. It made me pull out of every moment of potential I had by telling me I wasn't good enough. It told me not to go for the promotion, because they would all see I shouldn't have been there in the first place.

The monster told me I shouldn't do anything to make myself visible, because they would all see how little I knew, how little I was and how ashamed they should be of inviting me in. It told me to stay away from groups of friends, to stop thinking I should connect with people. Because if I was worth connecting with, they would reach out – they never did. Through all of this my monster felt vindicated. I felt alone, lost, weak, disempowered and worthless. The funny thing is, I didn't even think it was a monster. I just thought it was normal. I saw others out there being themselves and I thought it was because they were better. They had something more, something special. Like they didn't carry a dark side. But maybe they didn't realize, or maybe they were too scared to look. Like I was.

In May 1984, I was with a nurse looking at a small cut in my forehead. It was really nothing, but as a six-year-old boy, I'm sure, they wanted me to feel safe. I had been taken by ambulance to a local hospital after a car accident. My uncle was around somewhere, also unharmed. My father, however, was not.

The last time I saw him before I arrived at the hospital, he was behind the wheel of the car. Covered in blood from head to toe. I was told later his forehead had been struck with a rock roughly the size of a brick. For years after I told myself and those around me I had seen the rock. I don't know if it was true.

My father ended up with brain damage. From that moment on, he was no longer able to be my father in anything but name. He is still alive to remind me of the accident. Trauma can be so much and it can be so little. Depending on how much you attach to it. It seems to me it's whatever causes you to change your beliefs or dreams. For me, the dream of a father turned into a longing for the father I once had.

Now as an adult, we sometimes sit together after his lunch. I sit down by his table where he has his cup of tea and a chocolate biscuit. There are bits of food in his moustache and drops of sauce or soup on his t-shirt. He's holding my hand, tight. Looking at me. He doesn't say anything. In between, he takes his other hand and picks at some bits of food and eats them.

There's a faint smell of institution all around and on him. The room is almost empty apart from a nurse walking around cleaning the last bits from lunch. Another patient, client or guest (whatever they are called) another man, is sitting by a table with a woman and two children. I look over at them and the children are smiling. The woman is looking out of the window. She looks tired.

I notice my father again. He still hasn't said anything. But it's ok. I'm here to be with him. Asking questions is futile. He never remembers. He doesn't know, or at least the part of his brain that speaks doesn't. So, he says he doesn't know. Or he makes something up. It's exhausting, these one-way conversations.

Visiting when I was a child was particularly painful. I didn't know or understand that he wasn't coming back to me ever – until my early teens. I even remember asking the doctors when he would be okay. When he would be well. Despite that, I thought I had it under wraps. I remember a moment at age 20. I was so confident as I explained to a friend how I wouldn't have been the person I was now, without the car accident. The person who experienced this trauma was me – and I didn't know who else I would want to be other than me. The me, now, was a direct result of all my history. Good and bad.

Throughout my life, I've had two major emotional crashes every year. In spring, around the time the accident happened, then in November, around my father's birthday. Twice a year I would go into the darkness. I wouldn't realize I was there. The world just shifted. A sadness not strong enough to color the world. Not strong enough to make me notice it was there. The pain from my teens would return. The sense of not wanting to be inside myself. A sense there wasn't room for two of us and the monster was winning. The sensation was *this is pointless... it would be best to just end it all.* Why would anyone want to live like this? Is this life?

Everyone and everything turned into obstacles. The lights dimmed. Food was tasteless. Alcohol more and more tempting. Every time, I would have a sudden realization of what's going on. I remember periods of darkness for months, then realizing it was autumn. The clarity of sadness. The mood going from mild sadness to total breakdown. Hysterical crying followed by emptiness.

What's crazy is that this rhythm continues to this day. Only the darkness doesn't have the same power over me as before. The biggest reason why is probably awareness. I finally know that spring and autumn carry heavy weights. I allow myself to be sad. I allow myself to feel the pain. I'm starting to be kinder to myself.

This has left me with a deep sense of empathy. A feeling I understand what you feel. Your pain is mine. The deep cuts inside me reflect yours and we're together in this.

This ability to connect is the greatest gift I've received in life. Despite the pain, despite the moments of complete and utter darkness. Despite feeling abandoned, rejected and unworthy, I still believe my connection with others is worth it. At least when I'm feeling 'up.'

This empathy is my key strength. I've never felt entitled to have people do things for me. Even when I pay them for it. Being able to have support is something I'm genuinely grateful for. So, I show them. I always make those around me feel they are a part of the journey with me. We're in this together. I feel you.

It's created the deepest sense of loyalty. It made me realize I am a leader. I lead through empathy, through vulnerability and through allowing us to make it happen together.

The transformation to make this all happen came in two rounds. All my life I have been searching for a father to fill the hole. It was impossible, because my father is still alive. How can anyone take the place of a person who is still here?

At the same time, I grew up with a father only in name. A figure, a myth, an idol I never knew. I heard stories of his generosity, his anger, his love, his arrogance and his ability to make people feel amazing and terrible. Yet, I never experienced it.

Deeply connected to this was a sense of masculinity. In the period after my father was out of my life, I lived with women. Mother, sister, aunt, grandmother. These were the main people around me. Although later there were men in my life, these women were there at a defining young age.

So with women around and the image of a mythical masculine father, I was lost. I grew up with masculinity being a negative. Yet, a longing for something strong. A foundation. Something to push against, to give me boundaries. For decades I was searching for this masculinity inside me and outside. Wondering how much of us is nature, how much is nurture. Hoping nature would win.

Then I had a conversation with the dearest friend I have. She finally understood that I wasn't kidding when I told her I didn't feel masculine. At this point, I recognize I have a 'father' issue. It took me until 39 to realize not having a father does not mean I don't have a 'father' issue.

This was the moment when I realized I'm not just a man. I am masculine. I realized I could choose. I didn't have to find my masculinity. I had to embody it. The acceptance of my own masculinity felt like a sixth sense moment. When suddenly all the moments in your life are clear from a different perspective. I had to embrace the strong feelings inside me and stop fighting it all. I realized that being masculine is sometimes good, sometimes bad. I then saw the father I had been searching for all these years was inside me. I saw the good sides and the bad and I allowed myself to carry them all. I accepted me. As a man. As a son. As a son of the mythical man who is my father.

For days after this, I woke up crying. It was like something had broken inside me. Like after going to a chiropractor and despite the cracks, the initial shock, it feels better. I just didn't know what it was. A sudden confidence had appeared. A feeling of being me, being a man, and keeping my vulnerability in all of it.

The second transformation happened just over a year after the first.

In the period since owning my masculinity, my stepfather was diagnosed with lung cancer and died not long after. He was the man who was closest to me, he saw me, gave me a sense of connection. He was my intellectual sparring partner. He held me to a high moral standard. He drank brandy with me until 5 AM. His death was the second father disappearing from my life.

At some point in this process, a shift happened. I rethought the accident. Not in a sense of what happened. Just who it had happened to. All my life, I had been a participant in my father's accident. He was the one with the brain damage. He was the one living in an institution. I did not consider myself a victim of the accident, only of the circumstances.

For some reason, I started seeing myself as a survivor. I started defining it as my accident. I survived a car accident where my father didn't. I came out of it able to live my life. He didn't. From this point on, I could see myself differently. I was willing to accept myself in a different way. I could see how so many of my childhood memories were tainted by my victimhood.

As a victim, everything is an attack. As a survivor, you can choose your reaction.

The problems I thought I had with my mother, were suddenly my perspectives. The young me with victim glasses on, was unable to see how my mother was trying. This is not to say it was all good. Going from all bad to balanced is a big step, and after so many years, I'll take any progress.

From when I was in my teens I was in search of a solution. A way out of the darkness and into the light. I read philosophy, politics, religion, spirituality, self-help. I devoured masters and gurus, and none of them helped.

The most consistent desire was to find a way out, without having to face it. I wanted to take a pill and feel better. I wanted it to be gone. Now. I meditated, I prayed, I believed. But it didn't work. Nothing worked.

During this time I was writing fiction and journaling, but my writing was shallow. I didn't touch on the hard stuff. I was scared. I didn't want to wake up the monster. One of the defining moments happened because I could see the gap between what I wrote and how I wanted it to be. I wanted to feel something from my writing. But I kept myself safe. My writing stayed tame.

I didn't expect a writing course would change everything. But I found a course in Shadow Writing, a course that promised to go deeper, darker and truer. With the help of my teacher, Gloria Kempton, I finally managed to look at the monster inside. To open the door to the room where the darkness resides. I allowed myself to write out of me the fantasies of violence. The pain. The hurt. The guilt. So much guilt surrounding the feelings of inadequacy. I allowed myself to feel the pain of what had happened to me. I allowed myself to write about the abandonment. About the desires inside me, it made me shine a light in the dark room I had been avoiding all my life- until the only thing left was me. Inside this dark room was a little boy, aged six. Abandoned. Scared. Hurt. Screaming for attention in a way I couldn't understand until now.

I have learned through all of this that the worst thing has already happened. All we can do is look inside. Be brave. Jump before you are ready because you may never be ready. You'll find that the world is ready to accept you as you are.

Ignite Action Steps

The biggest mistake we make with our shadow is believing two things: 1) we can outrun it and 2) it will hurt you. If you can reframe these two concepts, you're already on your way. For me, writing has been the way in, and although we all have our different creative outlets, I believe writing with pen and paper has a different power. By using our hands, keeping the contact physical, we get a different connection to our brain. I don't care if it's scientific or not. Try it.

*Going forwards, I want you to write every morning. Make it a part of your routine. With coffee, tea, or even a cigarette. Any vice will do, as long as you keep the virtue of writing. You will feel stuck. You will want to stop writing. But you won't stop.

*Because you have these tools: Commit to a fixed amount of time or number of pages. This will help you go deep, because you can't run away from the heavy shit before you get to the end.

*When you get stuck, ask yourself these questions to get you back on track:

How do you feel?
How do you feel after writing that?
What are you avoiding to write?
If you were to burn this page, what would you write?
What's the most violent thing you've imagined?
What's the darkest thought you've had?
What do you want?
What do you fear?
What is death to you?

The power here lies in practice. Keep writing every day. But remember kindness is key. Allow yourself to cry when you write. Allow yourself to stop if it feels too much, then continue later or tomorrow. Just write. Don't make this into another stick to beat yourself up with. If you avoid writing a day, don't turn it into anything more than missing one day. Start again tomorrow. Be kind.

Another powerful part of this is the externalization of your internal voice. The voice you carry with you changes when you see it on paper. It almost becomes fiction. From there you can look at it in its true sense, and not believe it is the "you" you hear in your head every day. Most of all, be brave. We cannot afford to not shine the light. The shadow is you and it's *not* as dark as you think.

The worst thing has already happened.

Oliver Mann - Spain
Mentor, trainer and CEO
www.olivermann.co

MARK EGGIMANN

"Treat yourself as caring and compassionately as you treat your best friends. The universe will take care of everything else."

If you feel my story resonates with you, I truly hope my words inspire you to make powerful changes that will bring you peace and transform your relationship with yourself and beyond.

A JOURNEY TO SELF-LOVE

The couch is black, about the same luminosity of my thoughts. Not just for a week or a month. This has been going on for years. My gaze oscillates between the parquet floor and the window leading to the grey and soulless balcony of my apartment. It's a deep dark winter night in December; I haven't seen sun for a while. Neither outside the apartment, nor inside my own creation, which I'm condemning like almost everything else in the universe.

This could be the end, the end of a suffering that creeped in during my youth and did not dissipate. Twenty-five years of hardship inside, 25 years of remarkable achievements outside. "How come peace never settled in?" I question myself. I was the first of our family to ever obtain a university degree, climbed successfully up the career ladder, working for renowned companies as a Corporate Director earning a quarter million dollars yearly, whilst doing triathlons and composing beautiful music. I achieved all this, yet the challenges multiplied. Feeling utterly empty, separate and different from the world, experiencing back pain, sleep disorder and obsessive-compulsive thoughts about the sexual past of my girlfriend. These signs started recurring more than a decade ago, but their major offensive has left me weak and powerless for over a year now.

I hoped the scores of appointments with psychotherapists or their antidepressants I rejected for so long, would yield fruits. Maybe Tony Robbins' seminar or the Mindfulness Based Stress Reduction Course (MBSR) would initiate a healing process. Maybe my friends or parents would find a solution instead of observing my slow nemesis leading to the inevitable implosion. But they couldn't help. They were just as overstrained as I was.

10 steps. 10 seconds. 7 floors. Salvation from my pain, at last. Would heaven be waiting for me on the other side, or eternal darkness? I can't really care what's coming afterwards, I need to end this - right now. I visualize how to jump off the balcony to avoid sitting in a wheelchair for decades to come.

But there is this little flame burning, like a last guardian protecting what is left of my will to live, after the massacre that I inflicted upon myself for years. A tiny flame that could be blown out by the breath of darkness at any second. Fragile, yet persistently resisting its extinguishment, against all odds. That flame is the reason to live that my 10-year-old daughter gives me. The flame surges a last time preventing me from jumping, like a hand coming from the top of the cliff to grab me. My eyes fall onto the door leading to the balcony. What an unlikely coincidence, the balcony door comes with a lock that can be closed with a key. Is this a sign? Whilst keeping my inner eye on the flame, I take the key, lock the balcony door and put it far away, where it will remain until light penetrates my darkness. It's now 40 steps and 1 minute away, still 7 floors. The door remained locked for six months.

How could all of this happen? Born into an upper middle-class family, enjoying no financial worries, thanks to my hard working parents, things should have been smooth for me with all the amenities. My father launched his import/export company before I hit puberty. A persistent, gifted businessman, he traveled to countries where no comfortable Western man would set foot. His business grew, his financial risk exposure grew and his daily consumption of filter-free cigarettes. Our quality dad-son time was neglected. When my father did finally come home from travels or a hard day's work, his first words were often an observation of how his rules and standards were not met, in a loud, critical and harming way. It never seemed to matter who the culprit was, everyone should hear his point, ideally multiple times.

My father's rants became more frequent, his patience diminished, the solid foundation of my parents' relationship started to crumble. Extended emotional conflicts, often taking place in front of me, but far too often in front of guests, became a regular routine. The trajectory of my brother, older by four years, pointed south as he became rebellious. As a last attempt for my overstrained parents, my brother was moved to a residential school where he spent six days a week. I was now left alone to deal with the tension at home, since no relatives were living nearby--no role models, no mentor.

As a teenager I did not understand the concept that I was able to choose my own meaning and response to what happens to me. So, I started believing I was 'not good enough, not lovable and not important,' and my only chance to counter this was to achieve extraordinary things and be perfect. By doing so I would potentially avoid endless criticism and negativity from anyone. Unfortunately, these beliefs made me feel lonely, like I didn't belong anywhere, not to my family, nor this society or this universe.

Around this time I received two gifts which would leave their deep mark in my life. My father purchased me a personal computer when the popularity of video games started to rise. My brother left a couple of video tapes with explicit pornographic material, unattended in the cupboard below our television. No one seemed to notice or care. Naturally, I became addicted to both of them in my attempts to escape my negative feelings. Those addictions grew, perfectly timed with being put into a boys-only class for three years, not a great starting position in learning how to court and relate to girls!

The seeds of a miserable life were planted – years spent trying to fuel my esteem and confidence by impressing people, moving up the corporate career, outperforming friends or foes, providing my girlfriend with even more sexual satisfaction… My perfectionism developed an obsessive-compulsive nature on the grounds of a very unhealthy relationship with myself. I asked more from myself than anyone else. Any mistake initiated critical, harsh, unforgiving self-talk, demanding the best possible performance, necessitating I become a master in evading criticism from others. I'd constantly ask for early feedback to improve my approach and preempt blame. However, this prevented me from learning how to deal with criticism, regardless of where it came from, and it undermined my capability to nurture healthy relationships.

A psychotherapist called me a 'warrior' after realizing how many challenges I seemed to resist in my life. He saw strength and willpower in me, which I felt had dissipated long ago. Nevertheless, on that dark December night, I chose not to give up, for I saw my daughter's daunting future that would inevitably follow my disappearance.

Locking that balcony door, opened up space in my mind - a huge question appeared:

"Why do I treat myself worse than any other person, even strangers

on the street?" This question led to downright defying my entire belief system, turning around my destiny forever. *"Why do people unknown to me deserve more love, more compassion, more service and more attention from me than myself? Is it possible my suffering does not come from the outside world being mean and ignorant to me, but from how poorly I react? Is my reaction rooted in the alienated relationship between my body, heart, mind and soul? Don't these parts of me feel and behave similarly to members of a dysfunctional family as they meet up once per year for Christmas, merely enduring that day out of duty? If such a family would burn out within weeks, wasn't it obvious that I did in my struggle? Could it possibly be I would get a completely opposite feeling of alignment and harmony if I promoted myself to the top priority in my own life?"*

Having no better alternative, I set sails to the experiment and started treating myself as my own, most precious friend. Every once in a while, I was capable of interrupting my outdated response mechanism by acknowledging my negative feelings and asking myself: *"What can I do for you?"* or *"What do you need right now?"* My intuition's response did not make it consistently through the dense fog of my internal war. But over time, I would hear my inner voice. *"Call a friend." "Go for a walk in nature." "Try running." "Take the car for a drive."* Although I wasn't always able to follow the instructions, I allowed my feelings to exist. I started to hug myself, cry as a response to it and hug myself even tighter, caressing my own face. I showed compassion and received indications of what was needed, a giant first step.

Some days turned into okay-days, a place I enjoyed very much compared to the past months, a place from where it was much easier to assess the situation, to plan, to act appropriately and sail even further into this journey of self-discovery.

Somewhere down the road of transformation, I figured out my environment was filled with negativity as a consequence and reflection of my suffering, and it would continue to poison me if I did not upgrade my surroundings. Colorful items were seeded in my dark apartment, my playlist evolved towards more uplifting songs, personal growth books replaced meaningless internet time. Some items at home evoked negative memories and emotions; these items started disappearing. Some friendships were toxic. These started disappearing, too. Slowly, my days improved whilst difficult days still existed. But I developed confidence and courage to face those days, because I knew through the compassion and understanding I showed, the next day would likely be more cheerful.

Positive momentum built, and a critical obstacle on this healing journey appeared. If I wanted to grow even stronger, I had to tackle boundaries, an area I was completely unfamiliar with. The best place to start was on my own. I used to demand unrealistic things in a way that would inevitably lead to injuries. My disc herniation, cartilage damage and fatigue fracture were all witnesses to this unforgiving attitude. When physically working out, I would now apply a more intuitive approach. Goals were not set by an app but by me, based on fitness and state. As I trained, I observed how it felt. Discomfort was acceptable as it would lead to growth. But in the case of prolonged pain, I reduced or stopped the exercise at once to avoid further injuries. As a result, I felt better about working out. My body didn't need weeks to repair itself.

Observing how this approach was improving the relationship with myself and emotions in general, I was compelled to examine further. My hypersensitive nature allowed me to experience the feelings of others in my own body. So, their suffering would become mine by default. However, I felt *responsible* for the feelings of others, a consequence of my relentless desire to be recognized and admired. Thus, I realized my happiness could not depend on how people are feeling, even about me. I needed to change this mechanism if I wanted to win the war instead of just battles. My best course of action was to apply boundaries. This meant I would still listen to the opinions of others, but I would respect my own feelings and intuition more. I would not remain in a situation if I felt the urge to leave. I would not stay silent if I felt I had to speak up. I would not agree to an invitation just to please. Boundaries meant saying 'yes' to me.

All the years of desperately trying to fill the void with people, experiences and objects didn't work. Whatever I poured into that void depleted in a matter of days, and I would seek again. As I adopted new routines, I assumed accountability to fill up this emptiness, ending decades of illusion. My vibration turned highly positive. I suddenly depended on nothing specific to happen in order to feel at peace, as I *became* peace.

Paradoxically, focusing on me and applying boundaries wasn't an act of selfishness harming relationships. When I stopped taking responsibility for the feelings of others, my batteries replenished faster, letting me serve the universe much more effectively. Mistakes were still common, but I embraced them as a way of growing and apologized compassionately. The positive energy I radiated, naturally attracted more positive people and lightened up the hearts of those suffering. Mahatma Gandhi had a point when he said, "A 'No' uttered from the deepest conviction is better than a 'Yes' merely uttered to please, or worse, to avoid trouble."

My journey is far from over. Happy days are now the norm. Difficult days are welcomed as they remind me how grateful I am for the transformation. In healing my wounds, I could forgive those I felt had hurt or betrayed me. I forgave my father, understanding that providing for me was his way of saying 'I love you'. I became the light for my daughter who is the reason I survived. The balcony keys are somewhere, I never think about them anymore, it feels like an eternity away.

Most of my challenges have been mastered, a few remain. I embrace them, knowing they will continue to dissolve through my abundance of love and compassion. I aspire to inspire you to let go of the expectation to be perfect. Perfectionism can be the never-ending attempt of your rejected self to be loved. The rejection and separation is the illusion you may have adopted as a child and kept alive as an adult, nurtured through your own self destructive habits. It wasn't until I asked myself the crucial question that ignited my transformation through self-love that changed everything. It is an essential process I hope you and every human being can experience in the journey towards true enlightenment.

IGNITE ACTION STEPS

If you experience negative feelings on a consistent basis, if you apply dozens of rules onto the universe, how it ought to behave, only to be emotionally triggered by its lack of adherence, it is because you reject parts of yourself. Love for yourself is a mysterious blessing which is created and nurtured through the right thoughts, words and actions.

I offer you a list of recommendations that have helped me transform to self-love. Use it as an inspiration, complemented with your own ideas of proven positive actions. Start by adopting habits which come easy to you. They will build momentum, confidence and awareness. Be patient though. An increase of self-love will take time to manifest, the same way you need consistent action to rebuild trust in someone you let down. Be aware of your state. When you feel great you naturally choose better words and take better actions. What matters is what you think and do when you feel negative.

*Quality nutrition. Any engine needs quality fuel, yours is not any different.

*Exercise. Start small (10 minutes) with an activity you enjoy. You will expand.

*Explore breath. Your breathing may be shallow as a consequence of your heaviness. Your body will not flourish on low oxygen. Explore and apply deep breathing techniques.

*Meditate. It raises your awareness, your focus and your connection with your intuition. Alternatively, spend time in nature where air is free from noise and pollution. What matters is to shut down the constant feed of messages and signals. Consider doing a retreat like Vipassana for an all-in approach. It marks a milestone for most attendants.

*Recharge your batteries.** Use power naps and strive for quality sleep, where you heal, repair and grow. Turn off electronics 30 minutes before sleep.

*Establish and sharpen your morning and evening routine.** Most of our actions are habits. If you upgrade your habits, you upgrade your entire life.

*Upgrade your environment.** What we see, hear, and read affects our internal ecosystem. We take on the energy of what we let in. Upgrade what you take in.

*Detox from negative habits.** Identify & adopt healthier ways to scratch the same itch.

*Appreciate personality before action.** Praise for who you/they are relates to the personality and is clearly more meaningful than praise for what you/they do.

*Improve your communication.** Listen attentively without the urge to respond, rather ask questions. When you understand you develop compassion. Compassion leads to acceptance. Acceptance leads to forgiveness. Forgiveness leads to gratefulness.

*Crisis management.** When a dispute is breaking out, call for a time out and retreat to a secure place. Stabilize through breathing techniques or anything else that brings you back to calm. Be aware that the pain commonly originates from the past, triggered by the counterpart, a suffering that yet remains to heal. Your counterpart should do the same. Return to the scene and talk from a calm state. As an example, the Non-Violent Communication framework helps manoeuver through difficult situations.

*Hug plentiful.** It creates bonding and connection, especially on rough days. Hug and caress yourself if no one else is around; an infinite source of healing.

Always treat yourself as if you were the most important being - because You Are! You can serve the universe effectively only when you feel good. You may even want to adopt the marriage vow for yourself, as you are going to be married to yourself for longer than anyone else. "I promise to be true to you in good times and in bad, in sickness and in health. I will love you and honor you all the days of my life."

Mark Eggimann - Switzerland
Positive Transformation Catalyst
www.mindkatana.com

ROBERT VIG

"Don't search outside for what you can only find inside. Stay in the light, live from your heart and everything else follows."

As a man I learned early that I need to be tough and stoic. That opening up and being vulnerable equals weakness. Yet, vulnerability is where the magic is. It's really a superpower that creates deep connection and allows for true love and an authentic life. My hope is that by being vulnerable, I inspire you to open up and embrace your superpower, so together we make this world a better place.

OUR DEEPEST PAIN IS OUR BIGGEST TEACHER

It was the dreaded morning. I tried opening my eyes, but my eyelids refused. They felt heavy from all the crying the night before. For a moment I was wondering, was this all just a bad dream? But as much as I wanted it to be, the reality was cruelly settling in, pushing out any last hope. This was it. This was the day.

In a last try, the ever-optimist part in me pushed back: it's only a week, things might get better after it's all over. But the thought quickly crumbled on the deaf ears of my subconscious, which already knew this *was* something bigger.

I felt rejected with my heart broken in a million pieces. The thing I wanted the most and even had it briefly, was now completely shattered. I felt helpless, lost and confused. Lying in bed with my eyes still closed,

I wondered, "How did we get here? Were we destined to fail from the beginning?"

Just a few days before, I was enjoying the sunny beaches of Maui with my wife and our one-year-old son. Now thinking back on it, even my happy memories lost their color. "Was this our last trip as a family?" I worried. Maui was supposed to fix it all and it failed! We went there from rainy and cold Seattle for an entire month, hoping to reconnect, to find again what we had lost. But we only left the rain behind, our pain and sorrow followed us. At the beginning of our trip, I felt things were going in the right direction yet, on the last day, my wife broke my bubble of hope, telling me she wanted to separate. It hit me like a brick! She used to question our relationship at every little fight, and had threatened to leave before, so I initially hoped we would get through this one, too. But the more we talked, the more apparent it was, this time was different. She really meant it now.

So, I laid in bed, knowing that I had to get up, pack up my stuff and leave our nest we built together. Walking into the unknown by myself – this seemed daunting and scary, as for the last 12 years, we had walked together. Who am I without her?

The most painful thing, which filled my eyes with tears, was the thought of leaving my son behind. I felt I failed to be the dad I always wanted to be, the dad I didn't have growing up. I didn't know how this would affect him.

Finally, after much resistance, I crawled out of bed. With a heavy heart, I started packing. I wanted to leave before anyone woke up. I left that morning feeling broken, rejected, with my ego torn into pieces.

Our relationship started so beautifully; it could fit into a storybook...Two young lost souls meet in a foreign country after both leaving the comfort of their homes behind to take on a new adventure. They not only find the lost comfort in each other, but the newly found love gives them magical wings. They don't have anything, but they are happy, explore and enjoy life with passion. They support each other to go back to school. They are a great team – she helps him with English, he helps her with math and chemistry. He teaches her to ride a bicycle and to drive, she teaches him how to trust and open up more. They explore the world together and make many great friends. They get married and have an amazing baby boy. Life is wonderful. The story of us is only missing the part of living happily ever after.

She was everything I'd ever hoped for and more: smart, sexy, funny, super-creative, the list could go on and on. It's just too bad the initial high from the love hormones didn't last forever... But even after a few years, after our love matured a little, we still had a good relationship – or at least that's what I thought, or wanted to believe and hold on to... Several people raised red flags around me, but I easily discarded them. I was so good at finding excuses for her. "Oh, she only reacts like that when she is tired or stressed." "She doesn't really mean what she said!"

I was holding on to a vision of a happy family, one that I didn't have growing up. My father drowned himself in alcohol and my parents divorced in my teens. I wanted to have what I missed growing up. I held on to that vision with teeth clenched. We married, had a beautiful wedding and an even more beautiful honeymoon. After a few years, our little angel came into this world. So pure, so beautiful, so innocent! I'll never forget the first moments of his life, the first time he held my finger. We were filled with love and joy! The picture was finally complete, everything I ever wanted, my dream came true! I finally had it, and it felt amazing! But it only lasted for a little while; this picture quickly broke into pieces along with my heart...

The initial one-week separation after Maui we agreed upon, quickly turned into two, then she told me she's better alone; this turned into a half-year separation. Eventually, we decided to give it another shot, so I moved back. But we failed to heal all that was broken already, and things got even worse. We decided it was best to separate again and started planning the divorce.

This wiped me off my feet like nothing else. I was drowning and had to learn how to swim. I was into personal development and reading books before, but nothing could have prepared me for this.

I was holding onto the image of the happy family. I saw this as the biggest possible failure in life, especially after having a child. He was one and a half when we first separated. I knew the last thing I wanted was to be like my father, who used to escape in a drunken haze. For me, it was now a priority to figure out how to be present for my son, when I wasn't able to live in the same home. I wanted to be the father I didn't have. How was I going to be able to succeed now?

There is enough literature out there to make you feel guilty about how disadvantaged kids are who grow up in separated families. I remembered how my brother and I begged my mom to separate from my dad when things got so toxic and violent between them. The thought that kept me afloat was that instead of growing up in an unhealthy family with lots of tension, my son would be better off with two separated parents who are always there for him. That was and is still my strongest commitment. Even though we are separated, it is a rare day when I don't spend several hours with my son and put him to bed. He is my highest priority and now that he is almost three, we have more and more fun together and enjoy a special relationship. I'm very grateful for my wife being an amazing mom, too. I feel at peace because my son gets the best of both of us.

Initially, I saw myself as the victim; after all, I was hurting. It was easy to blame the other person. I found my true growth started when investigating, how I contributed to this situation. What was my role in this? From asking the questions, came answers.

We both grew up in dysfunctional families, therefore we came into the relationship with lots of scars. She had grown up 'not being seen', with a mother completely disconnected, emotionally lost in her own pain; her father was too busy working several jobs to provide for the family. My wife was hypersensitive to any signs of disconnection on my part. Anything that wouldn't go through this very sensitive filter, would trigger her pain. Next, I would be met with an onslaught of verbal abuse, withdrawal, complete disconnection to the point of her questioning our marriage. Me, coming with my wounds of seeing so much discord in my family, was very sensitive to conflict, and even though she was the person I was able to open up to the most, every fight, every time I got hurt, eroded that trust and made it harder for me to open up again. Most of our relationship was a rollercoaster: things would be beautiful and rosy for a while, we would get really close to each other, then I would do or not do something, use a wrong word, the wrong tone, not respond enough or pay her enough attention, anything would trigger her pain. She reacted emotionally, becoming very loud, calling me names, then completely withdraw and question our relationship. I would become defensive or frustrated with "Here we go again," or sometimes even become angry. I tried different things, like just hugging her in those moments as suggested by a therapist, but I would be pushed away. No matter what or how hard I tried, we'd always end up in the same space of complete disconnection. So, I never really found a good response to this and felt powerless most of the time. No wonder I ended up walking on eggshells around her, trying to avoid anything that would launch us back into this downward spiral. We would need days to slowly reconnect, and after a short while, we would repeat this whole scenario again. This constant up and down was drowning me and I felt like our relationship required a ton of effort just to stay afloat.

In the beginning, we would have these downward spirals around once a month, which felt manageable. After having our son, our vicious cycle, probably aggravated by not sleeping enough, would repeat on a daily basis. Many times, we wouldn't even have time to reconnect before the next thing would trigger us.

My biggest lesson was learning to let go, to surrender and trust. I had to let go of the image of the happy family, of feelings of failure, of not being enough, of anxiety and fear about the future. I had to go down to some pretty deep places before I saw the light. My ego was not only bruised but completely broken. And maybe that's exactly what I needed... When I met my wife, I was confident, set out to conquer the world, but also pretty superficial. Moving to a different country shattered some of my previous mirrors – people who reinforced my self-image. My wife became my main mirror and slowly the image I was getting back was one of "not enough."

I thought it was my job to make her happy and since I was failing, that meant something must be wrong with me, which I heard from her repeatedly. How naive to think that I can make someone happy? It was like trying to fill up someone's leaky cup. Yet, when my cup would become empty and I would ask for it to be replenished, she said she would do it as soon as hers was full. Guess how often that happened? So, there we were, two lacking souls with empty cups. No wonder we crashed to the brink of divorce. How different would it have been if we had known how to take responsibility for our cups, for our feelings, for our own happiness?

Trying to make her happy, I became a pleaser – not a good position for me because I knew I couldn't do that forever without becoming depleted, and eventually, filled with resentment. Especially when I knew no matter what I did, it would never be enough. I would always be walking on eggshells. It's not good for the other either, because by always protecting and shielding, you take away from their opportunities to learn and grow. Plus, I think it's just not loving towards yourself to always put someone else first. I can't be fully, authentically me, if I'm being so fully on for someone else. Self-love is an ongoing lesson for me – one good question I found to ask all the time before a decision is, "What would I do if I truly love myself?"

How easily I gave away my power! For what? What did I really want in this relationship? All I wanted was to be loved and appreciated for who I was. One eye-opening realization that came to me was the deep, unconditional love I feel for my son; I realized I could direct that love towards my inner child also – that part of me which sometimes feels alone, scared or little. I also realized the best thing I can do for my son is live a happy, meaningful and joyful life. My way of being and fully living will influence him the most. Staying in a relationship that was becoming toxic, where my frustrations and powerlessness would certainly have leaked out, wouldn't have allowed me to be the best version of myself and a good model for him.

This seeking brought me awareness, knowledge and transformation. Yet, one of the best finds was meditation, which helped me find something I didn't know existed: a deep peacefulness, a natural sense of inner joy. A place within that's always there, that I can always return to – regardless of what's going on outside. It's like having a safe-house – storms don't scare me as much anymore. It's very empowering. Experiencing that inner joy bubble up from this place of deep peace, proved to me that we already have everything within to be joyful and happy. Look at a child, that's our natural state. We just need to make space for it to come out.

Before, my focus was mostly on 'doing'. I lived by the model that if I accomplish enough, I prove to the world I'm worthy and lovable so I can be happy. The problem with that is 'it's never enough'. There is always a next thing to do. It's a life of chasing, 'maybe' with small bursts of happiness, but we never really arrive. Meditation refocused me on 'being' and acting from this place of inner peace and joy.

The painful "gift" of the separation invited and insisted I go deep and seek for answers. I could continue to be in pain or I could go searching for the lessons. It was very hard when I was in the midst of it. Looking back now, I'm grateful for it, because it was exactly what I needed to become the person I am today. Those lessons helped me find myself and experience more peace. I know every lesson has its reasons. I encourage you to do the work to find yours.

IGNITE ACTION STEPS

*When you have pain or something 'bad' happens, investigate it. Look at pain as a messenger or a teacher. Avoid labeling things as 'good' and 'bad'. Ask yourself, "What is the Universe trying to teach me now?" "What is the meaning of this?" If you're not familiar yet with Ajahn Brahm's farmer story on this, please look it up. Years later, I look back at events I judged as 'painful' or 'bad' and see they turned out to be the best thing that could have happened.

*Find a purpose, set a goal and go for it. It is too easy to sit around and lick our wounds, or even go into depression when life hits us. Albert Einstein says it best: *"Life is like riding a bicycle. To keep your balance, you must keep moving."* It might be hard at first and you have to push yourself but working towards a goal can give you a new focus and help you move ahead, instead of being stuck in your pain and victim mentality. For me, it was redirecting all that energy that I was putting into our sinking relationship into preparing for an interview with Google. Getting a job with my favorite company was a much-needed change and reboot.

Course correct when needed. Don't be afraid of the unknown, the uncertain, let it be your indicator that you're in a good place, that you are growing. When making a decision, ask yourself: "What would I do if I would truly love myself?"

Make a morning routine that works for you. You can start simple and keep adding to it if you wish. Even something as simple as making your bed each morning will give you the first wins of the day. Experiment, see whatever works for you. Mine are make my bed, have lime water or a smoothie, exercise or QiGong and meditate.

Invest in your relationships. Try to surround yourself with people who bring out the best in you, who energize and uplift you. Take your relationships to the next level. Go deep, by being vulnerable, show your struggles and the real you. That creates authentic connections. Even just having one or two of these relationships is priceless.

Be mindful of what you feed your body, mind and spirit.

Body – Eat well and hydrate, exercise regularly.

Mind – Read or listen to audiobooks. Try to understand and know yourself – why you do the things you do, what patterns you have, good or bad, what energizes you, what draws you. You can't change something you're unaware of. I find journaling helps with this a lot.

Spirit – Find a spiritual practice that resonates with you. For me it's meditation. I'm doing a combination of Sahaja and Love and Kindness meditation.

Invest in yourself, it's the best investment you can make. Try out some immersive experiences, I find them very transformative. I highly recommend the Hoffman Process and for men, the Mankind Project's New Warrior Training Adventure.

Robert Vig - USA
Software Engineer

ANDIS MELNGAILIS

"There is a diamond in every shitpile!"

My intention is to provide You with a tool to turn your losses, pain and sacrifices into the wins. Something bad happened to You. And? What are You going to do about it? Be a victim or use that experience to strengthen and enrich yourself? You've always been a winner. Sometimes You just don't know it yet.

YOU ALWAYS HAVE BEEN AND ALWAYS WILL BE A WINNER

It's a small village, population around 500 in 1992, which includes residents living rurally nearby, where the occupations for its inhabitants are mostly in agriculture and forestry. Everyone knows everyone. A small boy, with his rucksack on his back walks home from school. He's sad and upset, because of the bullying and harassing he had to experience during class breaks. A neighbor expresses concern, "What happened?"

Boy stops, considers and decides to explain, in a matter of fact tone, "I was bullied at school and I couldn't do anything about it."

Neighbor, "Why don't you catch them one by one unprepared and have your revenge?"

Boy listens, looks at him for a while, says nothing in return and starts to walk again. He ponders the neighbor's proposition. In the beginning, it felt tempting. He thinks, *"Hum, wouldn't it feel great to experience total control and power over someone else and the sweet sensation of revenge and justice for a moment at least? But what if I'm caught off guard and unprepared? Do*

I want to live in fear of an attack which might come as a retaliation for what I've done? Possibly it will become an ongoing blood feud and revenge will spiral where things can escalate and get out of control. Chances of a lethal outcome in such a scenario are high and even if that's not the case, all the pain and hurt during all that process... Is it worth it?" Seeing where it might go, boy shouts to himself, *"No, it's not! Better not start it at all!"* This is his first decision: defining the path he wants to walk in his life.

That boy was me, during second grade, at the age of seven. I was going to school during the '90s and those years were not easy. This behavior from my peers at school continued through twelfth grade. It was difficult, but I made it through. I had to. I wanted to. I wanted to show them, there's a better way. Years later it came to my awareness, they simply didn't realize what they were doing and what impact they were leaving.

That was the time when former Latvian Soviet Socialist Republic regained its independence from the Soviet Union and became known as the Republic of Latvia. During the Soviet Union reign, people had limitations on freedom and were not allowed to be individuals, to express themselves. Every person's activity was monitored and compared with the communist party accepted ideology. On the bright side, the state took care of the people. Most of the matters were controlled by the state, such as economics, companies, education, health care, media and social life. Education and healthcare were free and unemployment was close to zero. Those who didn't want to work were forced to in one way or another. After retirement, there was a state guaranteed pension, enabling one to live decently. As long as people obeyed the rules, they could have an acceptable life; and many were happy about such a deal.

But then it all came crashing down. The system, upon which so many relied, collapsed. Fear of the future, uncertainty, high unemployment and the rise of criminal activities grew. The mood in the society was not the brightest. So many with families, stable jobs and income, needed to adapt and learn how to live their lives in the new system, where state support was decreased to the minimum.

A very decisive event happened to me in 1995. Summer was coming to an end and it was a cold and rainy day. I was chilled and I noticed in one of the rooms a big window in a wooden frame was left open to let in fresh air. When I tried to close it by pushing it at the bottom of the frame, the top of the frame stuck and a crack ran across the glass from one side to another. "Oh man, I'm so screwed," I thought to myself. There was no way to hide or run away. I knew I was going to face the leather belt. It fell heavily and relentlessly on me for at least half an hour, which seemed like an eternity. I felt so much anger and frustration projected upon me when the crack was noticed. Nobody wanted to listen to my explanation-- it was an innocent mistake. It seemed like my words were fueling the rage even more. I felt helplessness and fear. I felt the pain and the only thing I wished for was to make it stop. Eventually, it did.

From the very beginning, in my earliest memories, I was an observant child. What I noticed, I analyzed and processed. Curious, my attention was drawn to the various events during my life, always with the question, "Why?" What caused that particular event to happen? What caused that person to behave that way?

There I was, a week later, sitting outside the house, looking at the stars and thinking about the broken window. The conclusion came to me that all this fear and anger arose from the financial insecurity which plagued the people around me. Then I made another significant decision. I will create an environment around myself with financial and material security and such worry will never occur in my life when I grow up.

A year later I ran across an article in a newspaper. It said there's a lack of officers in merchant fleets across the world and such a profession also offers good income. That's it! It was a golden ticket for me. I used it. I'm grateful for the support from my family, who helped me to get through those difficult times. They provided me with a strong foundation, so I could use it as a platform to achieve what I wanted. I was keen and willing to live my own life independently and differently.

After graduating high school, I joined the Maritime Academy. Amazingly, everything was coming easily. The studies were funded by the state and I also acquired a scholarship both from the state and the Shipowners' Association. Miraculously, relationships with peers became more friendly and pleasant. With some of my mates, I've kept friendships to this day. All the doors were opening easily. I guess that's what happens when *You* walk *Your* path.

Three years after high school, I earned my certificate to work as an engineering officer on a chemical tanker. Early in the spring I embarked on my second contract. The life on board that ship was all but easy. There was a huge overload of work, unpredictable hours during the nights, heavy seas with the ship moving from side to side, seasickness and sleep deprivation. After two and a half months, tension was mounting. I wanted to leave, but I didn't want to lose my position. I was close to the breaking point and a relief came to me in a way I least expected.

The ship was in a southern port of Norway to discharge her cargo. It was a hot midsummer day afternoon, June 23. We were receiving big spare parts for the main engine. I was crouching near the hatch outside on deck and watching how one of the parts was being lowered down to the engine room workshop. Out of the corner of my eye I saw the hatch door start to fall above me. I instinctively reacted, reaching out with my arms, trying to stop a half ton of metal. There was no stopping it. In a split second … WHAM! Soaring, burning pain in my right foot. My toes were a bloody mess. I could see my bones. My fourth toe on my right foot was hanging on only by a thin strip of skin and my right hand middle finger was bent backwards, broken, with bone showing. The hook holding the half ton hatch had broken loose from the vibration caused by the crane's cable lowering the engine parts. I had to wait an hour for the ambulance to arrive, take me to a doctor and finally, be given painkillers. Until then, my foot felt like it was burning and on fire; there was no way to get away from it.

After three operations and losing four toes, (two completely and two partially) plus three weeks in the hospital, I was sick of lying in bed – not able to go for a simple walk. I felt restless, anxious and angry, because of my limited mobility. Then out of this anger and helplessness, I exclaimed to myself, "Hell, no! I'm not going to be limited by this!"

Once again, a decision changed the course of my life! Needless to say, after rehabilitation, I returned to study to earn a higher ranking in the Maritime Academy and continue my career as a ship engineer. In addition, I wanted to prove to myself I was still a whole person. I engaged in various activities: geocaching, running, fencing, scuba diving, horse riding, snowboarding, orienteering, hiking in the mountains, ballroom dancing, yacht sailing, motorcycle riding and even bouldering. Obviously, that trauma was not limiting me in any significant way. I still could do whatever I wanted.

In 2009, I met a wonderful woman, Anne, who turned my world upside down. She and her family broadened my horizons both literally and figuratively. It was a huge leap, on a biblical scale. So much so, I look at my life like different eras – before and after 2009. They showed me it's possible to live in an environment full of peace, love, harmony, compassion, deeper understanding and higher awareness--something I had only dreamed about before. Instinctively, I had been looking for this all my life. Then there it was, like a sanctuary, a safe house, a home, where I could for the first time in my life, feeling fully safe and protected. An environment where drama, anger and negativity were not tolerated and transformed, if ever they did happen. It was a joyous and wonderful time of adventures and journeys. But…unfortunately, it wasn't meant to last.

You see, I was so cozy deep inside this comfort zone, enjoying myself and my life, I forgot to keep on growing. I didn't want to. Why should I? Everything was great, there was no need to change anything. Thus, the distance between Anne and me started to increase. It took four years and I felt it coming. Another decision. I, along with Anne, agreed – it's not working anymore for us as a couple.

Oh boy, if only I knew what was coming next. I was so attached and in love with her; detachment hurt like a hundred arrows had hit my heart, especially seeing Anne embarking on new relationships. This threw me out of my comfort zone I had been so used to, setting me adrift. The whole year I was depressed, suffering a lack of motivation and inspiration. Luckily, I was deeply involved with Anne's family, especially her mother, Christina. She supported me very much through this period. Miraculously, at the end of the year, I grew out of the attachment. The connection and love between me and Anne's family remained. In this way, we transformed our relationship from a couple to a brother-sister relationship. Her family became my family and has stayed that way until this day. Anne later married, and her husband, Daniel, and his family also accepted me as their family member. For the first time I learned what it means and how it feels to love unconditionally and transform affectionate relationships into pure love.

Years were passing by and I had several relationships, but all of them broke down. From one of them I gained a daughter named Elsa. Back then I didn't realize what a blessing parenthood actually is. Having her in my life allowed me to project my deepest love and energy to her and to harness my hidden strength and resources. It came to my awareness, when I was holding Elsa in my arms one evening while waiting in the emergency room. We had been celebrating her 4th birthday at a waterpark, when Elsa suddenly slipped and fell on a waterslide. She landed rather badly on her right shoulder. After the initial pain subsided and she calmed down I thought it's just a bruise and it will pass. But when we returned home, Elsa kept lying on a sofa and was unusually quiet. I asked her, "Does it still hurt?"

She replied, "No, no, everything's okay." But my gut feeling said we need to visit the doctor. As we were waiting for the doctor to see Elsa, I was holding her in my arms, entertaining her, doing my best to keep our spirits high. Then I realized the immense lengths I was willing to go to for her. It was already late evening, but I found so much determination and resolve, I was willing to hold her the whole night if it was necessary. The doctor sent us to X-rays and when we walked back into the doctor's office, I saw Elsa's X-ray on the screen. Oh, crap! Broken collar bone. I realized, Elsa kept quiet about her pain, not to be a nuisance or to cause any inconvenience, out of her love and care for others. That was so overwhelming and heart breaking; such selflessness. She gave me strength, resolve and motivation to push forward, to achieve more. Of course, in a month or so, she fully recovered and was as joyful and active as always.

Before that incident, I noticed Elsa's personality develop in observable ways. She possesses the same lighthearted, open, loving and positive energy I saw in Anne. Which come to think of it I noted, I too, had similar qualities at an early age. I'm very happy Elsa has inherited those tendencies from me along with developing those traits even more.

My commitment to Elsa after her mother and I split-up, continues to this day. I make sure they both have everything they need, including clothing, furniture, apartment costs, a car and financial security. My daughter will never be without. This I take as my responsibility and pride as a father, to create a safe, loving and positive atmosphere around her as much as possible. This is non-negotiable for me.

In my adult relationships, I was losing hope. Will I ever find a woman to connect with deeply and create a loving, positive and lighthearted energetic union? One with whom I can build a lasting relationship? Thankfully, I met her – Heidi. I rejoiced, I was so happy, like a small child about to jump in the air! There is one!

The energy which poured out of her turned me dizzy; it was really hard to keep my cool. I fell deeply in love with her in a moment and alas, my attempts to get closer to her failed. I was too intense and moving too fast, but thankfully, we kept communicating. One day she mentioned a month-long event that she joined, taking place in Pula, Croatia, called Mindvalley University. Heidi had me intrigued, "The people, the events and the atmosphere are amazing. If you're interested, you could join next year."Here again, not hearing the cue of taking time, I thought, "Why should I wait for next year? I'll sign up as soon as I return from the ship." It was true; the Mindvalley event was amazing even though I was only able to attend for the last five days. The people, energy, events, love and experience were so close to my heart. This environment was similar to the environment in Anne's family, so it felt like returning home.

During Mindvalley, I met a Rapid Transformational Therapist, Katarina Amadora. With her help I managed to get access to long forgotten memories and we worked to transform them. At the end of a session Katarina asked me to remember myself as a sad and hurt six-year-old boy. Then she told me to be my adult self approaching my younger self. She then asked, "What would you do, what would you say?"

"You're going to make it, look at me, I made it, I'm here, I'm alive, I'm happy." Then it struck me! So many revelations came at the same time! A truly Ignite moment, where everything became so clear. All the events of the past made sense to me now. I found the diamonds in the manure. Leading me to finding myself, I found my spirit. As long as I live and breathe, I will love myself and love the simple fact that I am alive. It has become a concrete foundation where I can safely land always, no matter what happens in my life. I now know self-love had to come first and everything else good in my life would follow. That day was my birthday. What can be a better present than feeling like being born again?

Here's my message, my dear reader: *There is a diamond in every shitpile!* I looked back at all my past events and found a treasure in every single one of them. It didn't matter if the event was pleasant or not. Every event was a turning point which led to a choice, "What path will I walk and where will it take me?" Through pain and suffering, I learned love and compassion. Through hardship and loss, I found strength and dedication. These are the diamonds You can find in every event that happens or has happened in Your life.

P.S. As for my true soulmate, this chapter remains unwritten… I welcome whatever will come.

IGNITE ACTION STEPS

***Write** down all the memories that torment You.

***Acknowledge** them.

***Look** for a value or a decision or a change in attitude or behavior.

*After finding it, **embrace** it and use it as Your strength.

***Turn your losses into wins.**

Andis Melngailis - Latvia
Chemical tanker 2nd Engineer Officer
www.facebook.com/andis.melngailis

JON-OLAF HENDRICKS

"In one moment of courageous vulnerability, simple tears can successfully ignite your freedom."

The truth here is this: He who cannot cry is left but hindered and weak. A man who is incapable of embracing the truth of his emotional state of being, serves himself in only one fashion - as an inhibitor and blockade to his own potential. On the other hand, he who unwaveringly opens his heart, extends himself beyond all limitations.

THE GENTLE FEROCITY OF A VULNERABLE HEART

I was still too young to properly understand the function of sunglasses, but this was one of those days where you were sure glad you had a pair. My most recent prized possession, these bad boys were just simply *too cool for school*. Some off-putting shade of bright green, or neon pink, I can't remember. Either way they certainly fit right in with the vibrancy of this day. There was laughter off in the distance and a hurried excitement encompassed the general surroundings. With a deep breath, I did my best to take it all in. A smell that found itself quite perfectly balanced between the sugary sweetness of an 'elephant ear' and that of a three-day-old petting zoo.

There was so much joy within me I could hardly contain it. This soon became apparent, because although we'd been waiting in line for the past hour or so, the fun of the upcoming ride was something we were simply not going to experience. My attention had been catapulted elsewhere. Just at the perimeter of my eyesight, a massive collection of what I can only describe as 'ninjas' were up on stage, breaking wooden boards, punching and kicking one another with ease and even performing some variant of acrobatics as they repeatedly screamed "kee-yaw!" I was fascinated, in fact so much so, I had hurriedly and with great force dragged my father all the way across the fairgrounds to witness this unfolding. As I looked towards the stage, looming some infinite height above my 4-year-old head and back to my father, equally grandiose, I began to wonder. Then, without filter, out it came, "Daddy, I want to be a Ninja. Daddy! I want to be a ninja like them!"

As I glanced up at my father, subconsciously praying that he would say 'yes', I was met by a speechless man. He didn't have to say anything though, I could see it in his eyes. An overwhelming sense of pride permeated from every quadrant of my father's being and I knew, beyond any doubt, I was going to become a Ninja.

To make my father proud – a rather simple concept, isn't it? One which seems to inherently become the underlying mechanism of action within the far corners of every young boy's mind. Here I was, not yet five years old, having had explicitly acknowledged my accomplishment of this mission.

"Great. Noted. I'll remember this forever" – and I have.

After all, this is how we learn, isn't it? Trial and error. Failure after failure and success after success. A perhaps never-ending journey of ours, trying to figure out exactly what actions are approved and which are not. It's a reactive process many men have succumbed to and one, which I might argue, is long overdue for an upgrade. Nevertheless, for better or worse, it's the reality I grew up within. Actually, it's the reality that many of us have grown up within.

React. Figure it out.

In my experience, it's a reality where our youth are only ever positively acknowledged *after* they manage to figure out how to fit the status quo. Only *after* they understand how to successfully fulfill the vision of positivity which has been set forth before them. Only *after* they comply with how to make the adults *proud*. A reality where free and creative expression are both numbed and narrowed towards an unfolding, which can only be as it would align with that of the adults' approval. Which sadly leaves us here, where even though the status quo is in itself a failing system, we subconsciously train our youth to assume the role nonetheless.

From a very young age and throughout the duration of my life, I've always seemed to defy this normality. I've remained stubbornly in pursuit of a grander understanding and have generally found little to no proper guidance, as if the vast benefits of a more proactive system of learning have yet to be acknowledged.

This aside, as a young boy I knew one thing was for sure. My father and this pursuit of making him proud, was the greatest teacher this world currently had to offer. My father taught me about hard work and sacrifice. He taught me about respect and honor. He demonstrated how to take care of myself and how to *always* be a man of my word. He showed me how to treat women – simply by looking at my mother in the way which he always has. My father encouraged my curiosity, or at least he didn't discourage it and so it is from my father I repeatedly found myself pushed to pursue and accomplish whatever it was I currently thought myself capable of. In simply being a young boy who wanted to grow up to be just like his dad, I found myself empowered and ready. My father lived the example, I reactively followed along and as a result, he taught me nearly everything I would ever need to know. Enthusiastically, I would find myself fully prepared to embark upon this journey of becoming a man – or so I thought.

You see, the major problem with this traditionally reactive learning process, is that if your role-models do not present something to you, then you naturally assume it must not be a beneficial component of existence. This opens the door for us, as young men, to neglect and forget about certain parts of ourselves. Parts of our being, although we were born with an understanding of their essence, we subconsciously wind up letting go of them. If we are not taught, we forget and unfortunately there is one thing my father never taught me, the same thing most fathers refrain from teaching their young boys. An unaddressed aspect of our being that rather sadly leaves nearly every single one of us feeling as though we are still missing a very important part of ourselves – and we are.

My father never taught me how to cry.

My father is A MAN, like his father before him and his before him. And like all good men of the centuries past, they did not cry.

Men don't cry. Or so it has been told.

However, as a young boy I must have cried and I can only assume that I cried often. I'm sure I sometimes cried over relatively pointless things, like the cut on my leg that didn't exist, or the fact that my little brother was sitting in *my chair*. But you know what I'm also fairly sure of, that in moments of great emotional turmoil... when I felt sad or angry, confused or neglected... or when I was perhaps demonstrating more love to the world than it was returning... you know what I did?

I cried.

Why? Because on an intuitive level I knew it was something healthy and productive. I might have been young, but I was also subconsciously highly aware of the emotional release mechanism that is crying. I didn't want to let all those emotions just sit inside of me, it made me feel uncomfortable... and so I cried. But then, somewhere along the line, I assumed the role and was shown what would soon become the most detrimental ideology I might ever choose to operate within.

Men don't cry.

"Great. Noted. I'll remember this forever" – and I have.

You see, I'm the type of guy that falls in love 'way too fast'. I live with an open heart and I see the good in people. I like to express myself as I pursue an open, honest and truthful vulnerability. This sadly, throughout the duration of my life, has provided me with nothing but heartbreak – after heartbreak after heartbreak.

For most of my life I found myself in an emotional slump, where I often felt as though I simply could not leave the door to my heart open any longer, but simultaneously just couldn't figure out how to close it either. To this end, I have experienced a great deal of emotional pain and for the longest time, I had always allowed it to manifest itself as suffering. To the outside world though, I was fine. There was no need to talk about it. I didn't need to express myself to anyone, verbally or otherwise. I had everything under control. I was strong and brave and courageous. I am a man and damn proud of it! Heartbreak, what's that? Tears? Not for me. No way.

Men don't cry.

A lifelong paradox, which has led me to where I am today, a grateful and astute recovering drug addict and alcoholic. A game which I drew to its bitter end, one where in that final year or so I found myself inebriated almost 24/7. There was too much of my life that I was unwilling to face. I couldn't handle it. I needed *freedom* from this pain. Sobriety was not an option.

Truth is, the drugs and alcohol were merely tools – ones which I repeatedly employed in order to continue hiding. What was I hiding from? Well, in the simplest way I can possibly say, I was hiding from the fact that I needed to *fucking cry*!

I was nearly 26 years old and I had never, not once, shed one single emotional tear in almost two decades. In fact, the *only* tears I can remember shedding since I was a *young boy*, occurred one winter when I shattered my leg in three places. That moment ended up requiring surgery, a titanium plate and 7 one-inch screws, plus 5 months in a cast. I allowed myself one tear, maybe two.

I was carrying around a lifetime of unaddressed and unexpressed emotional pain. The result of an ideology I had always chosen to operate within, an ideology that consumed me – that is until, the day came when I had finally had enough. I couldn't possibly bear the suffering any longer. I didn't know what lay ahead of me, but I did know that what was behind me could no longer be. On this day, I brought myself to the hospital, and within 24 hours, I had also checked myself into an intensive 28-day rehabilitation center. Four days then passed before I found myself capable of getting out of bed. It was on this morning, I found myself sitting in a room, chairs in a circle, facing what was to become the most beautiful group of strangers I have ever met in my entire life. At this moment in particular there were only men in this room, and my new male counselor had begun to ask me some questions. His intent was simply that I introduce myself to the group, but his word choice and the overall energy behind his inquisition, were pushing me into an emotional corner that I had absolutely no desire to be in.

What the hell was I doing here? My mind began to race as I could feel the energy within me escalate. I was resistant, and angry – *STOP!* But this was my choice, I checked myself into this place, this is what I want. Isn't it? Fine, *I surrender!*

I have no idea what I actually said or how long the moment actually lasted, but it felt like I was screaming for at least 10 minutes. By the time I was done, I was crying so profusely the damned Niagara Falls themselves might run away in shame.

Crying. Me, a man and in front of a room full of men, nonetheless.

I was scared and nervous as I finally brought my head up to look around the room. What a coward I had been, showing my petty weakness to all these men whom I had just met. What would they think of me? How could I ever regain my honor? This was the most 'unmanly' thing I had ever done in my life... "What the fuck?"

But you know what I found as I scanned the circle, gazing into the eyes of this room full of men? Compassion. I saw raw, unadulterated, honest compassion and love. These men were sitting there, half of them also with tears in their eyes, and just looking at me in this way that screamed, "You are not alone!"

An entire lifetime of resistance had just been lifted. This unbearable weight, which had kept me buried deep within myself for so long, was now gone. To think, in one moment of vulnerability, one instance of wholehearted crying, I successfully captured the freedom I had spent an entire lifetime seeking.

Emotional freedom. There was no more hiding, no more pretending. I was sad, I was in pain, and I no longer cared who knew it. I've cried thousands of times since that day, and each and every time I do, I feel a sense of release. I become lighter, yet more grounded. I am less confused, and resultantly stronger. I realize I am actively defying the norm, and with this, I often evoke a great sense of bravery and courage.

Nowadays, when I cry, I feel *POWERFUL*. More so than ever before, *I feel like myself.*

I sit here now and look back in bewilderment. I wonder how many of my brothers currently sit where I once sat? How many strong, powerful and beautifully empathetic men have simply pushed themselves into a hard and cold corner of emotional neglect?

How different a world we might live in, if it were one where instead – men cry. A world of open expression and vulnerability. A place of understanding and compassion, filled with a true and genuine embodiment of love. One where we do not belittle ourselves, or others, for simply being who we are. A reality where we have embraced our sensitivities, and instead of pretending like our emotions somehow make us weaker human beings, acknowledge that this is in fact our *superpower!*

Men do cry.

If we look back on history my friends, and deep within ourselves, we can deduce one thing is for certain! It is up to the masculine energy of our race to push the collective forward. Although the feminine is both capable and powerful, without the velocity, and the ferocity, of that which is masculine, we inherently stagnate.

And so, to the men of this world, to my brethren in arms, and to the forebears of our future, I ask you this: Are you brave enough to allow vulnerability into your life? Are you courageous enough to be openly expressive with your emotions? Are you a proud enough father, mentor, or teacher, to swallow this pride and instead do what's best for the young men of this world, for your own son? We must lead by example my brethren. Times are changing and they are doing so at an exponentially rapid pace. This notion that men can embody, assume and demonstrate their strength through a complete lack of emotionally expressive empathy, is outdated at best and flat out wrong in its worst.

The truth here is this: He who cannot cry is left but hindered and weak. A man who is incapable of acknowledging and embracing his own emotional state of being serves himself in only one fashion – as an inhibitor and blockade to his own potential.

I can assure you my brothers, it does not have to be this way.

Stop ignoring your emotions. Stop pushing yourself away from yourself. And for God's sake, stop pretending like this somehow demonstrates how much of a man you are.

IGNITE ACTION STEPS

Why allow those tears to build up inside? What good does this actually do for you?

There's an ever-growing assemblage of male support groups out there – ones filled with men just like you. Reach out to one! Or perhaps more simply, reach out to your male friends, your coworkers, cousins and fathers. Push through the discomfort, the resistance, and allow yourself to enter a place of vulnerability. Open up your heart, express yourself freely, and stand proudly in your new role of truly infinite potential.

I say, cry like you've never cried before and when you're done, go ahead and cry some more. And do so knowing this – you are *NOT* alone. I and many others like me, are here with you. *We* are here with you!

Will you cry with me brother?

Jon-Olaf P. Hendricks - USA
www.jonolafhendricks.com

FARAAZ ÃLÌ

"If knowledge is Potential Power, then Curiosity, Courage,
and Action are the keys to unlocking that Potential."

Let me invite you to uncover the greatness instilled within you. I believe we are often hiding our true selves behind masks of cultural norms in a world full of distractions. May my story inspire you to remove those masks and find your deeper purpose. Allow me to remind you that You matter, Your voice matters, Your ideas matter and Your time to take action is Now!

WITH TIME COMES PURPOSE

The consistent sound of crickets singing across the jungle, with the occasional interlude of rustling branches and leaves from the wildlife and wind was the soundtrack to my midnight experience. I was covered in insect repellant, sweat poured down my temples into my eyes and drenched my face.

With the little light I had from the moon, I could see and feel all sorts of insects flying and crawling around me, occasionally landing and getting stuck on my sticky skin. Usually such a scene would be something I would experience watching *National Geographic* from the comfort of my sofa but on this night, I was deep within the jungle, experiencing discomfort in darkness which evolved from a time in my life which felt far darker than this night.

Luckily, the jungle monkeys sleep at night but what if that one insomniac monkey planned to drop by to say "hello". To add to this evening episode of my adventure, there was also the awakening of the sleeping volcano, Mount Agung, which came to life a week earlier with strong smoke activity and warnings of a possible eruption.

Now you are probably thinking, Why am I out so late? My duty-filled reason justifying my midnight jungle walk will be revealed later, but for now, let's just say I was being of service to my commander-in-chief.

My adventure of being comfortable in discomfort was one of the many learning experiences I had come across in my spiritual journey. This journey, starting 11 years earlier in Norway, was at a time when I was very lost and in search of meaning.

It was August 2006 and I was living in Oslo after taking a giant leap of faith moving from New Zealand. I had chosen love over uncertainty. The hot Norwegian blonde was *my magnetic pull* and I assumed finding a job in a new city would be challenging but not impossible for a foreigner.

Eight months into my journey there proved to be a bigger challenge. In my struggle to secure a job, I had depleted my savings and maxed out my credit cards. My girlfriend was working three jobs to keep us afloat and I was embarrassed to ask her for more support. I felt like a burden. My pride and ego stopped me from reaching out to anyone for help. I felt shame in my lack of success and weak. Applying to over a hundred jobs online, every "rejection" received ended up adding to my giant snowball of negativity. My calls back home to New Zealand became less frequent. Starting a conversation disappointed and leaving it further dejected, kept me away from all communication with family. All my relationships were suffering, since showing up with negative energy was not really attractive or inspiring to be around. My stressful mood meant I avoided engaging with others. The gym was my only salvation to de-stress and reap rewards from my rigorous training.

Alone, broke and emotionally devastated, depression ruled. With my pride forcing a fake smile and pretending everything was okay, I was manifesting suicidal ideations. My internal self-love flames had become wisps of smoke. I had left a successful career, loving family and friends to pursue a new start with love, marriage, family, an alternate career and potentially many awesome adventures. Here, alone with my mind's darkest manifestations every candle of hope I had lit was snuffed out.

The disempowering thoughts eventually took over and one morning I found myself sitting on a bench at a railway station in Oslo. Tears carrying my last dreams streamed down my face, my eyes hidden behind sunglasses, and my mind drowning in thoughts, "Why is life so difficult? Why am I not good enough? Maybe I should end it."

I sat there for what seemed like an eternity, thinking of my family and their unconditional love and support. Leaving home to go live on the other side of the world seemed like an exciting adventure for me, but for them, it was the hardest thing to say goodbye, knowing they would see me less often. It had me thinking that by choosing death, I would be committing a selfish act in a victim mindset; I would cause pain to my family, my girlfriend and friends. As the late afternoon sun gleamed on me, I realized that despite this dark space in my head where rational thoughts had stopped and emotions had taken over, I needed to crawl out of this dark hole of victimhood and come up for air. I needed to grab hold of any snippet of positive self reflection and re-interpretation of my life.

I caught myself speaking out loud, "Get the f@#k out of this victim mindset!" and began self-coaching. I knew I was not meant to go out like this. "Find the light. Seek the hope and allow an answer to unfold," was the stronger message which came from within. Although I was talking to myself like a madman, my appearance was the least of my concern. My ego and pride had finally departed. I got some clarity and recalled a conversation I had with my friend Aaron, with whom I used to play university football. The conversation occurred three years earlier, a few days before a semi-final match. Aaron was on the opposing team. Concerned about my recent ankle injury, he asked, "Do you think you will take the field on match day?" My response was, "As long as I am breathing, I am fighting."

That memory ignited thoughts, clearing the smoke of self-doubt. I should be grateful for what I had in that moment: I had good health, a loving girlfriend who was going above and beyond, a supportive family and friends and the chance to create a life that served a meaningful purpose. Putting these gratitude pieces of self-love together was like stacking hot coals to burst forth my eternal flame. Gratitude lifted a weight. I could breathe and think clearly again.

I left the railway station that evening with a burning desire to pursue life to its fullest. I did not know HOW but I knew my WHY. My positive shift in mindset extended my thoughts to understanding that everything I have experienced in life was a lesson. I had to take control of my future. I needed to take potential new opportunities and transform them into something real. That meant doing things differently to get different results. More importantly, it led me to realize creating life's momentum was far more possible using positive foundations of gratitude.

My gratitude practice became habitual, and I made the extra effort to verbally extend my appreciation to people I engaged with, letting them know their time was valued. Unknowingly, this positive practice had become my HOW and within a month I found myself in a job resulting from a conversation at one of the engagements. By the end of 2006, my career journey in Norway continued its trajectory to better opportunities. The new start I had envisioned a year earlier was finally coming to fruition.

Gratitude practice had saved my life and now life was blessing me with its rewards. The challenges of 2006 strengthened my romantic relationship, evolving into marriage a few years later. I had a robust network of friends and communities that helped me create stronger foundations in Norway. My flexible work and travel obsession allowed me to discover new places and friendly faces all around the world, with the added advantage of working from New Zealand when visiting my family biannually.

All of this happened so fast that my struggles became a distant memory. Back then, my human need was to survive, and now it was to thrive with this growing curiosity to discover there was more to life. The curiosity that makes one desire that something more – it leads to the ultimate achievement which transcends everything. Historical literature calls this: one's **destiny** or **purpose** or **northern star**. There are many names to describe this element in life. I was ready to embark deeply into finding It.

As life unfolded, I was looking for **It** out there, that **something** which would fulfill the hunger inside of me and help me discover my purpose. In my quest to find **It**, I first made a bucket list of things I wanted to do and set about taking action and ticking them off. Financially, I was satisfied with one good comfortable job that took care of us with income, growth and flexibility. Spiritually, I was curious to learn but not making a gallant effort, as distractions and the acquisition of materialistic items took precedence.

My complacency grew, as I lived a familiar past and predictable future, avoiding the concept of being uncomfortable. This resulted in splitting my bucket list into two and favoring the fun over the responsible grown-up goals such as starting my own business, or a family or focusing on my personal growth. My fear of failure and judgement locked me into a semi-state of denial; "I am not procrastinating," I told myself. I was succeeding in achieving but not yet thriving in life. I was only taking risks when I was travelling. Everything else seemed to be on autopilot. I had slowed down my rate of self-evolution by not investing time in myself emotionally, spiritually and intellectually. I spent a lot of time on entertainment rather than education. I became that person who thought he knew it all. Although I felt lost without a guidance system, I was still cocky enough to be like the man who never asks for directions.

Ten years after that life changing decision at the railway station, becoming a father was my second magical moment. Holding my daughter Nicola in my hands as she looked at me with her little grey eyes and placed her small hands across my chest while falling asleep, was a powerful igniting experience. Being *of service* to her made me realize I needed to do more *and be of service to this world*. As her father, I vowed to bring about positive change for her future and the upcoming generations.

I chose to do something different! I would take action, get focused to achieve bigger results and embrace the ideology that the outcome extended beyond me. I knew I could create better communication between human beings and build strong communities. This was the ignition of my powerful purpose that shook me to the core and made me ask myself, "How can I bring change to the world while changing myself?"

This question led to some deep reflection, sleepless nights, research and journaling. Eventually all analysis led to one outcome – **I needed to change my way of thinking.**

I realized that I must first discover myself through unlocking my mind's potential by nourishing it with new information and systems to optimize my way of life. I needed to become the action taker, the student and the teacher. I had to step up my game, discover the best me and then become a better version of that.

I needed to let go of my self-esteem issues, my fear of failure and judgement. I decided to map my life's objectives and fulfill my life's pursuits.

Having travelled to 70 countries, people often asked me, "What was your best trip?" I used to answer with my top three adventures, but now I have only one answer, "The greatest journey I ever took in my life was the expedition I took inwards into my mind." By immersing myself into the continuous pursuit of knowledge and action taking, my intellectual, spiritual and emotional skill sets were nourished. I would read a book a week, do monthly courses and find mentors to guide my learning experience.

Adding learning, meditation, journaling, visualization and action taking to my rituals of gratitude, self-reflection and self-love helped me find that inner balance. Within three years, I saw life improvements beyond my imagination. I finally had control and direction of my destiny. My internal discipline of transcendence practice allowed me to be more present and focused, creating high equanimity where the rational mind overcame the emotional mind. I was now ready to serve the world.

Working as a mentor and thought leader were my first steps into creating something beyond me. My life mission became: to empower others so they can enjoy their journey on the way to discovering their northern star.

We all get distracted in life, in my case a few too many times, but now I have found my purpose. I had always been a late starter in life, but know that the most important thing is to **start**. I want you to know there is no right or wrong way to uncover your purpose. Every individual has their own unique path to life's continuous lessons. The only thing that changes is our interpretation of events and the choices we make.

Your mind is constantly evolving through learning and interpreting life experiences. Your perceptions are changing, your ideals are changing and the correlation of the decisions connecting the two will always be changing. Therefore, you must be willing to make decisions based on what you know to be true versus what you think might transpire. Knowing this concept will create new manifestations and allow you to evolve.

This brings me back to my night in the jungle where **I was leveling up in life**, being in service to my commander-in-chief aka my 10-month-old daughter, who was sitting comfortably in a pram behind a mosquito net, being kept cool with a portable fan installed inside, thanks to Daddy's innovative MacGyver skills.

She was in the routine phase of being walked in the pram and sung to at night to put her to sleep. (Did I mention I was singing as well?) Luckily, for the first few nights in Ubud, Bali she fell asleep without the need for an evening walk. But, on this night I had to muster the courage and do the walk I was avoiding, not wanting to become one with nature and its habitants. I realized I had to get uncomfortable to make my daughter comfortable. Venturing out into the jungle at night is not recommended anywhere in the world but her needs superseded mine. My courage and devotion meant my daughter was my priority and has been my plus-one, travelling to 23 countries in 23 months but that story is for another book. I looked beyond myself and knew my true purpose was in giving to others through empowering myself.

Sometimes things become difficult and unwanted, but with perseverance and determination we prevail. Metaphorically speaking, every path we encounter in life will have its rewards and challenges. The latter might cause pain and suffering, but through it we grow stronger. So always be curious to find a new path to explore, always have the courage to follow it and finally, have faith to take action and overcome the obstacles along the way.

IGNITE ACTION STEPS

ThE SEvEn Extraordinary StEps to SElf-Evolution: To awaken the mind to discover your purpose by creating systems to achieve it outside of your comfort zone:

1. Explore: New places and people mean new possibilities. Choose places that mix adventure with education. Examples: a transformational retreat, an educational opportunity in a foreign city, etc.

2. Execute: My "ZeroHT" concept means Zero hesitation time. Make that list of tasks you have been procrastinating on. For an hour a day, take action to get items on the list marked as done. Going forward, make "ZeroHT", 2-4 hours of your day.

3. Elevate: Rise above self-limiting beliefs through self-empowerment exercises with daily positive affirmations, meditation and visualisation. Have a daily journal so you can write your gratitudes, your goals and your daily lessons learnt.

4. Experience: Learn by doing with repetition. Reading the Karma Sutra, and doing the Karma Sutra are two very different things so live your life to experience it.

5. Educate: A reader lives a thousand lives, a non-reader lives one. Knowledge is one of the best tools we have. Read and listen to books and podcasts, watch videos and never stop learning. More importantly, take action on what you have learnt.

6. Empower: By being of service to others you also have the chance to empower them. By empowering them you empower yourself and the student can become the teacher.

7. Enjoy: Have fun and be happy. Live in the now and be happy with all you have in your life. Enjoy the process of getting to your goals.

The above looks simple, but be careful of distractions in life. Have the seven points in your journal and tick them off as daily tasks. Small steps on a daily basis lead to big gains in a lifetime.

Faraaz Ālì - Norway
Chief Empowerment Officer, Speaker, and Explorer
www.faraazali.com

ALEX STEFFEN

"Life is simply many individual moments united.
Uniting confidence and kindness *in an individual*
puts life *into simple moments."*

I choose to demonstrate how even the most disadvantaged person can grow into a true leader with a trait called *Kind Confidence*.

KIND CONFIDENCE

I found myself crying inside a glass phone booth at the edge of my school's courtyard. This was not the first time. Tears were rolling down my young face in a never-ending stream. My whole body felt miserable. Familiar faces rushed past the glass windows staring at me. Like every other day, I received weird looks. Their judgement was nothing compared to the overall sadness that held me prisoner at age twelve.

I held the greasy receiver to my ear as if it were my life-line to a better world. "I love you, too, Dad," I said before I hung up. It was the emotional nourishment I needed each morning and over the phone was the only way I could get it. Walking back the 100 steps to the school building was the hardest task in my day. I felt like the entire world was against me. I would enter the class, late as always, everyone staring at me – another huge embarrassment. No one ever dared say anything, but everyone knew. I was the kid suffering with the weird mom and the absent dad.

My parents spent years divorcing, us kids in the middle of it all. Mostly, I grew up with my mom and two older brothers. Although my mom pampered me, her undiagnosed bipolar disorder caused unpredictable outbursts of anger to come down on us like the wrath of Zeus. Every day we were exposed to strange requests. She'd toss the organized contents of a shelf on the floor and tell us to clean it up. My brothers ran away one by one to live with our dad. At age 11, all her aggression focused on me. Although she tried to give us a good upbringing, her illness made her fail miserably. There was no guidance to be found there.

I saw my dad every two weeks for the weekend. There was very little time for learning the life lessons a young man requires from his father. It never appeared to me that he saw mentoring as a priority. My parents had so much fighting to do and in the off days, earning a living was their next priority. My brothers and I were left in the firing line. So, I ended up socially incapable. An undeveloped character who resembled everything that an evolving young man is not. No confidence, no initiative, no taking a position. Simply put: no identity. And without getting clear on what I wanted, saying "no" was hard! I was never able to take a stand. I became a people-pleaser.

Growing up in Germany in its 'know-it-all' culture, everything has a label and an explanation. What that meant for the weirdo I was, is that I always had to justify myself for being different. My underdeveloped character would not allow me to own my differences and build a strong identity. When confronted by other people, I would buckle under. In search for some safety I started to micromanage the few conditions that I had control over. In short, by age twelve I was an insecure, anxious, control-freak. This added up to being unhealthy, inefficient, and unattractive. Life was miserable. In human relationships, I always lost. In relationship to girls, I always failed. In groups, I was never able to distinguish myself and lead with confidence. All this caused a downward spiral which eroded my self-confidence even further. I hated myself. There seemed no way out. I wanted to be a great man, but I didn't know how to achieve it.

I remember the day things finally changed, my *Ignite Moment*. It was after school. Lost in dreams of a better future, I cycled along a familiar, long stretch of a downward-sloping bend. With a well-paved, memorized path in front of me, I took my hands off the handlebars, my eyes off the track. It felt good to feel the rush of air on my face while the bike was gaining speed. I enjoyed those brief moments of freedom from an otherwise grey and dull childhood. I glanced to my side, "A circus tent? What's that doing there…" Before I finished the thought, there was the sudden impact. I was launched off my bike, which had been completely stopped by a thick power cable laid across the track.

Flying through the air – then hitting the dirt – I heard a massive crack. I remember thinking, "Now it's really over. Yet, surprisingly...also, not so bad." It was like the feeling of ultimate freedom immediately before death and was strangely comforting! It felt kind of good. Almost like a last wish had been granted, compared to the contrast to my life's routine. When I opened my eyes, I felt like weeks had passed. A voice above me kept asking if I was okay. It belonged to a girl my age I had seen at school a few times. She held a shattered object in her hand that I didn't recognize, as my brain seemed to work in snail mode. It took what felt like an eternity before I connected the dots. The black object in her hand was my bike helmet, or, what was left of it. The helmet, not my head was broken into multiple pieces. Now it made sense to me: Mom's daily stringent demand to wear it, PLUS loud crack on impact, PLUS girl holding helmet in terror, EQUALLED I've had an accident, this isn't heaven. I realized my body had landed on a hard stretch of gravel road and I was in a lot of pain, but a knowing in me had been shaken awake.

My first thought, "Thanks Mom, for insisting I wear a helmet." I escaped death by a whisker. My second thought was, "I'm leaving Mom." During those moments on the ground, weeks passed in my head – I put order to my life. Everything felt different. All misery gone. Clarity and joy in its place. I made a definitive decision to run away and start a new life. This set in motion a tremendous change. First, I started living with my dad, and within a mere two years, I left behind the culture I grew up in. I set off to live outside of my home country for a full decade, consciously relearning what I lacked by exposing myself to the world. It meant self-discovery and it meant life.

My *Ignite Moment* stopped my downward trajectory. The shift that came out of it turned me into a confident creator of my own life. It came as a blessing to rescue me from a future of lost identity and a life which lacked happiness. What I did not realize then was that this was the deciding moment that kickstarted my discovery of my mission. Over the next few years I would break down my lack of control over my own life and develop a powerful meta character trait, which I call *Kind Confidence.*

While researching masculine qualities, I discovered that few things are more attractive to humans than kind, confident control. Control in the sense of holding space for the creative, soulful and spontaneous energy that we commonly call feminine. Kindness for the grace and dignity that honors that container. What nobody seems to teach men is to be the "container". That defining and pursuing the where, when and how of any activity, or taking the lead on a major decision allows the feminine part to be in effortless flow. To a woman, a man in control demonstrates that he is in pursuit of his mission, despite the noisy distractions of a complex world. It's proof of intention as opposed to random impulse. The young, undereducated me could not possibly display this grounding energy. I needed to seek out this treasure in the world first. Once I started being in full control of my life, I stepped into my true masculine power. The bumpy, yet, rewarding road led me past three fundamental ideas that helped me establish kind conference in every area of my life: Identity, Exposure and Serenity.

1. IDENTITY: A strong identity supports every decision you make. You can't be pushed, pulled or manipulated if you have a crystal clear picture of who you are and what you stand for.

Before my *Ignite Moment* I always avoided taking a stand on core questions of life because I lacked an identity. In order to be liked I had become a 'maybe' person and a people-pleaser. Too many of us copy others and then feel disappointed for not living our own life. We don't take a stand and be our own identity.

I have learned it takes immense energy to make up your mind about hundreds of micro decisions on a daily basis. That's where a strong identity is required. Making better choices effortlessly starts with good macro decisions. They are the product of a strong identity. And they create consistency in your actions. They save you time and energy every time you need to make a decision. I started by asking myself "who am I in relation to *health* (e.g. no sugar), *personal time* (e.g. no meetings before 10am), and *energy vampires* (removing people who are chronic complainers). My strong macro decisions enabled me to change my experience from hustle and worry to effortless flow and growth. Identity is so powerful because it simplifies complex choices and thus makes everything else easier.

2. EXPOSURE: It is not just theory that teaches us. Conceptualization alone is relatively powerless compared to being in the bliss and the boldness of real life. We need both, yet what we need more of in our logical world, is exposure to new things and experiences. With my flawed upbringing I was socially less experienced than other kids. When interacting with people, I often felt unbearable stress. Any time someone addressed me, I blushed as if I had just been found out. What truly happened was that I lacked the *experience* of interaction. I realized that I can conceptually understand standing up to a bully. But when actually facing the bully, I always chickened out. I knew it in theory but lacked the ability until I put it into practice. This helped me see that life is a chain of individual moments that have to be mastered one by one through doing.

Looking for a potent catalyst I learned if books are gold, experiential learning is platinum. Many people in our logic-driven society become fascinated with pictures and words and end up forgetting the power of experience. This is what I call the curse of "book smarts." No book in the world can teach a kid the smell, taste or feelings life has to offer. It was only by *facing* the world that I was able to tear away the layers of insecurity. I found a white canvas underneath on which to create myself. Of all the personal development tools I have tried, *solo travel* is both the most underrated and the most powerful. It's exposure. All alone and far from familiar habits and norms, I was forced to leave my comfort zone and find myself. It allowed me to observe myself in social interactions away from the pressure of a familiar reference point. I discovered this when learning Spanish. Most people struggle with learning a new language. They follow the popular approach: learn the grammar first and make no mistakes. This is at odds with how the mind memorizes and reproduces information. Only immersion and experiencing mistakes or feedback gets you there. By immersing myself in the Peruvian society and not paying attention to what people thought, I had nothing to lose, so I dared more. This enabled me to go from zero to philosophical conversations in seven weeks. Because of its radically faster feedback loop, I consider this super-learning from exposure.

Experience is the true teacher. With each new situation we recognize patterns and build an understanding of who we are. As Patagonia founder Yvon Chouinard says, "travel alone and with intention. Otherwise you leave an asshole and you come back an asshole."

3. SERENITY: Acting from a grounded peacefulness and showing patience gets you so much further. People trust it more, because it's far more attractive, attracting and appreciated. Before my *Ignite Moment*, even though I had good intentions, many of my actions felt forced. This was because I lacked patience and the courage to be vulnerable. Without a strong identity I was constantly comparing myself to others. In addition, the fear of not being seen made me project a shiny facade of false confidence. I pretended to have everything figured out and by that I failed to show the real me - my scars, my fears and my desires. I was a control freak - angered when things didn't go as I planned. The unease must have been nerve-wracking for people around me. "You're so intense!" I remember a friend complaining. It wasn't the positive type of intensity, fueled by childlike joy. It was the type rooted in a scarcity mindset. It took me some time to become calm and soothe myself.

In a period of my life where stress and uncertainty were particularly strong, I went on a trip to China with my brother. One day, walking in the district of Guangdong on the Pearl River, we stumbled into a tiny tea shop. The old man inside didn't hesitate and asked us to sit. First, the control freak in me hesitates, "Is this a trap?" But then my curiosity took over. The man signaled us to pick tea from one of the hundreds of jars stored along the high walls of his miniature shop. With a generous smile, he engaged in a fascinating ceremony that must have been centuries old. I remember precisely how the tea leaves opened slowly as the hot water touched them. An incredible smell filled the room as the scene was captured in time. This is when I understood that the soul of the world can be found in the smallest things. Like watching the sea or the desert, they make you be there - only to be. Tea taught me the meaning of the Zen proverb "When walking walk, when eating eat." To live neither the past nor the future.

I see many men struggling with this idea. They want to control everything rather than holding space. Developing patience and sharing my true feelings helped me to react less and diminished my need to control. It directly affected my happiness. People around me started to notice a magnetic force as I gained more power to spread joy because I had become a source of joy. In the moments when others are agitated, confronting them with your own impatience can only cause friction, instead of building connection. The Buddhists say, "what you resist persists, what you look at disappears." Once I started not taking myself too seriously, I found a truer connection. Hiding behind social media or facades is easy. Paying attention is difficult. To me attention as a resource is more valuable than time. In fact, it can bend time. "If you pay attention you can improve upon the present. And if you improve upon the present the future will also be better." - Paulo Coelho.

Bending Time with Kind Confidence: Those experiences made me. They threatened the limited world I knew and demanded me to take a stand, to reconsider my priorities and then act according to my values. Most importantly they gave me my superpower: *Kind Confidence*. To understand its building blocks, imagine an alchemist who blends the three aspects of a strong identity, world exposure and complete serenity. It's a leader's winning blend of character traits. Balance is key. While many men exert too much confidence, others have forgotten its importance. On the other hand, countless men behave soft, fueled by their kindness, but lacking confidence. The synergy of kindness and confidence creates magic.

When previously I felt competition towards other men, *Kind Confidence* enabled me to control ancient emotions such as envy, greed and the need to win. From that place, I received more respect and acknowledgement. When it came to women, I was always incredibly nervous. By cultivating Kind

Confidence, I started to operate from a completely different space, more candid and vulnerable. Applying *Kind Confidence* as a leader allowed me to pay attention to people's needs and make them feel appreciated. It is a superpower because it speeds up your growth. Every intentional contribution you make towards your dream life using *Kind Confidence* activates other areas. It works exactly like the first domino. I started living these practices and at age 29, I became a #1 bestselling author, TEDx presenter, and was named Management Thought Leader of the year in Germany.

Many men find re-learning the traits of balanced masculine power difficult. They struggle because identity, exposure, and serenity don't grow on trees. They are the fruits of tremendous effort and willpower. Randy Pausch said it well: "Brick walls are there to show you if you really want something." The ones who care enough to draw from *Kind Confidence* will bend time and evolve not in a lifetime, but in a few years' time.

The first quality one-on-one moment I ever had with my dad was at age 28. It lasted for only 2.5 hours before he had to leave. My first impulse was disappointment. I was reminded how, as a kid, I was denied the stability I needed. But in an instant, I felt grateful. Fulfilling the traditional concept of a dad wasn't his strength, but he was the catalyst that gave me access to a much better type of education. I felt grateful for my father. Years into my journey of catching up, the brief meeting confirmed the hidden value of being left to figure life out on my own. He helped me stop needing that lifeline to a better world and creating magic for myself. It became the foundation of *Kind Confidence*. And it felt like a conclusion. I knew then: if I was able to conquer that chapter, I would be able to conquer the next.

IGNITE ACTION STEPS

*What I Stand for Exercise: Knowing your <u>identity</u> is a meta skill that makes everything else easier. In a notebook, draw a line down the middle of the page and state 1) on the left: what you stand for and 2) on the right: what you don't stand for. Find at least 5 points each. If you find it difficult, reflect on past moments in which life required a lot of effort and you persevered. You'll gain strength from remembering that.

Alex Steffen - Germany
Business Innovation Expert and Professional Speaker
www.alextsteffen.com

AUSTIN WOOD

"The more present we are in our interactions with other humans, the more deeply we are able to understand each other."

My intention is that you become intrigued by travel, immerse yourself in another culture, perhaps even learn to speak their language. And through these experiences that you may come to learn that, no matter where you are in the world, it is possible to meaningfully connect with others.

TRANSCENDING LANGUAGE

Learning a new language is like being given the keys to an exciting new world. Except the unveiling of that world is a slow and enchanting process. While exploring this world, nuggets of wisdom and alternate ways of interpreting reality can reveal themselves in a flash, but only after we've spent hundreds of hours committing new words to memory and contemplating the intricacies of verbal conjugation.

My first experience with one of these new worlds took place on day one of kindergarten. I wish I could remember the words my teacher spoke, but I couldn't understand her. None of us could. But that was the very idea behind the Spanish Immersion Program — throw kids head first into a difficult situation and they will adapt.

The Immersion Program was only available through grade five, but language continued to fascinate me. Before a trip to Europe with my high school orchestra, I taught myself enough French and German to order food and ask for directions. This wasn't required (we had local guides) and no one else did this (except my friend Jordan, whose shared enthusiasm created a nice feedback loop of motivation between the two of us). For most of the 200 students on that trip it was our first time abroad. We were all awe-struck by the towering cathedrals, quaint cobblestone streets, and interesting new cuisines. However, I unmistakably felt that even though we all were just barely scratching the surface of what these countries had to offer, my broken attempts at communicating with locals allowed me to go just a bit deeper than my peers who didn't know another language, or made no attempt to use what knowledge they did have. Most students studied a foreign language in high school because it is required. I studied them because I wanted to connect with people who were different from myself.

Even though I loved languages, I never saw them becoming anything more than a hobby. As I progressed through high school, I had many fleeting obsessions. At one point or another, I was convinced that I would go on to study music composition, architecture, or mathematics. I took my first physics course senior year of high school and within a month I knew that this was what I wanted to dedicate my life to. For one of our first experiments, we were given a spring-loaded device that shot a tiny metal ball. We shot the ball straight up and measured the height it reached, which allowed us to calculate its initial velocity. The challenge was to then use this number and the formula for projectile motion to predict where the ball would land if we shot it at an angle. I adjusted the device to a 37° angle on the table, performed the calculations, and placed a small plastic cup roughly 10 feet away on the floor. I pulled the trigger, and as if by magic, the ball sailed across the classroom and landed directly in the cup. "Wow," I thought, "If physics can predict this, what can't it solve?"

I chose to continue my education at The University of Maryland, in large part because of the school's focus on research. I didn't want to just sit in classes for four years; I wanted to get started as early as possible contributing to scientific progress. I was very fortunate to receive such an opportunity during my first year at The Joint Quantum Institute.

A typical university research lab might have two or three graduate students with one or two professors to oversee the project. Our lab had over a dozen people all working towards the same goal — to build a quantum supercomputer (or at least the beginnings of one). This was a very ambitious project and was really a collection of three distinct phases. I was tasked with the first (and simplest) phase. My job was to build a machine and write software that would take a fiber optic cable and stretch it out with a specific taper down to a thickness of 500 nanometers at its center (roughly 300 times thinner than the width of a human hair). These fibers were then transferred to another table where the optics team would shine red light through one end of the fiber and blue light through the other. As the light travelled towards the center of the tapered fiber it reached a point where the width of the fiber was less than the wavelength of light. At this point the light extended through the walls of the fiber creating an evanescent field in which the team trapped a handful of rubidium atoms. The fiber and atoms were then transferred to our half-million dollar freezer capable of reaching a few millionths of a degree above absolute zero (-459° F). This slowed the atoms down enough so that they could 'talk' with the quantum computer chip.

What excited me most about this project turned out not to be the physics, but rather the amazing collaboration that took place amidst our team. We had some of the brightest minds in each field working together, and what we were able to achieve was truly amazing, despite the fact that fewer than half of us spoke English as our native language. My mentor, Luis, came from México and was an expert in optics. Zaeill came from Korea and was in charge of the final stage with the freezer. One of our brilliant graduate students, Sylvain, came from France. We also had collaborators from Germany, China, Russia, and other countries who were all instrumental to the project.

As a language nerd, I absolutely loved this environment. I enjoyed hearing the mix of accents at our meetings. When someone made an error in his speech, I wouldn't judge him or think it was funny, but I would rather contemplate what might be different about his native language that makes him see the world this way. I recall the day we were all sitting around the conference table heatedly discussing a heavy aspect of our project and I was struck by the magnitude of what we were trying to accomplish. As I listened to all the different voices, I realized that this project was possible mostly due to one key facet — all of our foreign colleagues at one point in their lives had had access to quality and affordable language education.

I loved physics, but I needed to more seriously start exploring this other infatuation, which had been a part of my life for so long. My personal mission has been to creatively contribute to the technological and cultural progress of human civilization. I latched on to physics in high school as my best option for fulfilling this objective, but the experience in the lab showed me that there might be another path on which I could more effectively pursue my purpose. No significant progress takes place in isolation. Each human has their own unique gifts and when we combine these talents in a spirit of harmonious collaboration, our potential expands exponentially. Since language is the primary medium for collaboration, it was now clear to me that this was my best leverage point for advancing scientific and cultural progress.

I didn't know where to start, but I figured the answer probably didn't lie within my own country, where most people already speak my native language. So I packed my bag and took off. I spent that first summer teaching English at a children's camp in Russia. I had been enjoying the experience so much that I gave no thought as to what would come next. On the day my visa expired, I showed up at Sheremetyevo airport and said, "Give me the cheapest ticket abroad that leaves today." That landed me in Latvia, from where I started hitchhiking around Europe for a couple of months. When my bank account had nearly reached zero, I used all my frequent flyer miles for a free ticket to Tokyo.

After landing, I spent the last of my financial resources on a sushi dinner and one night in a hostel, leaving me to sleep in the park for the following two weeks while I tried to figure out how I would support myself. Fortunately, Japan is one of the safest countries I know and the weather in Tokyo in September is quite favorable to sleeping outside. It is also home to some of the most hospitable people I've ever met. The elderly Japanese woman who ran the hostel where I had stayed offered to let me borrow a blanket until I worked something out.

My strategy for eating mainly involved scavenging hostel kitchens for groceries left by guests who had recently checked out. Occasionally I'd be hanging out in McDonald's using the free wifi and someone would strike up a conversation. After we built some rapport, I would humbly admit that I was broke and ask if they wouldn't mind buying me a coffee and cheeseburger. I vividly recall one lady, Yuko, who bought me a generous meal several days in a row. She claimed that she was happy to do so in exchange for the English practice, but I think she secretly wanted to score a green card. I was too hungry to care.

My streak of homelessness eventually came to an end when I became acquainted with a business tycoon, Aki, who had recently purchased an old building and wanted to convert it into a long-term guesthouse for backpackers. He agreed to let me sleep there in exchange for spending several hours each week renovating the place. In addition to being a serial entrepreneur, Aki also consulted for several large Japanese companies, and so he connected me with their top executives who wanted to practice English. He gave me an iPhone and said, "Sometimes the phone will ring. If you are free and want to meet with someone, answer it." In a matter of days I had gone from eating whatever abandoned food I could find in hostel kitchens, to dining in world-class restaurants multiple times a week, all in exchange for holding conversations in my native language.

After three months my Japanese visa also came to an end, and it was time to decide what to do next. If six months of vagabonding had taught me anything, it was that I certainly wasn't ready to return to my home country. I was, however, ready to settle down somewhere for a while and start focusing on some larger projects. I chose Russia, to both leverage my existing language skills as well as continue to improve them. I settled on Moscow because I already had a strong network there.

I started honing my teaching skills by offering private and group lessons. Finding the available teaching resources to be inadequate, I started to develop my own curriculums. After a year of this, my schedule and classrooms were both full, but I still had a desire to help more people. So I began hiring and training teachers from the United States and organizing their travel and accommodations in Russia. That business grew steadily for a few years, but there were still limits to growth. I had started by helping a couple hundred people, and I was now reaching thousands of students each year. Growing to ten thousand would be a challenge, but certainly possible. A hundred thousand? Maybe. One million? Probably not. And there was no way that my current business model could ever bring quality and affordable language education to any significant percentage of the world's population.

I realized that the only way I would ever scale to reach as many people as I wanted was by leveraging technology. I had some experience programming from my days in physics, but nothing as deep as I would need to make my vision a reality. So I moved back to the United States and have been spending the last several years honing my technical and entrepreneurial chops in the startup capital of Silicon Valley. I still feel that there is so much to learn about software, business, and language. Yet, after a decade of experience and exploration since I entered my first physics lab, I am finally approaching the point where I can leave the classroom known as 'someone else's business'.

In order to efficiently teach a foreign language, it's imperative to take into account the student's native language. The biggest fault I see with most existing educational software is that they use a cookie-cutter approach to writing curriculums — teaching the same thing in the same order with the same emphasis placed on each common difficulty. Each language is a model of reality, a viewpoint unique to each culture, and it is useful for a teacher to understand how two models of reality are likely to conflict in a student's head. It is my aspiration to build this kind of thinking into educational software, adapting to and even predicting each student's individual needs.

Ignite Action Steps

Undertake to travel: Isaac Watts in his 1885 book *Improvement of the Mind* advises: "Acquaint yourself therefore sometimes with persons or parties which are far distant from your common life and customs: this is a way whereby you may form a wiser opinion of men and things."

I learned a great deal in college, both from formal instruction as well as through informal observation and conversation. Even though the College Park campus is only two hours south of my hometown of Lancaster, Pennsylvania, it provided a greater diversity of minds and personalities than I had ever encountered during my first 18 years of life. Still, my years spent traveling and living abroad did more in terms of opening my mind to new possibilities than time spent in lecture halls, research labs, and late-night dorm room jam-sessions.

Strike up unlikely conversations: My experiences also taught me that I can learn from anyone, even those, who by all standard measures, are less 'successful' than myself. During an overnight layover in Brussels, I decided to head downtown and check out the city. I passed a homeless man begging for change. As I walked away, I heard him curse in Russian. Only a year into my studies, I still jumped at any opportunity to practice my conversation skills. So I whirled around and fumbled for the right words, "Hey dude, I don't have any cash, but if I buy us a bottle of vodka with my card do you want to hang out for a bit?" He flashed a toothless grin followed by a resounding, *"Да, конечно!"*

Sitting on the sidewalk, I found out that Arsik had initially come to Belgium from Latvia for an operation, which the doctors messed up, leaving him crippled and in too much debt to return home. Despite his unfortunate circumstances, he never once complained, but rather focused on all the things he enjoyed in life. At one point his radio died. He picked it up and proudly handed it to me for examination. As I turned the crank, the radio came back to life. "Ah," he sighed in Russian. "I can't live without music!"

During our six hours together, I learned more from Arsik about life than I had from some of my professors in an entire semester. These lessons became available to me only because I had decided that I was willing to learn from him. When we think we know everything, we close off our minds to receiving new information.

*Transcend language: Paulo Coelho beautifully articulates one of my favorite aspects of travel in his story *The Alchemist*: "He walked slowly through the market. The merchants were assembling their stalls, and the boy helped a candy seller to do his. [...] When the stall was assembled, the candy seller offered the boy the first sweet he had made for the day. The boy thanked him, ate it, and went on his way. When he had gone only a short distance, he realized that, while they were erecting the stall, one of them had spoken Arabic, and the other Spanish. And they had understood each other perfectly well."

When I participated in this kind of interaction myself for the first time, I chalked it up to rational explanations, such as being able to decipher meaning through body language and vocal inflection. As this happened more and more, however, I began to wonder if there was something else going on. I only speak ten words of Thai, and driving my moped between rural mountain towns in northern Thailand I encountered almost exclusively people who didn't know any English. During those travels I learned that the more present I am in my interactions with other humans, the more deeply we are able to understand each other – even if we share zero linguistic commonalities. In those instances where I really connected with someone – joking and laughing together, each in our own tongue – it felt as if we were tapping into a universal language, one which transcends words.

"There must be a language that doesn't depend on words," the boy in Coelho's story continues to think as he ambles about the market. "I've already had that experience with my sheep and now it's happening with people. If I can learn to understand this language without words, I can learn to understand the world."

In my story about the physics lab I wrote that "language is the primary medium of communication." Is it the primary medium because it is the *best* medium? Or rather, is there another language which transcends our human languages, with all their words and grammar? A language which we have all forgotten how to speak? I am passionate about uniting the human race by leveraging technology to improve language education. I am equally passionate about learning languages myself as a means of getting to know other people and cultures, as well as learning to transcend these languages as a means of getting to know the universe.

Austin Wood - USA
www.austin.bio

VLADIMIR GONTKOVIC

"Go for it. Have a multi-color and diverse life."

Many of us are afraid to change societal stereotypes, whether it is to prioritize the career of our wife or consider the option to go for paternity leave. I hope to encourage all men to make unconventional decisions when it is best for your family as a whole, instead of just for you. Life can be a much greater and adventurous experience if you open up to all the colors it offers. Allow yourself to learn, to understand your wife and kids better. Everybody wants just one thing – to be happy. What about stereotypes and perception? Don't be bothered. Choose what is best for you. Everything can wait, your relationships and fatherhood can't.

MAN, BE EXCITED ABOUT BECOMING A DADDY!

When I was small, I spent my two months of my summer holiday with my grandparents on their farm. I loved it. So, I traveled there regularly.

My grandfather was born in the pre-antibiotic age in 1912 in Austro-Hungarian monarchy and died in the 2004 internet age in Slovakia. He was the youngest of nine children. During his life he lived in one geographical place but endured five legal forms of state during the 20th century. He survived two world wars. He had one wife, three children and six grandchildren. His life was strongly predetermined by family, the Catholic religion and common village habits. He worked in the surrounding woods at a sawmill. His job was to fell the trees, chop firewood and transport building timbers to the sawmill. In addition, he farmed his own land. His was the sole breadwinner.

His wife, my grandma, never had a regular job. She worked at home as a mother of three helping her husband on their farm. I remember they had a horse, cow, sheep, pigs, rabbits, chickens, one dog and many cats. The farm was not huge but in my child's eyes I perceived it to be big. With the villages, people and houses were spread out. In the 1700s, parcels of land were rectangular resulting in narrow, long fields. It took one hour to walk to the end of my grandparents' farm.

My grandparents lived nearly all their lives in the same village, Zdiar, in the mountains on the border between Slovakia and Poland. There were cold winters and short summers. Wolves, bears and other wild animals lived in the surrounding woods. Their village was founded in the 16th century, then covered by forest. During the next centuries people cultivated land and lived in small isolated communities. Their water source was a narrow mountain river running through the village, also used for sawing the wood. Their village was seven kilometers long, hilly and had several valleys. Life in this part of the country was hard but people were very proud. Strong rules and morals helped them survive. Isolated, the people developed their own language – a local dialect, which is a mix of Slovak and Polish. People from this region appearing on national TV need a translator or subtitles for the rest of the country. This region also has beautiful and richly decorated national costumes. They are still used for special occasions and religious saints-days.

I loved to spend my summer holidays there. I was free and adored by my grandparents. I liked their animals, the farm and appreciated the village life. I loved to hide in the barn and enjoy making a nest in the soft freshly packed hay. I remember sunny meadows full of colorful mountain flowers. We took day trips to the woods searching for and harvesting berries or mushrooms; talking about everything was especially fun. I learned to speak their dialect, which I never saw in a written form.

The isolation also resulted in many families with the same names so special nicknames were devised to easily identify family groups. I still find the practicality of this fascinating. My grandparents had such nickname, too.

On my visits, they both woke up silently, trying not to wake me, and started their workday before sunrise. If he was not working at the sawmill, my grandfather fed the cattle and went to the field with the scythe to cut grass, while morning dew disappeared. Meanwhile, Grandma would be cooking a farm breakfast and often, on the same stove she would be boiling some potatoes with corn for the pigs to help them put on weight. I often had warm milk or cocoa with some bread or eggs for breakfast. Hard work meant heavy meals.

When Grandpa was sawing, Grandma took care of the farm in addition to the house, children and later on, her grandchildren also. On Sundays, they never worked. They attended Catholic mass in the morning and had a rest for the remainder of the day.

In the village, after the Sabbath, I remember the men always did men's work. It could be hard work in the woods, sawmill, farms, work on the country roads reparation or they travelled to nearby towns to work more. My Grandpa never went to shop for food; it was his wife's job. Men worked hard and felt a moral right to engage in enjoyment. For them, it was a local pub, where they could stop for socializing with a drink. Thank God, my Grandpa did not stop there often, but not everybody was like that.

The life of my father was slightly different. He was born during the second world war. He spent his years working in communist Czechoslovakia. My parents, in comparison had a modern urban life, different from my grandparents, which still had its challenges. The role of a man and a woman was not so strictly separated as their parents but still, husbands did men's work and the wives did women's work.

In my family, men had men's patterns and women had women's patterns. When I was small, during the Communist regime, only women could legally take maternity leave. It was a common understanding and nobody doubted nor challenged it. As time passed, ideas were changing.

As a young boy I thought about being a chef, woodsman and even building roads. Later, I studied law, far from my idyllic summer holidays with my grandparents.

When I was accepted to the university, I wanted to become a judge. In the end, I became an advocate, working in one of the best law firms in Slovakia. The job was hard yet fun; I loved it all. I felt free, important, strong and I was following my family's pattern. I was the breadwinner. I wished to do it for the rest of my life. I did what I was good at and what I liked. In this profession, I worked to improve myself in many areas including crisis management communication. Attention to details became a part of my everyday life. This profession gave me the status of "Doctor of Law" and the daily assurance of being rooted in routine. Day by day, week by week, year by year, I loved the structure. Humans in general are inclined to love predictability and stability. Just like me. I am a perfect example of a human who loves routine.

I am from a Catholic country and family where God is important. I am proud of this strong cultural heritage. Based on the environment where I grew up and studied, I formulated my basic values which helps me to make the right decisions in many crucial life situations.

One year after university, I married my lovely wife, Andrejka. We thought we have been programmed to be happy. She always dreamt about an enjoyable and happy life. This led her to work in an international business company, where she had her first boss, an extremely entertaining and smart Englishman. I believed that fun was the main criteria for my wife to accept that job. Soon she understood that business was part of her nature. She was rewarded higher and higher positions in the company. We understood that further professional growth could be possible for her, but options were beyond our small country's borders. At this time, we had our first son Alex, so she took the one-year maternity leave delaying decisions about her career path. After nine months on her maternity leave, she got an offer from headquarters to return to a better job. It would be between one to three years and it was 1000 kilometers away. A big professional opportunity for her; potentially a huge destruction for my professional life and routines. The question arose, what do we do?

As a couple, we have always liked doing things together. We enjoy sports, mutual friends, sharing common ideas and values. We love and admire each other and cultivate our relationship. We discussed this offer seriously, but there were always questions. I depended on routine and now suddenly it was threatened. After years of studying and self-development, should I stop working from one day to another? What will I do? I was afraid to lose all my professional achievements. "What will happen to me as the breadwinner?" Questions driven by the dilemma. It was difficult to find answers.

We talked with our family and friends. They also did not have the answers or the experience because in the last decades of communist Czechoslovakia it was not possible to travel freely for work. We also considered splitting the family for the duration, but it was too long and too far. We knew that a long-distance marriage was not for us.

After some time, I realized, the questions, which I asked myself, were not complete. I forgot to include my wife and son. She is my best friend, the closest part of my life. She was with me when I was building my professional career. She has always cheered me up and has been my biggest fan. Now, we also had a small lovely boy. I realized I should ask questions regarding all of us, when considering our move: "What will we do?' Will we lose everything? How will we make our living?" Bingo! Suddenly, I started to see my future more clearly. My future was part of our future. I could see my values in this. I saw more options. The opportunity for Andrejka to grow in her professional life and for me an opportunity to spend time with my lovely son. I planned my maternity leave. Wow! No previous experience! Fun! Break! Free time! Freedom for my hobbies! Life in a new country, in the Alps and close to Geneva! This idea started to build new positive emotions and new ways to see the man's role, different from the one in which I was brought up. We started changing our opinion and this offer gradually became an opportunity for our whole family. We saw the benefits for each of us. For my wife, it was a work opportunity, which does not come often. It would help her to learn new things and grow professionally. For me it was a sabbatical break, an opportunity to be a father at home with my child, to see him grow. For my son, it was an opportunity to grow in his father's care and to learn another language. Finally, we said yes, and spent two beautiful years living this way.

My boss was unhappy with my decision to temporarily leave the job but understood the situation. She agreed that after my return, I could rejoin the company. She was fair and professional. We organized a couple of good-bye parties, packed and left.

The new country was really different. It was difficult to compare the nice apartment in the old building in the center of Lausanne with our house in Slovakia. Some things were better and some not. Everything was in French. One of the most peculiar things was washing clothes. There were only two washing machines and one dryer for the whole apartment building situated in the basement. There was an assigned time schedule for each resident. Moreover, it was a paid service requiring coins. No coins, no washing. Not enough coins, washing cycles were interrupted. The building was full of foreigners from all over the world with different ideas. Many of them decided to ignore the official washing-time schedule and washed their clothes when the machines were simply not used by anybody else. This turned the washing and drying clothes activities into a fishing exercise. Fish for free washing machines and collect small coins!

On the other hand, there were many benefits to this experience. The town was really nice, the streets were clean, the air was fresh and much better than in other big towns or cities in Europe. There were many creative playgrounds for kids, beautiful mountains and lakes with nice winter ski hills. While the landscape was very picturesque, I found the local people quite reserved and cautious. Even though one quarter of the residents in Switzerland are foreigners, the interaction and relationship between locals and expats were limited. It has been like that for many years and is not really changing. This is the country of referendum, country where women's right to vote was passed only in 1971.

The company my wife works for has its global headquarters in Lausanne. As she enjoyed her new job, her colleagues and our social networks started to grow. We built a new community and started exploring and enjoying this new country.

While my wife became a temporary sole breadwinner, I was looking after our son. Instead of sitting in the office, I became his main life companion. At the beginning he was just one year old. He needed my attention all the time. He was approximately 10 kilograms and 80 centimeters. He was easy to pack and transfer anywhere. At the end of my full-time parenting, he was 15 kilograms and 100 centimeters. Today, he is 16 years old and taller than me.

My days were full. I can say, much fuller than in the office. Sometimes I wanted to have a coffee break without anybody talking or requiring my full attention. We created a new daily routine and followed it thoroughly. Breakfast, playing, snack, walking, lunch, afternoon nap, snack, walking, dinner, shower, night, and so on and so on. Very demanding for a man's brain, especially when doing several activities at the same time. On the other hand, it was one of the best times in my life. I felt important, responsible, powerful and a real proud father. We spent a lot of time on playgrounds and walked up and down this hilly town. During the day, we were always together. In the evening, my wife joined us and then we had even more fun. Once I remember, we were doing the shopping and Alex was sitting in the shopping cart. I just trotted away to find something. He did not see me and shouted "Mom, Mom". I answered "Yes, my darling". Then I decided it was the time to teach him a new word, 'Daddy'. I enjoyed the time with my family exploring the country and nature on weekends and holidays. We had time for us.

When we moved back to Slovakia, my wife had expanded her expertise, and on her return, she was promoted. Our son joined a new crowd in kindergarten and I returned to my office. No big changes happened in my professional life during my "fatherly sabbatical". A new colleague came, and some old ones left but I had not missed anything major. I jumped into the everyday assignments and problems as life continued smoothly. I was absolutely sure that it was the right decision to have spent some time with my son while he was little instead of solving endless law cases. I have beautiful memories forever.

My paternity leave was a great experience and adventure and also perfectly timed. Before, I was afraid of what people would say if a man stays at home and his wife works. I was afraid I would forget what I had learned. I was afraid whether I could manage the gap and the return. These worries disappeared. I went for it, not letting doubts dictate my choices and actions. Society is changing. With me being firm and comfortable about my decision, people around me accepted it and we all benefited. My previous professional knowledge and skills were strong enough and I could jump back into my job without any problems. Comparing my professional job with looking after kids, I can confidently say that taking care of them is much harder and never-ending. It is one of the most difficult jobs in the world. I strongly recommend it. With changing roles, one also changes and opens up a new perspective.

Thanks to my wife, I could experience it. Thank you Andrejka.

If you have an opportunity to change your life, don't hesitate because it will open your eyes and create a wonderful new perspective. Break free of your routines. Be committed to your family in every way. Find the courage to do what will benefit everyone, and you will never regret it. You will have fantastic memories for life.

Ignite Action Steps

If you have an option to participate in raising your kids, do not hesitate. Go for it full speed. You will never regret it. It will open your eyes, widen your horizons and deepen your heart. If you have a family, look at the time spent with them as an opportunity to invest your time, care and love.

Put all your decisions in the family context, the huge rewards will come. Do not think just about you and your future. Build the future with and for your whole family. Do not be afraid. Nature will lead the way and you will learn it on the go. Your kids will give you so much in return. They will show you how they see the world in all its beauty. It is so amazing and so much fun to see your children grow, learn to walk and speak. These days this pleasure can be shared between both women and men.

Vladimir Gontkovic - Slovak Republic
Lawyer living in Prague

Bryce Malli

"Fear is energy we squander when it could be used to grow."

Mental health and suicide have a stigma attached to them. The pain and suffering I put myself through was because we, as a society, do not talk about them. It is my honest intention to do my part to open up this topic for conversation and invite others to understand more about mental health and suicide.

Rebirth of Self

I stood at the edge, looking down, hoping, wishing I was strong enough to let go.

I have had bipolar depression since I was a young boy. My earliest experience began when I was 10. I remember playing with my toys, finding joy in the simple act of indulgent creation. I built worlds out of bricks, made up stories for the sheer enjoyment of it. There were fantastical voyages in realms both familiar and alien. Heroes from the books I had read, or movies I had watched, having adventures in the saccharine, cliche riddled stories of my young mind.

And then...the next day I was staring at the ceiling, the joy of idle creation gone. I tried to pretend to do it. I pretended to play pretend with the stories which had once entertained me. I made the figurine climb over mountains of bricks, defeating whatever monsters were there. But gone were the heroes, now just shapes of plastic. That spark was snuffed out when I was not paying attention. There one moment and gone the next. The worlds

I created stopped *being* and were now toys just scattered on the floor.

I still remembered the stories I had made, but the sense of wonder and adventure was missing. The color had leached from my memories. I was unable to bring myself to do anything; everything seemed so pointless and trivial. I laid on the floor staring up at the ceiling fan, watching the blades spin slowly. While I kept circling the same problem, the same issue... I realized something was wrong with me. I felt a great emptiness, a great loss, something I could not articulate, something was clearly wrong.

Was this what growing up was like? I questioned. Did I put away such childish things without any choice of my own? I remember rather distinctly, going to my mother while she was working in her office, a cramped space with a laptop perpetually half buried under papers. I stood at the door way, staring at the floor, unable to articulate or even understand what was wrong, and merely, silently hugged her, mourning the death of this part of myself.

I do not know what happened to that boy, who once played with toys. Faint echoes of memories still rattle around in my mind of the laughter I once possessed then lost. I remember many a morning waking in my bed and lying there wondering why I had to wake up. I did not want to deal with everything else that followed. I wanted to stay asleep permanently. A longing for non-being, I did not know the name for it then.

I found a semblance of sanctuary in video games. Of course, I was called lazy, seeking solace and escape in the bright colors and 'Skinner Box' like sense of fulfillment that comes from video games. They allowed me for short periods, to ignore the hollowness inside. Video games offered a small slice of oblivion in order to silence my unquiet mind, but I did not 'enjoy' them. Whenever I finished playing them, I found I only lamented the hours wasted... I merely enjoyed moments when I could forget myself and not *be* me

In boarding school, I did no better. I always felt distinctly apart from my peers. I could play the part of the child, but everything else felt hollow. I struggled to make and maintain friendships, a fault pointed out to me many years later by a friend in college. One of my closest friends at the time, said she had no idea what I enjoyed. In truth, she did not know because I did not know.

I took no true pleasures in life, just going with the flow, be it hanging out with friends or even possible romantic interests. I struggled to enjoy anything. It is a curious thing in our culture. Back in boarding school I consumed media and found out about suicide. I understood its meaning and implications. Every single piece of information pretty much said the same thing. Suicide is wrong, it is bad, it is the worst of the worst. To an impressionable child who has had these dark thoughts for many years, it is perhaps not the best message to tell them. I now *knew* I was broken and people hated that broken part. Even more, people refused to understand or comprehend it. It was a subject one could not even approach obliquely. Nothing kills conversations quite like the term suicide.

The lesson I learned was if I admitted I harbored such dark thoughts, I would very quickly find myself in an asylum. Books and movies only showed the worst of what would happen to me there: white walls, padded rooms, enforcing hug jackets you cannot escape from. I wanted none of that.

In school, my teachers considered me a frustrating student. In Chemistry class I told my professor I had not done the assigned homework and apologized, ready to accept my punishment and move on. I expected the usual disparaging comment and I could go back to sitting quietly at my desk. Instead he went through my folder, found the worksheet in question and realized that I had completed it. He then explained to my parents I had an organization problem. He had no idea what dark thoughts dwelled within me.

My English teacher, at a later time, pulled me aside one day. She told me I was 'coasting', that I was capable of more. She was a teacher I respected a great deal, one of the few who told me to pursue writing. I protested my innocence but the unfortunate truth was, she was right. I *was* coasting. I was called lazy, idle, indolent. But it is hard to put any effort or energy into a task when you did not want to be alive in the first place. I was fine with that. Coasting meant lowered expectations, which meant less annoying, prying questions. I was content to coast, the minimal effort necessary to avoid repercussions. Enough to pass, but not too much that the bar was raised.

I survived for a time like that, just keeping my head down and running out the clock on this whole 'life' thing. Then, perhaps I grew too complacent, let my mask slip too much, made the wrong nihilistic joke at my own expense. I was put on suicide watch at school. I remember feeling insulted and angered by it. Telling myself that there is a vast gulf of difference between thinking about the act and carrying it out. I had dealt with those tempting thoughts and feelings for five years alone, by that point. I did not want attention, I just wanted to be left alone. Now I had to deal with well meaning, awkward conversations from people who did not know what I was going through.

I suffered through annoying questions asking 'how I felt' knowing full well I could not explain how I felt and still expect to be treated like I was sane. The moment I so much as admitted, "Yeah, I fantasize about leaping in front of a bus and greeting the sweet embrace of oblivion," meant I would lose whatever limited freedom I had as a child. There would be doctors, therapists, pills, none of which I wanted. If I still wanted to be treated as a person, as a human being and not some sort of china doll, I had to deal with it myself.

That is the unfortunate truth of this problem. Mental health is an alien subject to many. People do not know how to react or deal with it. Suicidal thoughts make it doubly so. I needed someone on my level, someone who could make nihilistic jokes with me. A therapist might have been able to do that if I could have found a good one.

By now, however, I had spent half a decade alone with my suicidal thoughts, we were old friends. They brought comfort, they were always there. No matter how hard things became I could retreat into them, nihilism became a safety blanket. The small cruelties and dramas of life did not seem quite so bad when they were weighed in comparison to the unrelenting void of oblivion. I did not want someone to take that away from me.

My darkest moment came when I was 17, already in university. The fatalistic whispers were becoming much louder and harder to ignore. I found myself rapidly approaching the logical conclusion. The sweet release of oblivion was looking to be more and more tantalizing with the mounting expectations and stuff I had to deal with. More forms I had to fill out to get things like financial aid or meals, more and more expectations of me to deal with, to care about.

Suffice to say I was not doing well. Leaving the rigid structure of boarding school and moving to the new freedoms of university did not serve me well. I was flunking out. I was also lying through my teeth about it because I did not want to deal with any drama. I still did not want to even be alive, let alone go to university. The only reason I went was because it was expected - because to not go would have required more energy.

I remember the car ride back to the dorms. My mother was driving. I was not in a good mood. Not angry, just empty, shallow, tired, petty, cruel...

To this day, I do not know why I said it. Whether some part of me wanted to inflict a petty hurt. Or if I was on the ledge, desperately trying to find a handhold. Maybe a mixture of both. Was I was hoping she would whisk me away and make things better?

I told her that I did not want to be alive. She did nothing. No shouting. No spiriting me away to doctors, therapists and the like. She remained calm, but I could hear the hurt in her voice regardless, as she told me she loved me very much. Then she hugged me. I went back to the dorms confused and numb, yet, internally relieved.

She later told me she cried the whole way home, not sure if she would see me alive again, but knew in her heart of hearts that this was something I had to face myself. She was right, of course, mothers rather infuriatingly are.

I found myself standing on the bridge overlooking the river. Staring at the rushing water, metal still warm from the sun, feeling the dusty air tantalizingly pushing me. And me, wishing I could just let go. If I could just let go. I would not have to feel tired, not tired from exhaustion, tired from life, lacking the energy to get up in the morning. I would not have to feel so hollow anymore. Nor would I spend so much time and energy playing the part of a *not-suicidal person* to my friends and family.

If I let go s*ome poor bastard's gunna have to fish my bloated corpse out.* It was an odd thought, not one I had thought about before. *Maybe weights?* I questioned.

Bodies rot, someone's gunna find 'Me-soup' eventually. Not the first time I had talked to myself. But perhaps for the first time, the conversation went on for so long, I finally lost the argument. But Only Temporally.

I had other thoughts. Hanging myself would be obvious, everyone would know I committed suicide, which would cause more pain than if I died from some form of accident. Stepping out into traffic would just traumatize whoever ran me over and there was no guarantee it would do the job. I could just wind up in a hospital which means forms I would have to fill out, crying people to deal with, and being in America, a large amount of medical debt.

In every idea I had, I found holes. I could not find a way of disentangling myself from the world without causing more harm than just suffering through it. It is an asinine truth that suicide moves the pain from the victums to the surviors. Before, I found it petty, patronizing, along the lines of, 'Finish your plate, don't you know there are children starving?!' Asinine or not, it is still the truth. I decided in that moment not to let go.

It was a fairly long walk back to the dorms, but I found myself back in bed nonetheless. A ghost of a spark ignited in me. I realized that I had to make a change. The fear I would somehow lose my free will, my humanity, by admitting to someone something was wrong was unfounded. I had wasted too much time and energy in fear of this perceived threat. I would knuckle down, do the right thing, and maybe feel better about this whole 'life' thing.

And so, I went to a psychiatrist. Which was the best/worst decision of my life. I was prescribed Zoloft. The doctor gave it to me like she was prescribing something for a cold. It all seemed so mundane. Like I had fooled myself into worrying about playing with my brain chemistry. It was just a small pill that promised to cure my depression.

In a form it did. The form it took was that I felt nothing. Not even the hollowness of depression. I... felt...nothing. I thought nothing and I became nothing at the thought of feeling and thinking nothing. I was a walking zombie. That sweet release of oblivion that seemed to beckon me for so long had embraced me, a small death of self.

I should have been happy, this is what I wanted. This is what I enjoyed about video games. I wanted to be free of being me and was granted it. I am thankful I was only in that hell for a few months. The prescription ran out and I did not find time to refill it. When I came out of that waking nightmare, for the first time, in a long time...I was happy.

I cried and laughed. A veil lifted from my mind. When I left that zombie-like doldrum, I realized I wanted to be myself. I wanted to be me over wanting *the sweet release of oblivion* as I now jokingly refer to it. For the first time, since I was 10, I was happy being me. It was after that time I took up writing again, rediscovering the joy of creating stories and worlds. Creating for the sake of it with a sense of wonder I had long since lost.

But alas, one does not win against a mental illness that easily. I am far from cured. But unlike before, I am willing to fight for it now. The truth of my story is this, I needed my mother to do nothing, though I am sure it pained her to no end. A part of me will always regret I had to inflict that cruelty upon her, but as she told me, it was a lesson I needed to learn. I needed her to do nothing so I understood my life was my own, not just acting to someone else's expectations. I needed to retain my autonomy so I could make my own mistakes, experience that little death of self, and reemerge able to love myself again.

Life can be cruel and strange, but without being able to love yourself, it is unbearable. Life saw fit I should lose the little boy I once was. I spent years as a ghost of myself, going through the motions. I do not know what that little boy might have become, what his hopes and dreams might have been. All I know is that spark died with him. Years later, a new spark ignited. Perhaps that boy one day went to sleep, only to wake up seven years later, older, hopefully wiser; one who hopes he will wake up others who may have lost themselves and want to ignite the spark within.

Ignite Action Steps

Talk to yourself, sometimes you need an expert's opinion on you. You have more experience being you than anyone else after all.

*To start, find somewhere you can be alone, preferably with white noise.

*Close your eyes, turn off the lights and just focus on the sounds around you. Let it fill you, let it drown out the voice in your head. Focus and be at peace being alone with yourself. Every time a thought comes unbidden, refocus on the sounds around you until it fades away. Slowly, relax, let the drama of life fade. Let yourself breathe.

*Now, in the silence of your mind, ask yourself a question and allow the answers to come. Do not ignore them, do not shy away from them. Let your thoughts wash over you, there are no wrong answers. Do not cling to them if they comfort you. Do not shy from them if they hurt, Listen to each of them

*When the answers stop coming, take a deep breath and examine all of them. Some will be comforting lies, some will be half truths, some you will not want to look at. *But all of them will tell you things you need to know about yourself.*

Bryce Malli - USA
Millenihilistic Writer
Mobiusgames.us

CRISTIAN AGAFI

*"A true warrior is forged out of the painful depths
of his past limited self."*

I hope my story will help you realize that you are so much more powerful than you believe. That having the courage to face your shadows will allow you to take your power back; power you were born with but forgot you have. The world has been waiting for you to become who you are meant to be. Shine brightly, authentically, unapologetically and let your light inspire everyone.

BEING MARRIED TO AN AWAKENED WOMAN

Madalina and I were having dinner at one of our favorite Cabo restaurants. It was our time. To be, to connect. We love Cabo – endless beach walks, horseback rides along the Sea of Cortez, sunset cruises at The Arch and sunbathing on Lovers' Beach. Every year we take a trip, no matter what. It's our relationship-building tradition. We intentionally set this habit from the beginning of our marriage to keep things fun and spicy. With the kids safe at home with trusted grandparents, we were relaxed, having fun, sipping cocktails and eating amazing food while a live band played on stage. Life was good, the night was young.

We were discussing our favorite topic – us. Reflecting on our struggles, the lessons, and successes leading us to this moment. Rejoicing in our personal growth, we looked ahead with hope and curiosity. These conversations were fun, yet I felt uncomfortable. Madalina would light up talking about personal growth and future potential. She had grown so much. She was truly an awakened, conscious woman. Her level of self-awareness was a wide net through which no unconscious action passes. Her higher self, reaching the boundless edges of the Spiritual Universe, where no man has dared to go before. Her sacred femininity filled with universal light, was a place I wanted to bask in forever.

My discomfort came from the fact that my personal growth was nowhere near hers. I did not feel as awakened. My self-awareness was a loose net rarely catching any familial patterns. My higher self, a myth deeply buried under dark shadows, a place filled with fear, shame and guilt. My sacred warrior masculinity – never heard of it.

Madalina's journey started with physical pain. She'd push her running, competing with only herself. She had applied the same attitude to her cardiology career, pushing through the wall, pressuring herself. A 'Yes' person, she climbed the career ladder ever higher. At what cost? Running one day, her body gave out. A sudden back pain forced her to limp home. She jumped from expert to expert, looking for 'the pill', the answer, the fix. The pill *was* a message; her body communicating, asking, begging her to change. She accepted her life had become unfulfilled. She then healed herself by going within. She was a product of her patterns. Pain motivated her to shine the light into the darkness of her unconscious. Her anguish reflected the gap between the authentic true self and the false self-created by patterns and limiting beliefs.

She had physical pain. Mine on the other hand was emotional – a gap between the true and false self was a wide crevasse. The depth reflected my perceived inability to break free from unconscious patterns I knew I had – but the fear of facing my shadow paralyzed me.

I felt frustrated. I couldn't connect with her on the same level or, rather, she couldn't connect with me on her level. Often my frustration turned into worry. Worried she would grow impatient with me, our paths would diverge, and we'd end up estranged, separated, another statistic. My fear was performing a balancing act on the thin line between her words, "I will always love you" and "I am not attached to any particular outcome." What does that even mean? I was too terrified to ask for clarification.

For some reason, personal growth felt like turning the Titanic on a river. It felt painful and slow, always opposed by a strong familial current, a relentless inertia. No matter how hard I tried, it seemed like I always reverted back to what felt familiar. Wounded memories crept up like little creatures lurking in the shadows of my unconscious, whispering stories, judgements, all based on fear. These voices projected my past onto my present reality. I was a lifeless puppet. The puppeteer was my subconscious.

My dad was a diplomat; my mom a physician. My entire childhood revolved around strict protocols of how I was expected to behave. I had to display a constant 'proper image,' be well mannered in every interaction. I did not have a clue what it meant to 'be myself,' since anything other than the expected was considered 'disobedience.' I recall when I was three years old, when my father was stationed in Cyprus, my mother took me with her to a brunch with other wives of diplomats. Sitting at the table, all eyes scrutinizing me, my mother leaned down to remind me, "...eat nicely." I remember the pressure I felt, afraid of making a mistake. At the end of the meal, around my plate was spotless, no crumbs and my hands were completely clean since I used the utensils properly. My mother was very proud of me and all the women were very impressed.

Now, as an adult, as a father, when my own kids run around with abandon and scream freely, my shadow comes out and whispers, "This is not ok, they have to be quiet, they cannot make so much noise." At the dinner table, it's an effort to restrain myself from yelling, "Eat nicely, use your utensils, don't be messy."

All I wanted was to be free. To choose my own feelings. To have control over the stories playing in my head; to act instead of react. I wanted to be free to be me. Instead, it felt like I was trying to move forward but kept in place by a heavy anchor. Progress was an immense effort for me. What made things worse was the perception that, while I was sweating and growling, pulling this heavy chain, my wife was effortlessly skipping around me like a little girl, and having so much fun doing it. For instance, we went to a mindful meditation. After, Madalina, glowing from the depth of her experience asks, "How was it for you?" Clearly the opposite – how frustrating.

That night, however, at the restaurant in Cabo, frustration visited my wife, and I was in her sights. I felt in danger, my very existence threatened. I knew this feeling all too well. It was not the first time I was in her crosshairs. I felt it in my body. I knew what was coming and it wasn't good. But I had a strategy. After all, my ego was creative and adaptable. I had had this conversation with her before and had learned her language. I could speak it fluently enough to come across as knowing what I'm talking about. Of course, I could talk a good talk but when it came to action, I lacked sorely. There was a gap between my burning desire to take control of my life and my belief in myself: the belief I could change. That evening my talk was cheap, my words transparent. Anxiety was building in my heart and I felt a tightening in my chest. The conversation was not going well. She let her hands slide out of mine as she leaned back against the chair and with a sense of disappointment, "I don't know how this is going to work out," she shared. I asked her what was going on, as if I didn't know. She proceeded to explain her frustration with me, her disappointment and even resentment towards me for not stepping up and being the partner she wanted, the man she deserved.

I did not have the energy anymore to keep up the pretense. The truth was that I was tired of myself as well. She shared with me how she felt we were moving in opposite directions and she was losing faith in our relationship. She even brought up the "S" word – separating for a while and how that might be a good idea to explore. It was hard to hear those words. I realized that the more uncomfortable something feels, the more rooted in truth it is. I had been hiding, telling myself and her that "I was doing my best," inside knowing well enough, I was barely trying. It's not that I didn't want to do the work to improve myself – I truly did not believe I could change.

Madalina was the master of change. She consistently puts 150% into the application of everything we learn. If she read some strategy or life-hack that would bring her closer to her vision, the next day she had a year-long plan of how she would implement everything she had learned to move her in that direction.

She'd say to me, with a snap of her fingers, "You can make any change just like that." The snap particularly annoyed me. It was the perfect antithetic visualization for how I was staying stagnant in my personal growth. I would defend myself by saying, "We're different people; you can change just like that, but not me." Every time I thought those words, they were religiously followed by Henry Ford's quote: "Whether you think you can, or you think you can't – you're right." My perceived inability to change, to become better, set me on a path of victimization. I threw so many pity-parties in my honor, I became an expert.

That night, after dinner, we took a long, silent walk on the beach. The full moon hung in the night sky as our only light source, guiding our steps through the calm evening waves. We sat down on the sand and watched the sea sparkle in twilight. Everything became a metaphor – the moon was the guiding light, the sand was the uncertain path ahead, the waves reminded of their consistent nature and their potential energy. Something was changing inside. An inner storm was brewing, electrifying every cell in my body with a desire to go within, to see, to shift, to take control of my own life.

Change was imminent. I had a choice to make remain the same, which clearly would lead to a life of misery, stagnation, victimization, pity parties, and eventually, loneliness. Or, I could take that first step, commit to assuming responsibility for my life – make the changes I knew would bring me closer to my vision. I knew I could become the man I wanted to be for my wife. The father for my kids and the best version of myself, for me. That night, I went to bed full of excitement at the prospect of how my life, our world, would change as a result of my new commitment. In order for my potential to manifest, I had to change first.

I awoke the next morning, my heart filled with hope, ready to start the first day of my new life. I was energized. I wanted change…now! I quickly realized that I had no idea what to do. How do I change? Where do I begin? Familiar voices played havoc in my head, "You really think you can change? Why do you need to change anyway? It's so much work." Previous doubts had me quickly sliding down the rabbit hole of victimization and guilt - again! Luckily, my fall was interrupted by my wife's voice, whispering in my ear, "The way you do one thing is the way you do everything. The way you choose to handle the first step will determine the way you handle the next and the next and eventually your life." I hadn't even said anything out loud. It was my blank stare into nothingness that gave it away.

My biggest mentor was my wife. I didn't tell her, but I decided to read every book she read, practice every technique she practiced – everything from morning affirmations, expressing gratitude, practicing self-forgiveness and so many more. Often times it felt silly and my mind resisted it. But I kept doing them. My car windows closed at the red light, me screaming so loudly, the old couple next to me thought I was crazy. I didn't care, "I am powerful, I'm amazing!" I shouted, "I can do whatever I choose to do, the Universe has my back." In order to grow inside I had to open up by becoming a vulnerable, authentic vision of myself.

First, I had to create a vision of the person I wanted to be, the highest version of myself. Guided by a process devised by my wife, I compiled a list of people I respected. Next to each name, I wrote all the things I admired about them, why they were great, and the reasons I wanted to be like them. The list was a few pages long. As we sat down to go over the list, I felt really good about myself. The same feeling you have when you know you've excelled on a project. She circled and underlined certain words, words I chose to describe these great individuals. At this point I was feeling proud of my work. She turned to me and said, pointing at the highlighted attributes, "All these things – you are not…" My heart dropped in confusion. She paused, "...yet!" she affirmed. "This is who you want to be. This is who you *will* become."

The vision I crafted that day has guided me since. Reading it out-loud every day, I internalized it, practiced it consistently. Soon my life started to shift. I was becoming someone I was not, someone I only dreamed of. It was not easy in the beginning but, with time, many practices became second nature. I learned that it's not enough to want to change. You have to actually embody that change. You have to take the actions that will move you outside your comfort zone. That's where you stretch and grow.

Einstein said, "You cannot solve a problem with the same consciousness that created it." To accelerate my inner growth, I immersed myself in experiences and processes designed to change people fundamentally, such as: 'The Hoffman Process', where I learned to forgive others, and most importantly, myself. 'The Mankind Project', where I learned what it truly means to be a man, not one rooted in ego but one soaring on values such as integrity, authenticity, responsibility and vulnerability.

In the process of healing my relationship with Madalina, I healed myself. In becoming a better father to my children, I mended the bond with my own inner child. While facing my shadows, I realized none of the patterns were mine. They were adopted from my parents, which were adopted from their parents... my life was controlled by a thread of generational patterns. I was able to recognize that the voice whispering, "You are not good enough, you are not worthy," was not mine. The voice came from the struggles of past generations, transmitted unknowingly yet with the best intentions onto me. *I was reliving struggles I had not experienced, from a time I never lived.*

I learned I had the freedom to choose my own truth. As Michelangelo used his chisel to reveal David from the block of stone, equipped with awareness, I started chiseling at my own layers; revealing my true self, in the image that I envisioned. I rejected society's false egoic portrait of man, rooted in insecurities and drawing its so-called power from strife and competition in a zero-sum game. Now, as a man amongst men, I claim my space and hold it sacred. I show up authentically and vulnerable. I do it unapologetically because I am in integrity with my values. I take responsibility for my own thoughts, emotions and actions. Everyone else is responsible for theirs.

Through my journey of awakening, I have learned what it takes to be married to an awakened woman. These attitudes helped me become the man I am today and have truly changed my life. Applied consistently, I have no doubt they can help change yours. I invite you to go within, to do your inner work, to have the courage to face your shadows, so you can be free, free to choose, free to live fully, from your heart. This is the best gift you can give yourself, your partner, your kids and the world.

Ignite Action Steps

*Create a vision.** When you start a new business, you start with an idea. Then you make a plan, set goals and take action. Apply the same formula to your own life.

*Be open and curious.** Suspend any limiting beliefs or judgments you may have and step into your power. Being judgmental toward others and yourself only imprisons you in a self-created box. Open the box, step out, get rid of it. Be free.

*Give 200%.** How can you give more than 100%? Your "100%" is relative. At every point check in with yourself and gauge what your best is at that time. Then, just double your effort. You may not always reach your full potential but, no matter what, you will consistently give more than what you think you can. You get out whatever you put in.

*Get rid of shame.** It's a social construct created to keep people obedient. It is not real nor natural. It doesn't serve you in any way. Let it go.

*You are David.** Hidden under layers of learned patterns. Be your own Michelangelo. Unlearn them, replace them with your own thoughts through daily practices and conscious action. Bring awareness into everything you do.

*Have fun.** Just have fun with life. Play with it!

Being in love with an awakened woman is a risk – there are no places to hide. Being married to an awakened woman is a choice – to have the courage to be authentic and vulnerable. It's hard and beautiful, all at the same time. You will finally experience the love you've been yearning for. You will live the life of your Soul's purpose. Take the risk! Your life will never be the same again!

Cristian Agafi - USA
Co-Founder of heartQ
www.heartq.com

DAVID MCDONNEL

"Dropping the armour we might have needed in our early years is the only path to true freedom and peace."

In writing this story, I came to an even deeper gratitude for being shown the way to love despite my flaws. I want to encourage the readers to not be afraid to show your weaknesses. Find that one person who can stand in your corner to cheer you on and help you find your path to peace.

THE COST OF WINNING

Months of my life were spent gathering and organizing all sorts of documentation. I was consumed by anything that could help justify my desires and strengthen my position in the inevitable upcoming battle. After coordinating with my attorneys to come up with the best plan of action, everything was ready. An unexpected shot was set to be fired across the bow. All I needed to do was give my attorney the word to send the letter that had been meticulously crafted over a good portion of the past year of my life.

I paused and asked the attorney to visualize the next twelve months. What was his best prediction of the events that were about to unfold? As I sat in my home office with a blank stare pointed in the direction of the final draft of the letter taking up most of my computer screen, listening to my attorney explain what my future held in store for me, I realized that I was standing at a major crossroad in my life. I had a choice to make and it was one I never expected to face.

In the not so distant past I seized on opportunities I could benefit from, especially when they also had the ability to make someone else look bad or feel less-than. That was the familiar way and it's what was fueling my plans. But in my pause I began to realize for the first time exactly what the phrase "winning at all costs" really meant and how subjective of a phrase it is.

I'm the youngest of three sons. My brothers are six and eight years older. I now know and appreciate how difficult it was for my mom, the only female in a house of five. I didn't make her job any easier. I had a few different examples of how I thought I should act. What did I need to mimic and what did I need to do differently enough to stand out? As the "baby" and being so much younger, my brothers reminded me how easy I had it growing up. They 'endured' chores and the work and scoffed at my light task load. My dad was a contractor. My brothers, on job sites pulled weeds and swept up sawdust as young as six. I interpreted I was supposed to feel guilty for these things I had been spared. Sarcasm was my defense teasing back, "That must have really sucked for you." I never saw how these interactions were shaping me on the inside. Guilt set in and I felt less than my brothers. I missed this rite of passage they experienced. I hid my guilt. I was the smart one for not having to do it.

Growing up I was closer to my brother Bill, who is the middle son and is six years older than me. We shared a room for most of my childhood while my oldest brother, Allan, always got his own room. In my eyes, Allan was at an entirely different, almost unreachable level of status within the family pecking order. Looking back on things now that I'm forty-seven years old, I realize it was pretty simple – when he was a senior in high school, I was only nine years old. The age gap and the timing of where we each were in life just didn't align very well. On the other hand, Bill was kind of forced into getting close to me. He was my roommate, chauffeur, babysitter and anything else my parents needed him to be if they weren't around. He was my idol and I thought if I could be just half as cool as he was, my life would be great. He was the high school quarterback; the point guard on the basketball team; he was a drummer with the coolest black drum set that took up a huge corner of our living room; he had a killer turntable with huge speakers (it was the '70's and early 80's alright, that was cool back then!) where we'd listen to records of his favorite band, Rush. Guess who my favorite band is and who I went to see play live for my first concert ever. Exactly.

As both my brothers went off to college, I was left to navigate things on my own. I always saw myself following in their footsteps – they both graduated from the same high school and both went on to become a "Tiger" at Louisiana State University, my dad's alma mater. But after Bill graduated from high school, my parents decided to pull me out of that school between sixth and seventh grade to attend a much better school. It was bittersweet for me at the time, but I understood the decision. It became obvious that the school I always saw myself graduating from wasn't the best at preparing kids for college. Both of my brothers struggled getting into college, and my parents wanted better for me. I ended up being sent to a school that had a stellar academic record, so it made perfect sense and I'm so glad I was given that opportunity. What I didn't realize was how much that decision would change how I felt about myself and how it helped shaped my behavior toward others.

My dad was very involved and influential in the school that I was pulled out of, where my brothers graduated from high school. I had been there since kindergarten and although it was a small private school in New Orleans, it was the only thing I knew as a kid, so I thought it was a big deal. I thought my family was a big deal – after all, my dad sat on the board and my brothers were really popular while there. So I got the idea that by default, I was a big deal. When I was in kindergarten, our graduation ceremony included a spelling skit performed by all of the kids in my class. One by one, my classmates walked up to the microphone, dressed in their white gowns and tiny tasseled caps, each holding a poster almost as big as they were with a simple picture and a corresponding word that they proceeded to spell for the proud, smiling parents. Each person said something like this – "I can spell cat, C-A-T, but I cannot spell hippopotamus!", while holding a poster of a cat. After all of my classmates took a turn spelling their word, I walked up to the microphone grinning from ear to ear. I was given the task of spelling hippopotamus, which I did accurately and ever so proudly. That memory was always recalled by my parents in such an innocent and cute way and I enjoyed hearing it every time. Looking back on things now, I realize it is the earliest memory I have that shaped so many unhealthy behaviors in my formative and adult years. My perception was one of being better. I was capable of doing something that no one else in my class could do. That attitude and misguided perception grew stronger and stronger as time went on. I was simply unaware of it as it became my reality.

Being pulled out of that small private school after sixth grade radically changed that perception. In my new school, I was a nobody. An outsider who's now trying to figure out a way to be accepted by classmates that have known each other for years. I was definitely in unfamiliar territory. I soon learned that not only did I not have any friends, but I was also from a part of town that wasn't popular by the other kids' standards. I also quickly learned why my new school prepared kids so well for college – it was tough! I was not nearly as smart as I thought I was. Getting good grades at my old school was easy, but things were radically different at my new school. Since spelling hippopotamus in kindergarten I was always better than everyone else in school, so now what do I do? The coping and defense mechanisms that I employed were sarcasm, ridicule and using every opportunity to cut corners and barely get by. If I became the best at exposing other people's weaknesses, then I'd never really need to deal with my own. It was much easier to hold the mirror up and shine the light on other people's faults, all the while keeping mine in the dark. As time went on, sarcasm and exposing other people's weaknesses became my identity and I proudly displayed them for everyone to see.

I managed to squeak by and graduate from my new school, but along the way had perfected my ability to deflect and overpower others. Opening up honestly and putting my own weaknesses on display to seek help or guidance is something that never even crossed my mind. After all, if I did that, I would become the exact thing I had spent a number of years making fun of and that kind of vulnerability equated to weakness in my mind. I couldn't let anyone think that I'm weak; no way! Looking back now I realize how arrogant and misguided that way of thinking was – I assumed everyone thought the way that I did and couldn't even comprehend the notion that vulnerability and connecting with others to work on your weaknesses was the epitome of strength. The one thing that I wanted to be all along was only possible by opening up to others and exposing my flaws. That concept completely eluded me into my adult years.

My parents couldn't afford to send me to college and for the first time in my life I had to get a real job. My dad and both of my brothers had graduated from college by this time. Yet here I was, a graduate of an exceptional high school, the place that was going to better prepare me for something that was a struggle for my brothers, and it was out of my reach. All of my classmates were headed off to some of the best universities in the country, and I was working night-shifts at a grocery store. This did not fit into what my picture of success was and I was many years away from understanding that wherever you are is exactly where you need to be. Instead of appreciating it and looking for the lesson in it, I was searching for something else, something "better".

While working I was also attending a local university, but it wasn't getting my full attention. I viewed it as being inferior compared to where my brothers and father graduated from. Was there anything in my life that

I could consider to be a success? Where could I divert attention to while shying away from the things that didn't make me proud? The one thing that I considered to be a resounding success at that time was my relationship with my girlfriend of five years. The realization didn't come until decades later that it wasn't a healthy view of success, rather a superficial one. Since everything else in my life was how I appeared to others rather than who I really was, a beautiful girlfriend by my side obviously meant that I was winning at something. My brothers married beautiful women, so at least I was on par with them in this area of life.

I then got a break in my work life that also gave me an opportunity to do something I couldn't do growing up – connect with my oldest brother, Allan. Following in my dad's footsteps, he worked for a local contractor and gave me an opportunity to work with him making more money and a long-term career. We worked together at three different companies over the next eight years and eventually became partners in our own company for another seventeen years. For twenty-five years of my life, I continued to hide my own insecurities and mask them under the guise of "hard work." I continued to feel less than and associated success with money and material things.

My wife and family only got what little crumbs of attention I had left to give. The company that I was a partner in was successful throughout the years and being a part of that success fed my ego and kept my insecurities hidden. Now that I had this connection with my oldest brother, I wanted to show him how good I was at something. The desire to achieve was strong, even if it meant ignoring my own personal evolution and ignoring my family. I chalked up time spent at the office or working from home as the price to pay for success. I was unaware of just how much I ignored my wife and my own family. I had been wearing blinders for the past twenty-five years and was only focused on achieving success at work. I was so caught up in "achieving" and over-compensating for the weaknesses I had been hiding all these years that I was completely unaware that I could choose a different path.

My wife, Kim, after enduring years of neglect in our marriage, went on her own personal growth journey and understood why she had called someone like me into her life. Once she woke up to what was a healthy relationship, boundaries were set and she made clear what was no longer acceptable. It was not something I welcomed and just like when I transferred to a new school all those years earlier, I was in unfamiliar territory. Personal growth and becoming a healthy relationship partner didn't fit into my own perception of success. That could only be achieved through one's career.

I would soon begin to understand what true success was all about. Kim showed unimaginable patience by holding space for me and she realized long before I did who and what I really was at my core. Through her own journey she could communicate exactly what and why I was feeling or behaving a certain way. She showed me unconditional love and exposed me to a number of different tools that I could use on my own personal growth journey. She knew that I wouldn't have the ability to truly love her, my kids or my grandkids properly unless I loved myself. She was determined to not have these unhealthy behaviors and lack of authentic connection get passed down to another generation. I will be forever thankful for her patience, love and understanding and I can't imagine where I would be today without her lighting this pathway.

Although I was new to the personal growth space, I realized I had to make a choice – either continue down the familiar path of success centered only around career achievements, or let go of the familiar and trust that everything would work out for the better. I no longer wanted to sacrifice my family and I was willing to take a leap into the unknown. This was the right decision, yet I struggled with taking action. Why? I didn't want to seem like a failure to my brother since he had given me the start in my career and an opportunity to be a partner in our company. But I knew I needed to leave to change me and I couldn't break my workaholism habits by staying. I didn't want to continue being what I now believed was an unhealthy example for other employees.

In August of 2017 I resigned and relinquished all of my duties within the company. I let my partners know that my life was headed in a different direction and I needed to make a drastic change. Although I was on my own personal growth journey, I now was using it as the justification for one last fight. I was still letting my insecurities get the best of me. I didn't have faith in myself and I didn't trust in the process I was going through. I hadn't truly given in to the unknown and I was still focused on how I could "win". Those old feelings of being 'better than' were still there, but this time it was okay because I'm now focused on personal growth and feeling pretty righteous about myself!

The fight I had been preparing for since leaving the company focused on how much money my ownership shares were worth. Listening to my attorney on the phone that day give his best prediction of the future, I recognized the choice I was tasked with making. What would the cost be to pursue this fight? Could I really consider that "winning"? In discussing the options with my wife, it became obvious that the cost was too high. Kim had already shown me what true love and forgiveness looked like, and fighting for the sake of fighting wasn't the answer.

I instructed my attorney to stand down and not send the letter. I immediately picked up the phone and called my brother. Together, we worked out a fair agreement that only took a few weeks to finalize for what might have been months to years and years of conflict.

So many doors have opened up in ways that I could never have imagined since then. I'm still in the construction industry as an independent consultant, but I now have a healthy, balanced work life with the freedom to work from anywhere, travel and spend quality time with my entire family. My wife continues to push us all to be the best versions of ourselves and I'm thankful to be on that journey with her. My definition of success has changed significantly over the years. I now understand that it requires being vulnerable and accepting of not only our own flaws, but of everyone's flaws, while loving them unconditionally. We can drop the armor we've been wearing and walk away from the fight.

Ignite Action Steps

* **Men**, it is time to step up and lead the way on the personal growth journey. We do not need to wait for our wives.

* **When** your wife does lead, drop your armor, follow willingly and find your own path where the two can intersect for greater joy and deeper intimacy.

* **If** you have a rift between you and your siblings or any family members, take steps to heal it. Again, be proactive and be the one to reach out first. Find the commonalities and even if they are few and far between and remember true connection isn't instant. It takes time

David McDonnel - USA
McDonnel Consulting, Chief Idea Officer
www.linkedin.com/in/procore-experts

Kunal Jamsandekar

"It's never too late to fulfill your dreams."

Have you ever wished to do something from the bottom of your heart and yet hesitated to work towards making it a reality? Doubt kills more dreams than failure ever will. By sharing my story, I invite you to be fearless in the pursuit of what sets your soul on fire.

The Language of Dreams

Born in India, moving to Oman as a child and returning to Mumbai around fourth grade, I have few memories of my childhood till then. What I do remember is the difficult time adjusting back in India – shifting from morning to afternoon school – no time to do much apart from homework – a convent for boys – bullies – a teacher who hit us with a cane – incessant rain in Mumbai – living in a one bedroom apartment with parents and grandparents – my father having a hard time finding employment… it was distressing.

In hope that things would take a turn for the better, my parents decided to move to Pune, around 100 kilometers from Mumbai where my father had purchased an apartment years ago. Things did get better, well, at least for me. I was back to a co-ed morning school and made a lot of new friends there as well as in the neighborhood.

However, a few months after we moved my father finally found employment – in Mumbai! After due deliberation, he decided to take the job while my mother and I stayed back in Pune; he would come every weekend.

I missed his daily presence, but eventually got used to us being a weekend family.

I was doing well at school and discovered my passion for languages amongst other things. I also realized I suffered from stage fright. I recall more than a few episodes of trembling knees caused by a fear of public speaking when asked to read out an essay or answer. This also meant that I was not exactly the most extroverted and outgoing person in class and had a few good friends.

Five years later, I was in the dreaded 10th grade which in India is academically, and therefore socially, an important year in one's life. Apart from the pressure to get a really good grade, one needs to decide on a career direction. For a teenager who might have never really given a thought to this, like yours truly, that was quite overwhelming.

Science, commerce and arts (in that order of preference and social approval) were the streams to choose from. Once you picked one, it was next to impossible to change over to another. In school, I was good at biology and good enough at physics and chemistry, but mathematics was certainly not one of my strong points. I was very good at languages, history and geography but then the only career option one had was becoming a teacher. Apart from being considered a boring career option in those days in India, coupled with the fact that I was generally shy in front of strangers, this did not seem like such a good idea. Little did I realize that I was making a decision based on common opinion and logic rather than my intuition. I believe my intuitive self always knew that I loved arts and would have excelled had I chosen the teaching field. Maybe I would have spared myself the unhappiness that this one decision unleashed into my life in the years to follow.

So, I decided to go into commerce because the subjects were unlike anything we had learned in school: economics, accounting and management. The two years after school are priming years in the stream of choice before one embarks on a proper undergraduate, bachelor's degree or professional training. All the new subjects were interesting and I was excelling here as well. In fact, I was selected for a shortlist of students with the highest academic potential.

One of my friends was following a popular trend in those days, going to the United States for higher education. Inspired by him and encouraged by my uncle in America, I seriously began to contemplate writing the SAT (entrance exam for admission to undergraduate programs) and applying to American universities. Outwardly my parents seemed to go along with the idea. The major reservation seemed to be that of financial funding. However,

I was fired up and confident of getting a scholarship.

Unpleasant stuff has a knack of creeping slyly around the corner and taking you off guard. I vividly remember every moment of one evening when I came back home from college. My mother did not answer the doorbell. The door was locked from the inside, so I knew she was there. After a couple more tries, I began knocking on the door, thinking it was an unusual time for her to take a nap. At first, I did not want to be too loud so as not to disturb the neighbors. As minutes passed with no sound from inside, I began to sweat, and a heavy sense of foreboding engulfed my heart. I started calling out loudly for her and banging on the door frantically. Neighbors heard the commotion and came out.

After what seemed like an eternity we finally managed to break into the apartment and were greeted by the sight of my mother lying on the sofa, foaming at her mouth and barely breathing. She had tried to take her life. I was paralyzed by the sight and I think I must have died a thousand deaths in that moment. It is said that major incidents (or even casual remarks) experienced in one's childhood have the power to leave lasting impressions on one's psyche and belief system way into adulthood. There was nothing in my childhood that came even remotely close to how traumatizing this particular incident was for me in my teens.

We rushed her to a hospital; she was immediately taken into the emergency section. I sat in the waiting room. My father arrived during the night from Mumbai; I don't recall much in between. I was numb.

The next day my mother regained consciousness and was finally out of danger. Later she was diagnosed with depression. I recall stray moments in the days after her discharge. My grandparents came to help. I was grateful to have them around. The very thought of leaving my mother alone again filled me with a sense of dread. She confessed one of the reasons she tried committing suicide was because I was going to leave her and go to the US. The idea of having her only child move away was devastating for her. I felt agony and regret, but also resentment. This incident crushed my ambition and desire to achieve anything big in life.

I made the list of top students in the state at the end of the 12th grade, in spite of the major setback. I had been seriously contemplating switching over to arts. But everyone around me said, "If you are doing well in this field, it has to be the field for you. It would be foolish to give up on something you are good at." So, I enrolled myself into the most predictable and logical bachelor's degree program – commerce.

I remember being unhappy and sometimes downright miserable with what I was doing in life throughout those three years. It felt like a compromise. The tight financial situation at home made it amply clear that I had to qualify myself quickly to have reasonably good employment prospects. I dabbled with two professional courses alongside my degree program and although I was doing well, I ended up leaving after the first year because I was not enjoying it.

At home, I believe my father was depressed as well. He admitted to having borrowed heavily. To our shock and dismay, my mother and I discovered that the apartment was mortgaged. Our entire family equation was heavily strained for the next couple of years with all of us blaming the other for what we were facing. It was a triangle of resentment.

I graduated with distinction and for a third time going against my gut feeling, decided to continue with the field I was in, though it was only filling me with misery with every passing year. I admit the idea of suicide did cross my mind a couple of times. But having experienced the negative impact it could have on the people around you, I thankfully desisted from doing anything of the sort.

My father resigned from his job in Mumbai and moved back to Pune. We should have been happy but due to our financial situation, it only added to our worries. I tried to spend most of my time outside of home, throwing myself into my first job. When offered a position in Mumbai, I jumped at the idea of getting away and shot off. The hectic life in Mumbai gave me a taste of what my father had gone through living there, but it was only years later I came to see this and empathize with him.

After nine months in Mumbai, I moved back in with my parents to prepare for MBA entrance exams. Bored by just sitting at home, I decided to join a French language course. After one week at the institute, I realized I was loving it *and* that I was perfectly capable of feeling happy and fulfilled from it. It was the experience I had been longing for. So, I parked the idea of doing an MBA and decided to study another foreign language. From the various languages offered, the Japanese course was full for the next six months. I wasn't sure what I could have done with Russian, so I rang up the German language institute, which was my last choice. Serendipitously, they had one seat available for a course that would begin the following week. I took it.

Thankfully, despite financial constraints, I persisted. Where my passion for languages would take me, I was not really sure, though suddenly, the idea of becoming a teacher didn't seem as horrible as it once had. In due course, I started offering language tuition for young students and teaching at a language institute on the side...and rather liked it.

Later, before I completed all the levels, I landed an opportunity to work on a German documentary being shot in India. I love movies. Filmmaking had always been a career choice I had considered at multiple junctures in my life, but I always gave up the idea due to the uncertain financial future in such a career. The opportunity to work on the documentary brought together two of my passions – language and cinema. The experience of working on the film challenged my comfort zone and I happily took it head-on. One thing led to another and I ended up working on two more German documentaries. It was one of the best times of my life.

To advance my German further, I joined a master's course spread over three years, which required me to spend two intensive months on-campus then send assignments by post for the rest of the year. At the same time, I took up an offer to work as a corporate language and intercultural trainer for Indian associates working with German customers. Teaching – the very career I had dreaded, gave me some of my most cherished experiences in my professional life; and helped me overcome my old belief of not being able to hold my own in front of a group. I felt like I had found my calling and I loved every minute.

Everything was well on the family side. In fact, in an interesting turn of events, my parents decided to move to the US. I helped them with a bit of the initial capital they needed to start out and they made good of it. Years have passed and through all our experiences, we are closer and stronger as a family than ever. I could not love them more and miss not getting to spend time with them as often as I would like.

There's a saying: 'too much of a good thing can often be bad'. The new job, albeit highly fulfilling, had crazy working hours and my desire to give my course participants the best teaching experience they could get, translated into me spending inordinate amounts of time at work. Between that and the master's program I had very little personal life.

By the time I graduated with a degree in German Studies, I had set my mind on going to Germany for further education, but I needed a break after the tightrope walk between work and study. I decided to wait for a year before applying to universities. As fate would have it, my first trip to Germany happened through work. I could finally experience the country for myself, which until then, I had only known through books and what I had heard from others who had been there.

The following year I happened to switch from an HR profile to an IT department within the same company and ended up being sent to Germany for a two-year stint. Though this was a conscious decision, it felt like the final nail in the coffin wherein lay my dream to study further. I told myself it did not matter, considering I was going to be in Germany either way. The switch gave me the chance to learn new things and the confidence I could be successful in anything I put my heart into. But I missed the quality of human interaction that teaching had offered.

The company had a very strict expat contract which required I stay for double the time I was sent to Germany or pay the equivalent salary, irrespective of the fact the job profile in Germany might lack application in India. This debilitating clause made me feel enslaved to the company as leaving would have meant parting with all my savings. A series of assignments ensued, with me never quite knowing where I would be in a year. It felt like being driven by river currents, not having any choice in my destination.

In my last year with the company, both my parents fell seriously ill. Due to complicated leave procedures, I was unable to visit them until my annual leave. I found myself questioning my rationale to continue with the job. It was neither allowing me to spend time with my loved ones, nor leaving much time to do things I was passionate about. I knew it was time to move on. When I did put in my resignation, it physically felt like something heavy and dense had left my body. I instantly felt lighter. I had given up financial security and everything else I had been clinging to. I had no idea what was to follow, but I felt liberated. I felt as though I had cleared 360° around me and was free to decide what I wanted to do in life.

With time off and deep introspection, which I fondly call quality time with me, I heard a voice inside ringing loud and clear, "It's never too late to fulfill your dream." I took the dive, found my dream course in Germany, put all my energies into applying and getting in – and was accepted! During the months between my last day at work and the start of my course, I spent time doing things I love and could not have been happier.

I am 38 as I write this and will be graduating soon. The experience at the university and beyond in the last few years, has exponentially fuelled my personal growth. I look back at how enriching my journey has been, ever since I finally began to understand the language of my dreams and acted on them. By tapping into my gifts and honing my skills, I believe I have come a long way from what I once was. I am making huge strides towards who I want to be. I urge you too, to find that one thing which sets your soul on fire, then leave no stone unturned to fulfill it. Be who you want to be and decipher the language of *Your dreams.*

IGNITE ACTION STEPS

*I discovered **breathwork** sixteen years ago It has been the best thing to happen to me since then. It helped me overcome anger issues, calm down, and cope with stress. It also has multiple health benefits like enhanced immunity and sleep quality. Breathwork brings me to the present moment and to myself by blocking out the noise around me. I consider this to be one of the most important practices you can have.

*Take time regularly to connect to yourself and listen to what your intuition is trying to tell you. Incorporating **meditation and mindfulness** practices in your daily routine will help greatly. Bringing your attention to your breath is one way you could do that.

*The things that excite you are not random, they are part of your purpose. Make a list of **things you are really passionate about**. Write them down on paper and then visit that list regularly! Incorporate as many things as possible from this list into your day, week, month and year. This can be easily coupled with **manifesting** tools such as a vision board. As you do this, you will start stepping into your most authentic self. Even the challenges on your path will seem like stepping stones because you will have the larger picture in sight. Take little steps before you try bigger ones.

*Work on **identifying and eliminating any damaging belief patterns** you may have. If you are getting caught in the monkey trap (search more about it online: 'hunter + monkey + peanuts'), let go of stuff that does not serve you. Deeper belief patterns could take more work and you might want to seek help from a reliable therapist or life coach.

*Take responsibility for your state of mind. Being **happy, content and grateful** can do wonders for the way you show up in life. The ability to see everything you have gone through, good or bad, as a learning opportunity, will change the way you look at things and open you up energetically.

*Ask yourself in which relationships and interactions in your life, could you show up with more **empathy, compassion and forgiveness**? Start with yourself.

These are not meant to be quick fixes or shortcuts. It involves doing continual work on yourself. Your results would be equivalent, if not manifold, in relation to the efforts you put in. Dreams don't work unless you do. I wish you all the best for your journey!

Kunal Jamsandekar - India

BENEDICTO

"It is in sharing our stories, along with all the emotions
tied to them, that our legacy is created."

It is my hope that this story inspires the next generation to not just dream, but act... to act with reckless abandon, act without fear, yet, to act with clarity and purpose. By doing this you can truly live your best life without regrets, DAILY.

BABY GOT BACK

My heart was pounding. My mind was racing. The sweat was beginning to take over my forehead, the back of my shirt, even my lower legs. It was a warm August day inside Gym 1 and despite knowing what my relationship with heat and sweat was, I still made sure I was the swaggiest looking dude on stage. It was after all, the annual Green, Gold, & White Drive fundraiser – the event everyone looked forward to. This was the day we, De La Salle Zobel High School students make it known that legacy, in the form of a nicely put together yearbook, was of utmost importance.

It had only been a few weeks prior to this moment that I decided I was going to choreograph, and of course perform, in front of my high school on the stage of Gym 1. I remember learning about the opportunity to perform, and even questioning why I, or anyone in my class would ever want to join me, in doing something so gut-wrenching in front of almost twelve hundred of my peers? Yet, something inside me, some sort of longing to be seen fully, over took the fear. So, without truly thinking of the how, I submitted my name to the committee to perform a dance...a hip-hop dance routine. There it was, written on paper, for all the world to see. One important fact to note during this period of time is that it was 1992 in the Philippines. The most popular form of music, as well as the prevailing pop culture influencer at that time was Heavy Metal/Rock. This was an era of tight black jeans and Metallica t-shirts. The awareness of hip-hop and R&B was very minimal, only popular amongst the Filipino-Americans (also known as Fil-Ams such as myself), who had access to this music and the culture it came from because of our connection and frequent visits back and forth to the United States. So, as you might imagine, I was quite unique among my high school peers.

With only two weeks to go before the actual performance date, a lot of work had to be done. I asked every potential classmate if they'd be interested in joining me on this extraordinary journey and, much to my surprise, I was able to convince a good number of them. Enough to create a "squad." There were six boys, six girls...and me. I wasn't too keen with the uneven number, but I rolled with it. Deep inside I had a feeling something magical would come out of it. That said, magical could be the only word that would describe what decision had to come next...choosing the perfect song. Although I made it seem as though I didn't know what it was going to be, I knew exactly what song was needed for this epic moment. A song provocative enough for me to 'blast onto the scene.' A song that would definitely put a stamp of both wonder and awe among my batch-mates, the rest of the high school population, and all the faculty and staff. What song did I pick, you ask? Sir-Mix-A-Lot's *Baby Got Back.*

The day of the big performance arrived, my heart was pounding. My mind began to create doubt. As I stated before, the sweat began to take over my forehead, the back of my shirt, and my lower legs. I didn't know which was worse - the performance itself or the anticipation of it. Being backstage, feeling the anxiety that at any moment, **The Moment** would be arriving. Then it hit me...five words that would define my life from then on, *I was born for this*! The big show, the bright lights, the big crowd... factors that would normally bring fear to many, became a driving force for me to perform at the highest level, especially under pressure. And to think I was only sixteen at the time.

Our turn was up. The announcer said our class name over the microphone. We stepped into our positions. The music blasted out of the speakers, with the iconic line "I like big butts and I cannot lie..." and we were on. Dancing our hearts out. No turning back now. Not for the group, whose choreography

I completed and fine tuned merely hours ago.

Not for me. Desperate to fillin about thirty seconds of non-choreographed song time, a unanimous team decision had me filling in – solo – in front of twelve hundred of my schoolmates. The three minutes or so it took for our group choreography to be completed felt like an eternity. Then, just like that, it was time... I was on. Inspired by Vanilla Ice's most recent video, *Cool As Ice* and MC Hammer's *U Can't Touch This* – I was possessed by the dance gods. The only thought in my head, "Let's Do This!"

With half the crowd cheering and half the crowd jeering, we finished the song as a group with a little bit of choreography in the end and exited stage right. The audience didn't know what to think. It was the first time in my high school that anyone, or any group did anything like it. In the age of heavy metal music and culture, having a group perform a rap song, let alone have some dude do a solo number, was unheard of. But now, they not only heard, they saw.

Leaving Gym 1 created a roller coaster of emotions I have never imagined before: relief from completing the task I set out to do; gratitude and joy from my classmates for pushing them out of their comfort zones and empowering them to perform in front of a crowd; admiration and applause from those who believed in my talents; shame from the many that didn't understand me, the music, or the culture that I found inspiring. Even fear from the possibility of being called names, being bullied, and being disrespected because I knew who I was and was not afraid to go against the societal norms that were present during that period of time in the Philippines. Did doubt creep in my head after? Of course. But would I ever do it again? Heck, yeah!

What followed after that day was destiny, not just related to dancing, but my life in general. I founded and became lead choreographer of a dance crew I named Da Meaning of Brotherhood, Da MOB. We were made of a hodge-podge of dudes from several batches within the high school. We even had my dear friend Michael Sicam create our logo and graphics for the shirts, so we looked official when we performed for the many events our school hosted. We were also invited to many all-girls private schools, to perform and teach "Hip-Hop," as well as some variety shows on local TV channels. My dance crew members and I also got invited to multiple soirees, high school dances, and even proms and balls from many of these all-girls private schools. Needless to say my social life flourished and still does to this day.

A couple of years after that fateful day in 1992, I once again found myself on stage... this time it involved the entire Southeast Asia. As a first-year student at the University of the Philippines, Manila, an opportunity caught my eye – an open audition to be the first Filipino VJ. It was being hosted by Channel [v], at that time a predecessor in the Southeast Asian market for MTV Asia. The task was simple: make a short video, introduce myself, explain why I deserved to be the first Filipino VJ. I asked my then carpool-mate, Katrina Palafox, to film me at an open field inside our village. Armed with a Hi-8 Camcorder, the now Eye Specialist filmed me doing cartwheels, dancing around like a madman and going into poetic verses. I had to hand it to her - although she found the whole adventure hilarious, I felt fully supported. No one believed I could pull this off more than she did. For that, I will forever be grateful.

So, I edited the tape using a VHS player, connected to my Hi-8 Camcorder, connected to my Phillips CD player, one of the first CD players ever created. The tone was light and playful, the theme adventurous and colorful. After a few sleepless nights and a lot of mistakes, I completed the tape for submission. I had the tape hand-delivered because the Philippine postal service had issues with efficiency at that time, and I prayed that it would be received and viewed accordingly.

A few weeks later, I got a call from a friend saying they saw my name on the television. At this time, I hadn't heard from anyone regarding my tape so hearing my name being announced on national TV was massive. I remember sitting in front of the screen waiting for the announcement to re-appear. Hours passed, I got nothing... Then, it happened. *"Out of 1000 submissions for Channel [v] search for the First Filipino VJ, here are the names of the top 100."* I was shocked when I saw my name. I couldn't believe it at first. But there it was, in front of me, coming from the bottom of the screen moving like a speeding elevator going upwards. Holy guacamole! I immediately called my videographer Katrina with the news. It was real, just like that afternoon in Gym 1 two years before. Once again, the roller coaster of emotions took over. Once again, I heard the words inside of me say, *"I was born for this"*

Days later I got a call from a representative of Channel [v]. They congratulated me for making the next round and invited me to come to some fancy hotel along Roxas Boulevard (the main road where the famed Manila sunset can be seen) where the auditions would be held. Although the location was close to my school, I was torn. I was going to miss classes. It may seem quite elementary today, but at that time, this Type-A Honor student couldn't fathom the feeling of missing a class, let alone two to three days! But thanks to the support of my classmates, my carpool-mate and my high school buddies, I decided I was going to push through it. If ever there was a #YOLO (you only live once) moment long before the hashtag was even created, this was it.

Off to the next round of auditions, Katrina and I drove from our village straight to a church close to both our school and the hotel. We prayed the rosary. Maybe even multiple times. My heart was pounding. My mind was racing. Again, the sweat was beginning to take over my forehead, the back of my shirt and even my lower legs. It was a hot summer day in Manila. I was more nervous than I'd ever been in my life. With a farewell hug and good luck wish, Katrina dropped me off at the hotel. I told her I'd be okay and that all she'd need to do at this point is pray. That's all I really needed. Everything else was up to me.

At the hotel, I was directed to where all the hoopla was happening. The elevators opened and I was greeted and asked to sit in a room filled with chairs. There were lights, cameras and famous celebrities and personalities I knew from TV shows and Ads. There were beauty queens and male models. There I was, an 18-year old kid, wearing my Cross Colors outfit, skipping school for something that had no relation to the world of Physical Therapy or Medicine. But for some strange reason, I felt comfortable in the midst of all these people of 'status'. At one point I found myself telling jokes for almost an hour, effectively creating my own comedy show. One person, who seemed to be laughing at everything I dished out, was Michelle Aldana. She was a former beauty queen winner who made a name for herself as a successful, mainstream actress. We ended up sitting next to each other for quite a while and I learned some valuable insight on what it took to 'win' in this industry. She would later become one of my best friends outside of this event and today remains a source of insight, guidance and support.

Armed with confidence, a room filled with a laughing crowd and by far the most colorful and swaggy outfit any young man could be wearing at that time in the Philippines, I completed all the interviews on and off camera that were required of me and the rest of the one hundred people in the room. Once completed, food was served, and judgement came. One hundred became fifty. Another round of interviews and tasks on and off camera. From fifty we became twenty. Another round of interviews and tasks on and off camera. Late into the evening...there were only five left. And I was one of them. "Holy guacamole!" I actually made it to the top five. "*Yes E, you were born for this.*" I felt like a superstar.

Just when I thought I had some time to process everything that happened, I heard the news. "Congratulations, now it's time for the final phase. Go home and pack some clothes, we'll have a car pick you up tomorrow. We're heading to Puerto Gallera." (A beach resort in the Island of Mindoro, a generous boat ride across Manila Bay where most city dwellers go for short weekend jaunts of sun, surf and sand.) At this point I hadn't yet told my parents what had just transpired. I hadn't confessed that I had skipped school to be part of this audition and was going to miss even more. Coming home late that evening, and leaving early the next morning, the inquisition incurred. Although my parents didn't approve of the path I was taking, they knew I would do it anyway. I was after all, already 18. All they wanted to know was that I was going to be safe, be taken care of and brought back home when it was all over. I love my parents for the trust they've always had in me, even if they didn't always approve.

"I can't believe I beat out Tom Lupton," I told myself, sitting in the car on my way to the ferry that would take me and the four other finalists to Puerto Gallera. When it came to music, television, radio, and fashion, Tom was the man. He embodied what it meant to be a music television host. He was a tall, good looking *'half-breed'* who everyone expected to be the first ever Filipino VJ, and here I was, an 18-year-old college kid, going further into the process than he did, one boat ride away from a beach resort for the final part of the competition. I knew in that moment, *"I was born for this!"*

The next two days in the beach resort were something out of reality TV. Our schedule was filled to the brim, each of us having separate locations where certain on-camera tasks were needed. It was up to us to determine how we wanted our backdrop to look, what outfit would match the shoot and overall direction we wanted our segment to be. We introduced songs, interviewed artists and celebrities that the channel brought over for us to speak with, figuring out our own method in making sure we were able to showcase who we were as individuals and future TV hosts. During breaks and at the end of each day, we would return to our own suite. I ordered room service and reflected on what I did during the challenges of the day and how I could be better. Even the fully stocked mini-bar fridge that we were entitled to use, something I've never experienced before, didn't stop my determination to be crowned as the First Filipino VJ.

When you're 18, there is a sense of invincibility that runs through your veins. I was adaptable, persistent and more innovative than anyone around me... or so I thought. Despite not fully understanding the entertainment world and the demands that it would possibly bring into my life, I charged forward and believed with all my heart that I was going to take home the prize. I was going to be able to show my parents that I didn't need to be a doctor, lawyer, or accountant to be considered successful in life – I would be handsomely paid to be a television video jockey. What I didn't consider right away was that I would have to drop out of the most prestigious Physical Therapy program in the country, move to Hong Kong and produce a show for the channel, *all by myself*. Like I said, I thought I was invincible.

My personal reality show ended like all other reality shows – standing in line with my four competitors, the host holding an envelope. With one major difference – this wasn't a popularity contest. This was purely a contest of on-camera look, confidence and the ability to make artists comfortable during interviews. "I got this," I told myself.

My heart wasn't pounding. My mind wasn't racing. I wasn't even sweating. It was as if I knew I had this in the bag even before I started. Angela Chow, a seasoned VJ for Channel [v] was hosting the event, like a sideline reporter in professional sports. "She likes me." I told myself. "I'm sure she's going to announce my name." As she began her on-camera spiel, I suddenly felt something I hadn't felt the entire time – doubt. "Is there a chance that I could actually lose?" I wondered. "Am I just an overconfident 18-year-old with no chance of winning this thing?" Suddenly, like a light switch, I was a nervous wreck.

"The first ever Filipino VJ is…" Angela Chow announced over the mic while staring into the camera, "Melanie Casul!"

"WHAT?!" I screamed inside. My heart dropped. A weird chill ran through my spine. I went pale and silent, with my gulp the loudest sound to come off by body. I was in total disbelief. Yet, despite experiencing the greatest disappointment in my life up to that time, a certain peace came over me. It almost seemed like destiny, despite its cruel methods, created this behemoth of a lesson to redirect me to the path I was actually born for. Where is that, you may ask? Exactly where I am today.

IGNITE ACTION STEPS

At what point in life do you begin to face your fears?

***Listen** to your intuition and take the leap. You will be glad you did.

***It's never too early** to make your mark in the world. Start now.

***Take the time** to truly know yourself. Invest in your personal growth.

***Think** of rejection as the Universe redirecting you to where you're supposed to be. Take nothing personally. Be open to what is coming next.

***We are all where we need to be** in this exact moment in time. Start every day with gratitude.

Benedicto - USA
Storyteller, www.erwinvalencia.com

GAVIN MASUMIYA

"When you courageously share your weird *in the world, you expand your capacity to* find *your kind of weird – those who truly cherish you for who you are."*

I share from my heart hoping to Ignite a renewed touch of appreciation for the 'forgettable' moments in life. It's when I put my foot on the brakes and slow down to honor a fragment of time, the people involved, the items used and everything it took for the moment to be possible – that life becomes more meaningful. My intention for me is to *never* underestimate the *power of my own voice.* I don't know who it might impact and I may never know. Regardless… me *expressing* who I am in this world is so worthy of me – and so are you and your voice.

SHY TO FLY

"Why are you a year older than everybody? Are you stupid? Why are you so shy? You have big ears." Those were the words I remember from kids in grade school. These words would nag at me like an itch inside my ear that I couldn't quite reach and rather than find someone who could help me, I left it alone and grew numb to the itch. I was the shy Asian boy in school with the blue braces and crooked bowl-cut hair, quietly tucked away on my little carpet square. I looked like a nerd but, in actuality, school was very hard for me. My mom held me back a year because I cried a lot and would pee in Tonka trucks but that's another story.

Although I was a year older than all of my friends and classmates, I had to exert a lot of effort and energy just to keep up with everyone else. Then there were my siblings: my older sister who reigned as the golden child with nothing less than a 4.0 GPA every year and a younger brother who didn't have a vested interest in academics but was highly intelligent. Then there was me. The one in the middle. The average one. The one who never spoke up. The one who kept everything to himself because he was afraid and ashamed of being an outcast.

It's interesting how a single thought, the thought that 'I am shy,' became an imprint which sculpted my identity moving forward. Everybody else around me confirmed that for me. Japanese-Americans are passive-aggressive anyway. It's a part of my cultural roots. Shy is who I am.

Then ninth grade rolled around. There I was, fifth period in Mrs. Carrabio's art class. Eliana was sitting next to me. She played on the soccer team and had a Kool-Aid smile where you could see her complete top and bottom teeth. Sprightly and very curious, she would ask, "What is it like to be Japanese? Do you like art? Where were you born?"

Who is this chick and why does she talk so much? It took some warming up before I slowly began responding back to her. "I'm more American than Japanese. I don't know if I like art. I live down the street." There wasn't anything romantic about our connection, though I was attracted to her energy. She glowed whenever she smiled.

During one class in the spring when we had a substitute teacher, I noticed Eliana's energy shifted. Her face drooped and her voice was more tender, and shaky. She slowly turned to me, "I got in a fight with my dad last night, Gavin. I don't know, I don't know... he just doesn't understand me. I didn't get any sleep last night. I don't know what to do. What do you think I should do?"

Why was she asking me for advice? I was flabbergasted. I've never been asked for advice before. What the hell do I know? I didn't want to leave her hanging so I just made up something, "Why don't you just tell your dad you love him?" was all I could think of.

The lunch bell rang the next day. I was walking to art class. I heard from behind me, "Gavin!" I turn around and it's Eliana grinning from ear to ear. She came up and wrapped her arms around me tightly. I was caught off guard as hugging was not something we did in my family. And why is she hugging me anyway? My wheels were spinning. It was like this polarity of discomfort due to being unfamiliar yet coming from such a loving place. And it felt refreshing. I didn't know what it meant or why she was doing it at the time. I'm not sure how my arms responded, but I do know now that physical touch is my top love language. That was the first "hug" that lingered in my mind, like Eliana's voice when she shared, "So I listened to what you said and spoke with my dad yesterday. He understands me more! It feels good to be understood, Gavin. Thank you for your advice!"

That was the **first** time my voice meant something. Does she even remember that moment? I don't know. But I think back on it often. Her joy from my words ignited the slow roll of leaning into my voice and sharing it.

Years later, after graduating from college, I went to teach English abroad and found myself at a Junior High School in Yokohama, Japan. I taught for one year. When my contract was up, I was asked to give a farewell speech. The best thing about it was, instead of shoving English grammar down the students' throats, I was allowed to share anything in those five minutes to bring closure and hopefully something of value to the students and staff. With the help of my girlfriend at the time, we put the speech together in both English and Japanese.

My final day came. There I was, inside the school gymnasium, standing at the podium staring into the sea of 800 Japanese faces. I had a piece of paper planted right in front of me. I looked up at all these Japanese people staring back at me, my heart beating like it was about to come out of my chest. I took a deep breath and glanced back down at the paper, "...there can be scary moments in life. A part of me was afraid to move to Japan. I didn't have any friends. I was away from my family. I didn't speak Japanese..." I stared back out into the eyes of a few students, some of whom were very shy and often never spoke, others who had dreams of living abroad and those who took the lead as the class clowns. I smirked and a wave of calm permeated from within, "...and yet, I knew this was the opportunity of a lifetime...and was a challenge worthy of me. It's so important to test your capabilities and limits. Challenge is the stuff dreams are made of."

I finished giving the rest of the speech in Japanese. To be honest, I don't know how much they took away from what I said. What I do know is here I was, thousands and thousands of miles away from everything I knew, and I had never felt more at home. In that moment as I wrapped up my final sentences, I gave one last glance into the crowd of students and staff. It reminded me of the first time I saw Tony Robbins live at his 'Date with Destiny' seminar in Palm Springs. I saw a piece of myself in him and I didn't quite know what it was then. In this moment, I got it.

I reflected back on the days spent hiding behind my classmates during a recital, terrified of being seen. Or the time I chose to be stage crew in fifth grade when we performed Lucy Whipple, a classic children's book because I didn't have the guts to play the main role I really wanted: Mr. Scatter. I would be in my room alone at night secretly studying Mr. Scatter's lines. "Beans and bacon, fish in cans, barrels of flower, sacks of yams, raisins, rice, salt pork and such, woods and cottons soft to touch..." I never had the chance to play that part. My secret dream.

During my time teaching English in Japan, I saw myself in a young boy named Takuto, who sat in the back of class. I didn't hear him utter a single word the entire year. I longed to know, is that who Takuto really is? My ancestral seeds were planted in Japan and I see that I no longer identify as a shy Asian boy. Why should I label him the same?

As a fourth generation Japanese-American, I never knew much about my culture until living abroad in the Motherland. I returned to my roots, the roots of my heritage and the roots of my self-expression. What I saw in Tony Robbins, I saw myself manifesting in a small way on that podium.

Within six months of giving that speech, I was coaching people in the U.S. Navy for free and some friends back in the United States. I'd spend my Saturday mornings starting at 9 AM, inspiring and igniting my clients' lives. To this day, I continue that path, supporting people in stretching their voice and spreading my *weird* as a speaker, reminding people across color, socioeconomic background and culture, that each voice is worthy of being heard.

That final moment on the stage, I knew I wanted to be a coach and a speaker. I decided thereafter I would spend one more year teaching and living in Japan and then head back to Los Angeles to pursue my dream. That moment ignited a self-validation in the power of my voice.

Upon returning to the US, I joined a Toastmasters' group within the first month and went on to win a few international speech and evaluation competitions. One of those speeches nourished my soul as I shared about a friend who lost his life in a car crash shortly after graduating from college. I didn't realize how much people related to that story and how much it touched the family of my dear friend, Hank McVicar; rest in peace, Golden Boy.

I later became a certified professional coach from one of the largest coaching programs in the country, the Institute for Professional Excellence in Coaching (iPEC). That investment signified my destiny as a coach and let me know there are people out there who resonate with my *kind of weird*. It showed me I have a right to be my weird and live it fully. Because of this, I was asked to be a TedXYouth speaker at one of the largest high schools in

Southern California. I shared my journey of transforming my shyness and any insecurities that came with it. That was the same month I quit my job in social services to become a mindset coach full-time. My mission is to support high performing, heart centered men to be confident, emotionally available and self-expressed.

I look back on wearing those blue braces from fifth to tenth grade, wondering why I didn't have the freedom and confidence to express myself like my other classmates – and I smile. I am so grateful for those days identifying as an inferior shy Asian boy, for it taught me how to observe and listen – two crucial skills for being an effective coach. I am also grateful for my 'shyness' as it sparked in me a passion. It unshackled my self-expression to empower humanity to believe that their voices, when spoken from the depths of their guts, matter.

There's a traditional Japanese saying that is often spoken before meals and it's *i-ta-da-ki-ma-su* (pronounced 'ee-tah-dah-kee-mahs'). When I was growing up, my dad used to say it and I would laugh at him. I thought it was foolish. I thought it just meant, "Thank you for the food and stuff." The only times I would ever say that phrase were to mock my dad.

Then I met Keiji. He was one of my roommates during my first year in Japan. He would always cook right before me. His favorite meal was noodles. When it was my turn to cook, he would move his bowl and chopsticks to the living room and place it on the round glass table with his chopsticks on the edge. He then would move his hands into a praying position, bow his head, close his eyes and say, *i-ta-da-ki-ma-su*. He paused in silence for five seconds. Then he would open his eyes, look at his chopsticks, pick them up and begin eating.

I would see him do that everyday. How dope (cool) is that? It's like the world and time stops for five seconds – to give a prayer for food that he prepared for himself. I started saying, *i-ta-da-ki-ma-su* before every meal from then on.

This word became even more important to me after attending my grandfather's memorial service. A Japanese reverend led the occasion. I had to lean in close to catch what he was saying as English was not his native tongue. I remember having a hard time keeping my eyes open. I was nodding off throughout the service due to not being able to understand. Then he said something that really struck me; woke me up. He began talking about the tradition of saying *i-ta-da-ki-ma-su* before meals. He then stopped, looked at each of us and asked, "Do you know what it means?" I thought about when I was a child, not really knowing what it meant and mocking my father. The reverend then shared in his broken English that *i-ta-da-ki-ma-su* roughly means, "Thank you for *Everything* it took to make this happen."

It immediately brought me back to Keiji's five seconds of silence after he'd say *i-ta-da-ki-ma-su*. I thought about the person who chopped down the wood for the chopsticks he was using, the person who decided to open up the grocery store where he bought the noodles and the cashier who made the transaction. I thought about every single person who had to come together to make every noodle in his dish and was grateful. What a powerful meaning *i-ta-da-ki-ma-su* has! I was overcome with a deep sense of reverence in that moment.

What had to happen in order for you to be here right now?

For me to be here writing this chapter right now, my friend Yoram had to reach out to me and connect me to the publisher. Before that, I had to have a conversation with Yoram at a coaching summit in the lobby of the hotel, asking him, "What does it mean to be a man in the modern world to you?" That's what had him think about me for this book. Not to mention, that when my friend, Ramin, shared with me about a coaching summit advertisement he found on Instagram, I had to buy my ticket, drive for an hour and spend the entire weekend to say yes to that opportunity... it's there that I met Yoram and formed a bond. I can look back and see that not expressing myself growing up led me to want to help others. This got me to Japan, up on that stage and transformed my communication which eventually sparked a curiosity in the coaching industry. In that sense, my shyness as a child led me to this book. And do you know what else? The universe was working long before that as my parents met on a blind date... and they decided to pursue a relationship together. And out came me!

All of that had to happen for this moment to happen. Just like you, reading this book right now, millions of fragments had to come together to get you here. Never underestimate the power of *i-ta-da-ki-ma-su* in your life. When you courageously expand your capacity for the reverence of the moment, you truly cherish where you are.

IGNITE ACTION STEPS

What if, *i-ta-da-ki-ma-su* wasn't just meant for meals? What if it was something you can incorporate at any given moment in time?

Here are some simple steps you can take to have an *i-ta-da-ki-ma-su* moment each day. You can also think of it as a 'Thank you for everything' moment:

*Just take a moment. Breathe in. Release. Think of where you are right now.

*What had to take place in order for you to be here? In this moment?

*Spend 2-3 minutes speaking aloud the different things that had to transpire.

*Think of all the people who contributed to you (parents, teachers, relatives, friends, nurses, doctors, etc). Who told you about this book? How did you get to the physical location you are at right now? Imagine the people that it took to build the physical space you're in. Even more ancestral, what brought your parents together? What had to happen to create you? It can go on forever. All of it played a part in creating this very moment.

*If you are with someone else, let them know you are taking time to appreciate this moment. Recount what had to take place for you two to be together. You can even recount it together – get them involved!

*At the end, place your hands together like a prayer, bow your head, eyes closed and say, *i-ta-da-ki-ma-su* (pronounced 'ee-tah-dah-kee-mahs').

*Pause in silence for five seconds. Take in a deep breath of gratitude for everything. Breathe out and release any tension you have in your body and mind.

*Allow yourself to be ignited by this renewed touch of appreciation. This moment is sacred. Give yourself the gift of an *i-ta-da-ki-ma-su* moment.

Gavin Masumiya - USA
Mindset Coach
www.GavinMasumiya.com

JAMES MCMILLEN

"Be You, Do You. Shine so bright that you inspire
others to do the same. "

I share my story to help you heal and then dream. I want to remind you that you are a divine being that has unlimited potential. Learn to step through the pain rather than burying it. Feel it fully and move beyond the story, become creative with how you want to live and show up in the world. I'm here to inspire and empower you to find yourself along the way, to embrace you as a whole and celebrate every moment, loving you and loving your life.

LIVING IN LOVE

Growing up was idyllic for me. I lived in the country on a family farm. I spent time in nature, playing in the mud, time with animals, had homegrown food and ate meals together with my family. My brother and I did everything together, working and playing on the family farm. We would build hay forts in the barn, connect with friends, fish in the nearby creek and see family often. I learned about the circle of life. Imagination was easy and I could dream and plan a great life ahead. I had a poster on my wall with a picture of a big house, a helicopter, a boat and a fancy car. It was a young teenager's vision-board before I knew what that even meant. I was barefoot and grounded into the earth.

When high school came around it became more and more apparent that

I viewed life and the world differently. I did what every teenager does – I embraced the social norm: played sports, hung out and did the cool things all the while suppressing the real me - the healer, the gardener and the mystic. I hid my voice in order to have the 'normal life'.

It was in summer break after Grade 10 my life was about to change and not for the good. I went to a party at a friend's place; there were lots of people, all having a good time. Everyone, but mostly the guys in my small town, were oohing and ahhing at this amazing red corvette convertible. All the boys wanted it and the owner, Steve, was a funny personable guy who everyone seemed to enjoy as he made people laugh and have a good time.

I don't remember why but weeks later Steve asked me if I wanted to hang out and go for a ride in his corvette. Thinking, "Here's an older cool guy with a dream car, who wouldn't say "yes?" In hindsight, I was naive and stupid. We ended up catching a popular movie at a drive-in. At some point during the movie, I was sitting there watching the screen and he started touching me. I froze, not knowing what to do or how to stop him. I was far away from home in a stranger's car with his hand in places I didn't want.

This was the beginning of almost three years of being sexually molested. Nothing all out and no penetrative sex but a toy in an older man's desires and games. Through this I shut down and numbed myself - feeling pain, fear and holding in my emotions. I was going along with things and keeping up appearances while at school - being the sports jock, not wanting any of this to spill out, especially in a small town.

On the inside, I hated myself, loathed my weakness and inability to stop him. I had lost my naive, curious and playful self, no more dreams, no self-love or respect. I was full of shame and disconnected from my true nature. I had no clue how to deal with the hurt and pain and intense emotions. Wounded. I had given away all my power and betrayed myself. I was empty. Everything I did was to overcompensate, mask and never be vulnerable again.

Finally, it all ended when he had to flee the country after crossing paths with the wrong people. What a relief. It was over. I could continue my life and forget about it. So, I buried that experience deep inside and locked away the pain, the hurt and the devastating emotions. I put up barriers and didn't trust or love myself. It was the beginning of believing I was damaged goods. It created the feeling 'I am not good enough' which took over my life.

So now what happens? you may ask… I started spending more time with friends, drinking, doing the guy thing and having awkward relationships. Feeling lost and on autopilot all at once. Everything for me was external. I wanted to be accepted and fit in and I did. Things seemed easy: working for a family business, having a car, nice clothes and people who loved me. From the outside, it looked as if everything was fine. Little did others know what was going on inside of me.

I always felt empty inside, needing to fill this void with external validation and experiences. I signed up with a modelling agency, did print, runway and extra work to find the validation that I was attractive and had something to offer. I created relationships for this same reason. I did everything I could to fill the void inside: partying, drinking, hanging out and doing stupid things. I had many friends and a best friend; we did everything together. Life seemed full. Yes, there were many amazing times and joyful moments. I don't want you to think the bad out-weighed the good. I just wish I'd been more conscious and aware as a human being. Even though being molested was a huge blip that I filtered everything through, I needed that experience to become the empathetic conscious Being I am now.

Relationships and communication were where I really sucked, having built up walls and not really letting anyone in. I would self-sabotage everything good in my life especially in the romance department. In college, I met the most amazing woman who I was with for 15 years; we share a beautiful daughter. Again the self-sabotage and lack of self-love damaged the relationship which ended due to me acting out and being a real asshole. Our breakup transpired through her pregnancy and the birth of our child. It was a horrible ending which created deep hurt and pain in another human being. Wow, I don't even recognize the person I was at that time. I have so much advice and wisdom to share now with that version of me. Being unconscious and on autopilot in a relationship is the worst thing you can do for yourself and the other person you are with. This goes for all relationships. We need to be aware, conscious, authentic and vulnerable, everything I wasn't.

It is not what we do in life but how we make people feel that they remember most. We shared some amazing times over those 15 years, supporting and believing in one another. Sadly, it was overshadowed by how we both didn't take it as a learning tool and instead resorted to anger and resentment. Today anger is rarely part of my life. If I do feel the emotion, instead of reacting to my triggers, I take three deep breaths activating my parasympathetic nervous system and respond in a calm and rational way, if I need to at all. I feel through the emotion and become curious about its origin, search it out and then release and heal the trauma that was triggered. When we do this, we gain back our own power and reconnect with ourselves and free up the energy that these triggers locked inside of us.

Communication and vulnerability are key and now, as a conscious man,

I just shake my head at my old self. I didn't honor the mother of my child and celebrate her light. Instead, I disengaged from her and turned to spending time online. The internet offered so much content to distract me and hide my pain. It was here that I met someone who later became a part of my life. It wasn't until after, we realized we had already met years earlier. With the disconnect I was experiencing, I felt lucky to have a special friend in my life who was there being supportive and helpful in my unconscious state. She was offering me validation that I was something good, I mattered and everything was okay. I couldn't see how my hidden side, the shadow me and my need for validation was affecting my judgement. The cycle started all over again turning into another 14-year relationship repeating my ineffective pattern.

Everything wasn't doom and gloom and I appreciate much about my experiences throughout these relationships. There were many epic moments, friends, memories and good times; starting my own business, purchasing a beautiful home, having a fairytale wedding and the birth of my daughter. I got to experience deep love from others, built a dream house, traveled to exotic places and explored other cultures. All beautiful memories I cherish and value.

Before I arrived at my present wondrous state and while in my second relationship, I started having panic and anxiety attacks. I'd end up on the floor, unable to breathe and blacking out. While at the gym and not being able to perform due to inflammation and weight gain from high cortisol levels, I had tingling in my fingers and toes. My chest and shoulders were so tight I would swear I was having a heart attack and had tests done at the hospital. On another occasion, I felt so much pain and hopelessness, I contemplated suicide and ended up on the high bluffs at the lake, with a bottle of alcohol, ignoring my phone. My addiction to internet porn and a virtual online game called 'Second Life' was part of my coping and numbing out strategy. Everything in my life was suffering; relationships, my business, my health... I would often ask myself, "Wow, how did I get here?" I was in pain and hiding it all, scared to be vulnerable and authentic and unable to fully open up and communicate what I was going through. I felt alone and believed no one could understand me.

In December 2012, the age of Aquarius began. The Mystic in me was reborn. I had a deep and profound energetic awakening that rocked me to my soul. It was like a veil was lifted and I was woken up. I knew who I was. I had been living with immense stress and anxiety and feeling deep sadness and confusion about life. My consciousness was activated. When I look back, it was a series of Ignite moments that brought me to this state: becoming a phoenix rising out of that darkness. I knew there had to be something more, something different, a better place and experience. I was becoming curious as to where this was and how I could live differently.

I began reading and exploring options and started to change my mindset. If I got myself into this, I can get myself out of this. I was becoming accountable to myself and where I was in life. I found tools that helped me change one thing at a time. I needed to destress and heal my body, mind and soul. I started becoming curious - why was I here? What was my purpose in life and in my relationship with internal happiness and prosperity versus the 'culturescape' and being accustomed to external validation? Life was becoming more exciting and fulfilling. I did a course called the Silva Method that helped me immensely and after this came an experience that would forever change the course of my life.

Awesomeness Fest was an application based, experiential conference and I decided it was for me and that I was going. I manifested an invite and purchased a ticket and then didn't go because of relationship pressures. I gave away my power, placing another's fear above my own. That didn't last long as I deferred my ticket to the next year and attended in Puerto Vallarta, Mexico. There I found my tribe, others who were on a journey of exploration, making things happen and helping humanity grow. We played, we partied, and we connected. It was amazing. The experiences there set my life in a direction of self-discovery and awareness.

Two Ignite moments really struck home for me. The first was a term created by Vishen Lakhiani called 'Blisscipline', the art of being in bliss. I resonated with this and made this a part of my life. No matter what is happening or what I'm experiencing, I'm always finding the bliss. The bliss in each and every moment of learning. The next Ignite moment came when we did an exercise called the 'Three most important questions.' We answered three questions in a timed manner: 'What do you want to experience in life?', 'How do you want to grow in life?' and 'How do you want to contribute to the world?'. Doing this exercise shifted my thoughts to the way I looked at life and what I wanted to do. One of the biggest, immediate takeaways for me was self-care and a deep love for my own divine sanctity. I want to be able to travel and to never stop growing as I explore daily what my best self looks like. It was in this moment, I realized that I wanted to be in service to humanity. I didn't know exactly how but knew that I would figure it out.

When I returned home. I started to integrate what I learned and experienced. Self-care was at the top of my list, so I started eating better and moving more; being aware of what I was putting in my mind and the limiting thoughts I was having. I started meditating to quiet my mind and going to yoga to manage the physical challenges so I could heal my body. Within that practice I found so much more as I became aware of myself and was breathing and feeling more deeply. At the time it seemed like another addiction and maybe it was but more of an addiction to feeling better. I would often do seven or eight practices a week and instead of it being merely physical, I started embracing the other areas of yoga: breathing, awareness, calmness in a pose, do no harm to self or others and so forth.

I started studying various healing modalities and holistic nutrition, all while exploring myself and integrating what I was learning. This path was intoxicating, and I dove into becoming the real me; all I wanted to do was learn, grow and heal. I was advancing and evolving. I became fully aware of the cycle I was repeating within my current relationship. Things began to shift. Grounding and integrating would come later.

The following year a friend told me about an event called 'Camp Reset'. I signed up. It was an epic experience, a digital detox with no tech, nicknames only and no talk about work. I was able to shine my light of self without any judgement. It was another pivotal point in my life. I found an amazing tribe close to home. Together with Awesomeness Fest and Camp Reset, I continually pushed my boundaries, explored within and integrated what I learned along the way.

My journey of self-discovery continues to shine the light on my blind spots and allows me to grow, expand and feel I Am Enough. This is where the need for external validation diminishes as I am now able to feel it from within. I deepen my exploration of self through authentic relating events, drumming circles, conscious mens' gatherings, Burning Man, Envisionfest, advanced spiritual studies and other trainings. Everything I do is designed to push my boundaries and discover deeper and deeper layers of myself, allowing my authentic light to shine. I now help others move through their stories and live more epic and optimal lives. I am about living from the heart as a conscious spiritual being and speaking my truth in an authentic way. I am feeling blessed in an amazing conscious relationship with a new and beautiful spiritual soul mate. I enjoy abundance in many areas of my life as I am finally me.

Many Ignite moments occurred in all my relationships and continue to occur, in both small and large doses on a daily basis. The 'blip' I once had, detoured me into an unconscious human, asleep at the wheel, living on autopilot. These Ignite moments propelled me into becoming the conscious, authentic man I am today, one who is vulnerable and shares his emotions. I am loving myself unconditionally and exploring deeply within. I offer my story because I want you to know a story is, just a story. It is a gift and a blessing all at the same time. If you are going through something, find someone who can listen to you. Find that one person who you can share with and will help you heal. See past the pain and know you are okay. It isn't necessary to do life on your own. As men we are told to suck it up and instead I suggest you be open and find the wisdom that is undoubtedly there.

IGNITE ACTION STEPS

*Get a journal or a notebook: Start writing things down and clearing things out of your head. For me, I use 'The 5-Minute Journal'.

*Read the book The Four Agreements: 1. Be impeccable with your word. 2. Don't take anything personally. 3. Don't make assumptions. 4. Always do Your best.

*Meditate and go within: I started with the 6-Phase Meditation. Create a meditation space in your home. Adopting a daily practice of gratitude is really important. Start walking slower and notice your surroundings as you find stillness within yourself.

*Start honoring yourself: In what you're exposed to. This includes food, thoughts, people and places. These all have an impact on us. Eat the best quality of food possible. Go to a farmers market or organic grocer. Start observing those around you: do they support you? inspire you? help you live life at your best? If not, find people that do and create boundaries that support you and your personal growth.

*Become aware of your thoughts: Never go to bed anxious or with a busy mind, especially if you're upset or emotionally triggered. How we end our day and fall asleep is how we wake up in the morning and how we wake up and start our day determines how the day unfolds. Limit electronics use to 60-90 minutes before bed and calm your thoughts and finish up cycles before turning in. Go to bed in peace to wake up rested. Start your day with positive thoughts and affirmations as it influences the direction of your day. You are the one who makes the choices – so start with what serves you best…Choose the best You!

Love Yourself so deeply that you inspire love in others.

James McMillen - Canada
CEO of James McMillen International
www.Jamesmcmillen.com

JIMMY NARAINE

"Your biggest fear can often serve as the northern star pointing to where you are meant to be."

You really do not need to wait for a life-and-death crisis, as I did, in order to step up. My wish is to inspire you to stop allowing your fears to sabotage your life. Read my story in the context: "What is still holding *Me* back?"

'LOST' THEN 'FOUND' IN THE HIMALAYAS

That day was meant to be a regular acclimatization day, to prepare my body for the extreme Himalayan altitudes. I decided to embark on a spontaneous adventure. The goal? Reaching the mysterious Ice Lake that lies 15,000 ft above sea level.

Purely focused on the mission at hand, I'm in a flow state. Determined to reach my destination in record time, I keep moving forward at a consistent pace, fully focused on the steps ahead of me. In the pain of the struggle, I feel truly alive.

I am in flow, I keep going. I feel powerful. The fascinating thing about flow states is that you simply forget about what is happening around you. Time stops and you are not even being you anymore. You simply become the "present moment". Flow states are powerful because they allow you to go deep inside and be fully engrossed in the now. Normally, all of this would sound marvelous, but not when you become totally oblivious to the swarm of dark clouds accumulating in the distance. In high mountains, the weather cannot be taken for granted and I seemed to have forgotten about this important fact.

After several grueling hours of steep ascent, I see it – my destination. Breathing heavily, I stop – surveying the rugged scenery. All my concentration turns into a sense of accomplishment and exhilaration. "Hell yeah! I made it pretty damn fast". I stroll around the frozen lake, savoring the mighty silence of the mountains. I am the only living being here and it's magical. I love every second.

Regaining awareness of my surroundings, I ground myself. Then, my perception shifts radically and a sobering thought pops into my head,

"Shit. It's getting pretty dark. No one is here. What the hell did I get myself into?"

Do you know the feeling when you realize your hubris got you into trouble that won't be easy to escape? "How come I didn't notice any red flags?" – I keep pondering. However, just like in other realms of life, hindsight can be a bitch. When you are in the fervor of pursuit, it's easy to become oblivious to factors that truly matter.

The emotions I feel are trepidation and disbelief. It's like a bad dream. The panic begins to overcome my body and mind and I have the distinct feeling of adrenaline rushing through my bloodstream. At this altitude, the weather can drastically worsen in a matter of minutes and each year the Himalayas claim the lives of people who find themselves in a similar predicament.

It took me several hours of uninterrupted hiking to reach this point and I was aware that merely walking down wasn't an option. It would simply take too long. In my anxious mental state, I begin to run down trying to pay attention to each slippery step. I feel the adrenaline coursing through my body – I'm fighting for my survival and feel panic lurking in the background. I know I can't afford to lose control… am I making rational decisions…? I calm myself, "I'm gonna be just fine. I just have to keep running. I'm gonna be fine."

Since it started raining the visibility became alarmingly low, and I hear lightning crashing far in the distance. My imagination runs wild. I'm fully aware that in such conditions, the probability of getting lost increases exponentially. It's one of those surreal moments when I know viscerally the danger isn't just in my head. It is real.

Suddenly I feel a strange impulse. It's not even a thought, it's more like an overwhelming feeling in my entire body which translates to, "Fuck, I'm in danger... I should feel fear – what about this other bullshit holding me back in life that I think is fear...? Does it even matter...?"

At that moment, I really felt how fragile and unpredictable life truly is. We often have an illusion that things will last forever until something bad happens. That experience on the mountain put things into perspective for me. I saw life as a fascinating game where we may impact, but not fully control, the ending. Am I holding myself back from fully exploring my potential, because of some self-imposed limitations? Sadly, the answer to that self-inquiry was a resounding, "I am."

At that stage of my life, I was already an accomplished content producer. I had published best-selling video courses which helped tens of thousands of people. I enjoyed presenting in front of a camera and felt comfortable doing so. After all, if filming didn't go well, I could simply delete the video. There was no "real-time" negative consequence to making a mistake. However, whenever there had been an opportunity to speak in front of a real audience, I would always decline. Initially, the justification seemed legitimate. I would usually respond, "I don't have enough time." Of course, this was rarely the case. In my own head, I rationalized that fully focusing on building scalable products was a better use of my time. Both activities were not mutually exclusive though. In fact, they complement one another. Clearly, something was wrong and deep inside I knew it. Running down the rabbit hole went significantly deeper than I initially thought. As I was realizing then, on the side of that mountain – many of my decision-making processes had been wrapped in self-sabotage.

Have you ever had a situation when you wanted to do something important that could dramatically change your life for the better? You knew exactly what you needed to do. Perhaps, you even knew how to get started. For some mysterious reason, however, you couldn't summon enough courage to embrace it. Something in you didn't believe you had what it takes. Perhaps, your negative inner voice kept whispering, "You could fail, and failure means embarrassment and rejection. Stay where you are. Be safe." Admitting the truth to yourself is hard though. It's often much easier to invent a story which helps you rationalize inaction.

'Imposter syndrome' is something few people talk about, but so many suffer from. It's the feeling you are not good enough, you don't truly deserve what you have. It's the pressure you feel when you are afraid you will not live up to some artificial expectations. After all, the moment you challenge the status quo, someone might realize you are not as good as you seemed. You may be "found out." Interestingly, after discussing this topic with many successful people, it became apparent that this issue is more common than I expected. 'Imposter syndrome' can manifest in different forms. For me, it was a tremendous resistance to anything that involved being vulnerable and putting myself in front of live crowds. In my fearful delusions, doing so would always lead to a negative outcome.

People assumed that a bestselling content producer must also be a compelling presenter. This awareness triggered an immense pressure to perform. Each opportunity I was given was always concealed by the heaviness of potential failure and rejection. The initial excitement would always gradually transform into paralyzing self-doubt, "What if my performance is less than what they expect from me? What if I embarrass myself?" It was easier to lie to myself rather than leave my comfort zone.

Think about your own life – do you spend way too much time stressing about things that ultimately don't really matter? Do you allow limiting beliefs to hold you back from becoming who you are meant to become? We often let imaginary fears dictate our lives. Sometimes you can deceive yourself for years, until something really heavy and unexpected forces you to recalibrate.

I like the way one of my favorite humans, the Navy Seal, David Goggings, puts it. He believes that right after your death you will have a 1-on-1 meeting with the creator. God shows you who you were really supposed to be and how you wasted your potential. This belief fueled Goggings to transform from an overweight and depressed person working in a dead-end job spraying for cockroaches, into one of the toughest men on the planet and an inspiration to millions. Cockroaches are something David and I have in common, but more about that later.

As I'm running down the mountain I realize, I haven't been even scratching the surface of my potential. I've been allowing fear to dictate my life. It has prevented me from pursuing things which truly matter to me. If I die today and meet my creator he most probably will tell me: "Hmmm, let's see… Jimmy Naraine… here is your file. It says that you were put on this planet to help millions of people overcome their limiting beliefs. You were meant to speak on big stages, write bestsellers and do whatever it takes to spread your message. You wasted all this potential..."

Our fears are acquired throughout our lives, mostly in childhood. We all have our demons and I'm pretty sure I know when mine materialized. I was growing up in post-communist Poland. My parents did their best but barely made ends meet as aspiring medical doctors. At that time in Poland, there was almost no money in medicine. In our case, this meant living in a flat infested with cockroaches. Till this day memories flood back when I see one. Since my father is South American, I am of mixed race and other kids made sure to remind me of the fact I was different. On top of that, I had to move schools several times and never felt a true sense of belonging. Everywhere I went I was an outsider.

Even though I had dreams about traveling the world and making an impact, I didn't truly believe that it was possible for a kid like me. I still vividly remember my teachers advising,

"Listen, kid, you are from a small city in Poland. Stop the bullshit; graduate and get a job. Maybe one day you will be able to go on holiday abroad."

This made me a very insecure kid and even though I did a lot of inner work, some of the old demons were still lingering in my mind. Apparently, I needed a potentially life-threatening situation to clearly see them for what they were. Fortunately, at some point I discovered personal development. I read stories of people who overcame odds much worse than mine. This sparked a tremendous inspiration to work on myself, as I realized that I could literally design my own reality. I learned one important truth about life that became my 'northern star' for years. The sweetest breakthroughs don't come easy. They are born from discomfort. If you want to accomplish something remarkable, you have to work your ass off for it and do things that scare the shit out of you.

This is why I consciously started putting myself in scary and challenging situations. For example, when I bootstrapped my way to a British university, I was terrified, having no idea how to cope with making ends meet in a foreign country. The challenge of not speaking the language was uncomfortable as hell, but the experience was invaluable. Eventually, burning all my bridges, taking a leap of faith and starting my own business venture, went way beyond my comfort zone. What those things have in common is chasing the unknown and accepting that nothing good in life comes easy. When I look back at my life, most breakthroughs were a direct result of pushing my comfort zone. I'd hear that inner voice whispering, "you can't do it", then do the damn thing anyway.

As I was running down the mountain, I had an epiphany. It was so simple, yet, I needed an extremely dangerous situation to open myself up to it. I realized that in order to fulfill my true potential, I needed to embrace extreme discomfort once again, just the way I had been doing it all my life. I had to get back on that fucking stage.

"Zzz-bam!" – the loud sound of the lightning interrupts my internal dialogue, snapping me back into reality. My predicament is still real. I keep running down, but the feeling is different. Something happened; I can't put my finger on it. I have a strange sensation that if I make it down the mountain, my life will never be the same again...

Soaked by rain, I notice houses in the distance, a sense of safety discharges the adrenaline. "I am safe." I feel a sense of relief that is impossible to describe. I'm fully aware I got lucky escaping a very dangerous situation. I barge into a random teahouse; everyone looks at me. I suspect they feel the peculiar energy of someone who has just escaped from harm's way. I find a table in the corner, "Namaste, can I have a ginger tea, please?" In a trance, I stare into the fire burning in a traditional Nepalese stove. To an external observer, nothing has changed since that morning. However, I clearly feel I am no longer the same individual. I have left some of my demons on that mountain. Sipping my tea, hands still slightly shaking, I can feel the doors of new opportunities opening up. Suddenly, I am no longer afraid. I know what I have just experienced was one of those rare Ignite moments – the course of my life is about to change dramatically! It's now or fucking never... Right there and then, I made a conscious decision to take massive, imperfect action.

The shortest route back to civilization was through the mountain pass, its highest point 18,000 feet. Those last three days of the Annapurna Trek presented further challenges but also solidified my new resolve. Just one week later, I was making calls and sending messages to various conference organizers. Several days later, I found myself training a small group of entrepreneurs in Bangkok. It was the best feeling in the world.

Those old fears, dissolving... I ride the momentum to schedule other speaking engagements all over the world. Since then, I've spoken on dozens of stages in 17 different countries and have never looked back. Nowadays, I help founders and company executives become more powerful presenters.

My entire transformation can be traced back to that one moment in the Himalayas. Whenever I think about where I would be, if I didn't take that leap of faith to dance with my fear, I get chills. Life is too short and unpredictable to live in regret of actions not taken.

What about you? What is that one critical thing you have been afraid to do? That you know could take your life to the next level? Are you allowing fear to prevent you from being the person you were meant to be? Embrace discomfort; push yourself. Make a conscious decision you will do whatever it takes to unleash your true potential.

IGNITE ACTION STEPS

*First step: I want you to take a couple of minutes to think about all the challenges you managed to overcome in the past. Go deep into the recesses of your brain and think about things that seemed impossible to you when you began. I know for a fact that you had situations like this. Everyone does. However, we often tend to underestimate ourselves and focus on what we lack. Once you have a few points, close your eyes and go back in time. Feel all the emotions associated with you accomplishing something seemingly impossible. How does it make you feel? This part of the exercise will make you realize how powerful you already are.

*Second Step: Jot down all the things that are still holding you back. Think about some of the biggest fears you experience that prevent you from taking important actions. Now, I want you to think about one thing you have been procrastinating on, because of one of those fears.

*Third step: Ask yourself: "what smallest step can I take right now?" It could be as simple as writing several emails to potential mentors. Perhaps, it's creating a short outline for the course you've always wanted to build, but have been procrastinating. Maybe, it's more challenging like signing up for a skydive to face your fear of heights. Whatever it is, commit to it **right now**. Before you start the next chapter, I challenge you to tell your friends exactly what you will do and when you will do it. Embrace the power of accountability and face the fear that has been holding you back. I can guarantee you magic will happen, and you will never be the same person. Ever.

This is crucial - once you have the momentum you absolutely have to keep it going. Remember, even the highest mountains can only be climbed one small step at a time.

Jimmy Naraine - Poland
Entrepreneur, Adventurer & CEO Speaking Coach
www.jimmynaraine.com

MARCUS
YOUNG KETTLES

"Go Beyond Reason to Love. It is Safe. It is the only Safety."

To live life fully, with passion and humor; to go beyond appearances to see the best in every person and situation. I find when I do this, I meet people at their highest vibration, and when I accept every situation as it is, it is perfect. I invite you the reader to find your own way to see yourself and others in their 'golden essence' and beyond their outer shell.

LOOKING INTO THE EYES OF GOD

When I look into his eyes, I can see how I'm doing, or more specifically, how I am connected or not connected. I am referring to the teacher Paramahansa Yogananda, a man who shows me how truly to be seen and see myself – or at least see myself through his full-sized portrait that hangs across from the double-wide mirror in my bathroom.

There are times his eyes are so alive. I want you to know you can *eye-gaze* with a portrait and not just a person. When he looks at me, it is the all-knowing eye of God and I just know there is no hiding from anything. There is complete transparency. It's a feeling of vulnerability, of being seen, laid bare and naked. Paramahansa Yogananda is there with his all-knowing, piercing omnipotence.

Looking at myself in the mirror and seeing myself reflected in his eyes, can make me feel uncomfortable. It brings me to question my emotional response to his gaze. What do I do when I feel this way? I take it as a sign, I need to evaluate how true I am being to my soul's course and daily path. Yes, I experience all of this looking into his eyes.

His eyes are alive. They are penetrating, communicating infinite degrees of meaning based on my perception of what he is telling me about myself. It is surprisingly powerful to lock eyes with a portrait and not a person. For better or worse, there is clarity.

This daily self-examination hasn't always been the case. I have self-medicated and bypassed many opportunities for true transformation while connecting with something bigger than myself. But I have learned that my past is my map to my future. I know that all of my experiences have led me to my personal expansion – to being (and attempting to be) the embodiment of Love in all things I do.

Born in 1963, I had an odd, yet magical childhood. I was brought up in two different worlds: traditional middle-class grandparents who held the beliefs of the past, while my parents were exploring and breaking boundaries in many ways. It was during a time energetically similar to what our country is embroiled in now: political and social strife, unwanted, lingering, painful wars. There were ideological differences that punctuated those times and made it impossible to find a middle ground rooted in ideals of peace, harmony and understanding. Some people were turning on and tuning out, while others were gripping tight to the past and safety of the norm, of how our culture has taught us to believe and behave.

My family of origin included my brother and me, my father and his two wives—his ex-wife, my mother, and his young bride to be. At his wedding, my brother and I were the best men and my mother was the maid of honor. It was an unusual constellation, but it worked for us.

My brother and I felt like 'strangers in a strange land' balancing between the two dimensions of realities. We were involved in anti-war protests, as children at six and seven, chanting down the street with Hare Krishnas. The Vietnam War gave way to trouble in the Middle East when American hostages were taken in Iran. It was a national trauma.

During one of our late-night card-playing marathons, my brother and I as teenagers, along with Dad and his two wives, were trying to figure out a solution to the strife, hatred and severe distrust facing our country and the world. It was a time to think out of the box and we did. We came up with what we thought was a brilliant solution to Middle East strife predicated upon flying an armada of aircraft filled to the brim with man-made plastic green frogs filled with nitrous oxide/laughing gas. We surmised that if we dropped all of them in the capital city, the plastic frogs would explode, like a million gas-filled water balloons, releasing enough laughing gas to awaken the leaders, soldiers and masses to the 'Truth'. The Truth that The Beatles knew, sang and ministered: All you need is Love…Love is all you need.

We created a chant we sang in rounds, full-throated and wholeheartedly, with all the passion and determination we could muster, until we all burst into uncontrollable laughter and satisfaction of our brilliant problem-solving capability.

The chant was simple: "Go beyond reason to love. It is safe – it is the only safety."

I was a child during the summer of love and was exposed to that world by my mom, with her loving spirit and wild Carol King shock of hair. Along with my trippy magical aunt and my Grateful-Dead-loving dad and his teenage girlfriend. They were experimenting, inspired by Timothy Leary and the electric Koo-laid acid tests. My brother and I were included. We traditionally would have Christmas Eve family acid-trips, so I was no stranger to projecting to other dimensions and levels of consciousness.

I felt fortunate being raised in the redwoods in the Santa Cruz mountains of California at the bottom of Jackass Hill, but I longed for more. At times, we lived on food stamps and dehydrated eggs. Growing up amongst hippies, with little to no limitations pressed upon us, my brother and I joked, "How do you rebel against ultra-liberal parents? You go to USC – the elite, The University of Southern California (referred to by some people as the University of Spoiled Children)". And both my brother and I did.

From the redwoods to the city streets of south Los Angeles, I found myself at a crossroads at the end of my freshman year in college.

I was enjoying my newfound life at the University of Southern California. I even gave myself a preppy nickname, Tripp.

I had been a straight-A student in high school. But it left me exhausted. I really struggled. I didn't have the discipline necessary to counter the over-the-top fraternity row experiences available at that time among the prestigious, rich kids of Beverly Hills, San Marino and Palos Verde. I routinely fell asleep in class, even the small ones. I was almost kicked out of school when I was caught cheating on a math test by my professor. I failed my first class ever. For a non-violent person, I found myself storming back to my off-campus apartment in a blind rage to the point that I literally punched the lights out of a wall sconce with all of my might, almost breaking my hand.

I was definitely burning the candle at both ends. I managed to survive my freshman year and decided to stay in Southern California for the summer and work at a swanky new restaurant in Newport Beach, called The Ritz.

I was living with my grandparents in their guest room in Laguna Beach, one block from Shaw's Cove. I thought I had made it, until I came down with hepatitis. Not the run-of-the-mill kind, but the really bad Type B that kills your liver and debilitates your body and immune system for life – or so I was told.

I remember lying in bed, completely sapped of energy, of Prana life-force and for the first time in a year, or many years that I could remember, I was being still. Not by choice, but by necessity. By the Universe putting the hammer down on me – really hard.

As I settled into this unfamiliar territory, I noticed a book on my grandmother's shelf, *The Autobiography of a Yogi*, by Parahamansa Yogananda. I had seen the book before, but that day it was like a beacon of light. My latent intuition surged; I knew I had to read this book. I was told I would be laid out for 8-12 weeks, so what else was I going to do?

I delved into his life story timidly, not sure why I had such a calling, such an imperative feeling I must read this book. Even though I had been steeped in unconventional spirituality, nothing prepared me for the experience I had reading, breathing and living this book. I would read a few pages, succumb to exhaustion, ponder, sleep, and repeat.

Yogananda had his own healing journey which he described in his autobiography. He told how he found his peace and pathway through meditation. I was beginning to understand how to tap into this energy, but I could only remember always having done so in "altered" states. I started to put into practice the techniques and focus on his meditation teachings.

Not two weeks into my convalescence, I finished the book and came to the profound belief that by implementing what I understood from his meditations, I could heal myself. On a balmy summer night, I prepared myself for the meditation experience. I had been sleeping 10-14 hours a day, was pampered by my grandmother; her simple, delicious, made with love food and forced solitude and isolation.

On that night, I focused my energies and connected with Source as I had understood how Yogananda had done it. It was a somber moment as I consciously asked God for help with this sacred ceremony I was giving myself. As I dropped deeper into meditation, the midnight moon checked in on me through the narrow window of my room and I centered myself. In my mind's eye I saw a blue light emerging. It wasn't a sky blue or pastel in any nature, but a vivid, powerful, thick, bold color. It came into my mind clearly that what I was seeing was 'Universal Energy Blue' healing light.

As my mind accepted its presence, the light entered me at my crown chakra. As I breathed and released resistance and fear it flowed down into my head, through my shoulders, into my torso and all my internal organs, flowing down through my hips and legs and to the bottom of my feet. I was in the energy. It was in me. I was the energy. There was no separation as I lost all sense of me or my body, until I started to shake, subtly at first and then more violently. It felt vital to me to embrace this as I felt something important was happening. Powerful, pulsating, surging, energy cascaded over me as if I had just been pulled into the backwash of an enormous ocean wave.

I struggled to quiet my mind as the flow increased. I had to tell myself to stop thinking and then had to tell the thinking to stop thinking and go deeper into the feeling. I felt my eyes roll back in my head, I was prone on the bed, sweating profusely, unable to move, vibrating in every muscle fiber and inch of my body. I experienced a mental quickening and an overflowing rush of joy and bliss. I was connected to my Source, to All I could conceive or imagine. I was floating in the arms of God or so I sensed. Just as that thought crossed my mind, I lost all consciousness and passed out cold.

I awoke the next morning with the sun radiating onto my body from that same window as the moon had shone in the night before. I could hear voices in the living room. For the first time in weeks, I had no pain, stiffness or nausea getting out of bed. I went out to the living room to see my grandmother speaking to her friend Lucille who had an enormous yard that was perpetually overgrown and out of control. She was lamenting this fact when out of my mouth, I said, "I'll help. I'll come and clean your garden." Over their protests, I assured them I felt fine. And I did.

In fact, I couldn't believe how amazing I felt. I worked for eight hours in the heat of the July sun in her yard with no undue fatigue or consequences. From that day forward I had all my strength back and more. I had a bond. A connection to the Universal knowing of my Being. I resumed college, flourished, finished on time and with honors. The chant I learned as a teenager came back to me: "Go beyond reason to love..."

Soon after that life-changing experience, I was visiting my aunt on the Big Island of Hawaii. One afternoon she took me out kayaking to see if we could find some dolphins. We paddled out and off on the horizon I saw them. With almost military-like precision, they were spread out wide in an expansive line of dorsal fins coming right at us. "Are you sure they are dolphins and not sharks?" I questioned, my heart in my throat. "There's only one way to find out" she replied with twinkling eyes and a wry, sage-like smile on her face.

So, we slid out of the kayaks and into the clear blue water of Kealakekua Bay. The fear and trepidation I felt turned into exhilaration as my snorkel mask enabled me to see them approach. I was amazed at their speed, grace and agility. Soon I was surrounded by the entire pod, enveloped in their playful curiosity. I was face to face with them and as I slowed my breath to take in their magnificence, I caught the eye of one of the magical creatures. I had a fleeting eye-gaze that, in what seemed like a split second, was a full connection to another species of life. I felt such benevolence and love from them. Pure delight spilled forth from me. I was literally under the water, dancing with dolphins as a continuous uninterrupted flow of uncontrollable laughter spilled out, the bubbles like an upside-down waterfall of joy rising through the tropical waters to the surface. For the life of me, I have no idea how long it was. Time stood still, but my heart was forever expanded. You can never undo those kinds of experiences.

I spent the next twenty years expanding my heart and views on life while growing as a spiritual individual. I took life by the horns. I moved to Washington, D.C. working at a lobby group, recruited to New York City, and became a VP of Business Development. The financial crisis gave me the opportunity to shift. I finally did what I wanted to do: begin a career in entertainment… and yes, I became a bartender…and eventually a producer and program director for a metaphysical new-thought church.

Decades later, while living in Manhattan, I was having a medical check-up and in the past history of the form, I checked that I had had hepatitis. The doctor ran a bunch of tests. When the results came back, he brought me back into his office to tell me that my body showed no signs of ever having had that disease or even having been exposed to any variation of the virus. An overwhelming wave of gratitude, humility and joy swept over me as I heard the news. Tears gently fell for the divine healing I had been blessed with.

As Life would have it, I finally returned to live in California, and it was no coincidence, I came across the oversized lithograph of Yogananda in the gift shop of the Encinitas Self Realization Fellowship Temple. His eyes represent a constant reminder and gauge on where I am, in relation to my connection to myself, to the Universe, to Truth and ultimately to Love.

I find that the more I surrender to Love, the more fulfilled my life becomes. I am a father, a partner, a friend, and although life is not without struggles, I have the faith and knowingness to face those challenges. To go toe to toe and eye to eye, going beyond reason to see the best in all situations, going beyond reason – to Love. I invite you to search inside and see yourself through the eyes of God. Connect with the deepest part of you and dance with the Universal energy of life.

IGNITE ACTION STEPS

*Journaling – I had the privilege to know and work with Julia Cameron, the author of *The Artist's Way* book and journal. Three pages a day and an artist's date with yourself are great ways to stay open and connected to yourself. It is Healthy and Fun.

*Time alone – Taking time for Self and to be in silence and solitude is a game-changer for emotional well-being. Take time alone in a quiet place or go commune in nature.

*Meditation – However you manifest meditation, do it. Try a moving meditation where you consciously connect your body, mind, and spirit through breath and movement.

*Connect through eye-gazing – a lot can be said for being able to look at yourself in the mirror and be okay with you, just where you are. Acceptance is the first step to transformation. Assess. Accept. Move forward to greater self-love. Or, find an image of a guru or entity that you connect with: it could be Jesus, Mary Magdalene, the Dalai Lama, St. Germaine or any image that gives you a quickening of your Soul. You will feel the connection and the Power. Nurture it. Explore it. Surrender it. Go to Love.

Marcus Young Kettles - USA
Owner, Founder
ministeroflove.com & fitbuddha.com

ØIVIND GRYDELAND

"Do what you can today, tomorrow it might be too late."

Healing one person at a time affects many. It is my hope that my story has a healing effect on you and has a ripple effect on many.

BREAKING THROUGH THE BARS

Madeleine entered the room. I still see the image of her in that purple dress. A swarm of butterflies danced around in my stomach. My whole body went numb. I was *obsessed*. Only one thing mattered: to have her realize she was the woman of my dreams. This became a long, winding path that altered my whole point of view of life.

Before her, life was an open road. There was no steady girlfriend insight. To pick up women out on the town was in another league for me, beyond my confidence level. Therefore, on a late October evening, long before Madeleine, before social media apps, *before I got to know myself*, I logged into a popular Norwegian dating site. Click... Clack... Click... Clack... dyslexic one-finger typing. Fortunately, as an electrician running my own company, I didn't have to write too much.

The dating site paid off! I got a reply from Lisa. *"Shall we meet?"* After two days, we met to play pool and the following week, she had almost moved in. Lisa was about my age, a little round in her body shape, sweet, lived nearby and loved to cuddle, the same as me. She fit perfectly into my life. She liked me. I was a "happy guy" who didn't think too much about what I wanted in a girlfriend, except she should have nice assets, and Lisa did have those and a beautiful face. She also made me feel useful. Her life was in financial chaos and I liked cleaning up other people's messes. *Maybe because it made me feel better about myself.*

She was happy to leave her moldy, crappy apartment and move in with me. I taught Lisa about economics and we established a practical life with routines. Every day was not exactly ecstatic, but we were a little in love and enjoyed ourselves. She went to her grocery store job while I set up wires and gave people lights in their living rooms. In the evenings, we sat close to each other on the couch and watched movies. Our happiness lasted about half a year. The difficulties started when we were forced to move and decided to rent an apartment together. I really got to know my new life partner well, discovering qualities that weren't easy for me. She was anxious about doing laundry, she wasn't happy cooking and she struggled to do everyday, practical things. Social situations made her anxious. Communication broke down. Every time I tried to talk with her about an issue, she slammed the door and went outside to have a cigarette. "You're impossible to discuss things with. You always have to be right."

I did feel like I was always right. In my view, she was incapable of seeing things from a logical perspective. Without noticing, I became depressed. Everyday life played out like a colorless pattern without a start or stop. Getting up, eating breakfast, going to work, eating dinner, sitting on opposite corners of the couch to watch TV and then sleep on opposite sides of the bed, was all we did. My brain raced trying to figure out if it was time to break it off. Weeks went by, then months – I still didn't have the courage or energy to end it.

Life in the colorless, foggy ocean lasted until I had a long conversation with my dad. He commented on how powerless I seemed, and that I hardly ever smiled anymore. I spoke about how difficult everything was with Lisa. "You need to get out of that relationship," Dad said with a determined voice.

That same day, I called my mom to ask about the guest apartment she had in her house. Her summer guests were moving out, a sure sign the time had come to leave Lisa. I pondered how to break up with her. We'd promised we were never going to leave each other. Everyone who's been through a break-up knows how liberating it can feel when it's finally over. Still, I felt totally lost. Fortunately, the conversation I had with my dad became the starting point for a long list of coincidences that put my life on a new course.

Late that evening, she said, "We need to have a proper conversation about our relationship." I felt a rush of joy. This was the opportunity of a lifetime to tell her what I thought and felt. We agreed we should talk. We sat down on the couch, and Lisa started the dialogue, "Our everyday life is quite exhausting, Øivind. My suggestion is, we each make a list of ten things we like and don't like about each other. Then we can figure out what to do." The confrontation with Lisa went easier than I expected. Except, I was totally determined things needed to end. I could barely manage to think of anything positive. There was only one thing on the positive side of my list. We usually had a nice time while we ate dinner together. With my heart racing I anxiously took the leap, "Lisa, I've thought about this for a while. These lists won't help us at all. Our relationship has completely died. I want to break up."

She went into shock; tears flowed down her cheeks. This wasn't how Lisa had envisioned our conversation. To end our relationship was totally unacceptable for her. It seems she was for the most part satisfied about things and didn't see the problems I struggled with. It was probably because I was a safe rock of financial security for her and one who could do all the everyday practical things.

It wasn't easy for me to sit there and watch her cry. We had lived together for almost two years by then. Her anguish made me feel forced to accept a compromise. We would take a break for two weeks to think about it. During that period, she would continue to live alone in our place while I'd spend nights at my mom's house. But there was only one thought in my head, "Our relationship is finished." She cried and slept alone on the couch with me sleeping in the bedroom. Even though I got a knot in my stomach listening to her tears, I felt an incredible relief to have made it this far. I knew when I went to my mom's place the next day, I would never return.

Neither of us said a word the next morning. As soon as Lisa was out the door, I packed my most important things, rented a van and drove three loads to my mom's residence. As agreed, we met two weeks later. I was dreading it, fearing she would convince me to return. Fortunately, I managed to stand my ground. It was over. She stood there and cried, but two weeks on my own had made me even more certain than ever before.

It took a bit of time but slowly, my energy came back. I woke up in the morning feeling a sense of joy I hadn't felt for a long time. Of course, I had some bad days now and then. Sometimes, my conscience would sneak up on me for Lisa's sake. But over time, those days of guilt became fewer and fewer.

During the fall, I decided to look for a permanent place to live. My uncle, a real estate agent, recommended I buy my first apartment in an area outside Oslo, Norway. As a chain reaction of positive energy, a lot of pieces of the puzzle started to fit together. I found the perfect apartment for a reasonable price. Right after that, I bought a new car for a bargain. To top it off, water damage in my residence led to a refund amounting to the total purchase of my apartment. Suddenly, I had some extra money to remodel the bathroom. I felt life was in a really good flow.

I was quite content for six months. I wasn't ready to look for a new relationship or replace what I was enjoying. Then one day in March, when the sun had started to end the winter, I met the woman who would have a huge impact on my life. I will never forget the moment this colorful creature pranced into the party, while the song 'Womanizer' by Britney Spears was blasting on the speakers. This unknown woman was dressed in purple from head to toe: purple shoes, purple dress, purple sunglasses, vivacious red hair and a glorious body. I was pulled towards her. Everyone else at the party became invisible. I was a little drunk, and in very high spirits so I didn't hesitate to go straight up to her. "Hi, my name is Øivind. What's your name?"

"*Madeleine,*" she answered in a playful way. She was five years younger than me and had just moved from Sweden to Oslo. I thought, "Perfect." We laughed, danced, sang and talked for hours. Madeleine had the qualities Lisa lacked: cheerful, full of life, energetic, confident and with an enchanting laugh which made me feel completely free. The 28-year-old me transformed into a teenager with a crush. I was filled with an indescribable rush of joy! Every time I accidentally touched her, it felt like small electrical shocks tingling throughout my body. As the night fell, the whole group from the party took a large taxi to the center of the city to check out the nightlife. Madeleine had already found a seat and shouted, "Øivind, come and sit next to me!"

I was surprisingly happy. The fact that she spoke Swedish made her even more appealing. During the taxi ride, we made fun of the couples around us, who were smooching in their seats. On the inside, I was very jealous of course and noticed I admired Madeleine's lips when she talked. Suddenly, she grabbed me, leaned in towards my face and gave me a long, deep kiss. I blushed like an overripe tomato. Madeleine just laughed, "We have to smooch when everyone else does it!" she stated gleefully all wrapped up in the moment.

The butterflies in my stomach whirled around. When we reached the center of the city, we held hands and pretended to be a couple while we skipped up the main street. I was more affected than ever before. I don't remember the rest of the night. We got pretty drunk. Madeleine got sick and went home. So, the romantic goodbye with a phone number exchange didn't happen. Luckily, I knew her name and could find her again on Facebook. I could barely sleep since my body was tingling so much that night. I ate dinner with my mom the next day and I told her how completely lost I was in Madeleine.

I felt as if my system was overloaded and energized by her. It was one thing to flirt a bit at a party when I was tipsy, but it was completely different to take the initiative and put myself out there with someone so amazing. Yes, I did manage to take the lead with Lisa, but it was more her initiative that steered the course. I didn't do much myself and this time wanted to be different.

To say it bluntly: Sharing my feelings was never my strength. Except, I'm a very emotional person. I was often insecure and nervous. It was typical for me to feel happy and relaxed after having a few beers. Otherwise, my feelings were hidden deep inside me, in a prison. I've always been terrified of saying or doing something wrong if I release too much emotion.

Before I tell you more about Madeleine, I have to go back to my early childhood. The feeling of being closed in is something that has been a part of my life in several ways. From the day I was born, my mom told me I fought against coming out of her womb. The labor went on for many hours and my arrival was traumatic for both her and me. As a baby, I spent a lot of time *behind bars* in a blue metal crib. As a toddler, I had so much energy I'd wake up at 3:00 AM when my parents were asleep and I was left to myself. I was fascinated with electricity even then and they were afraid of me breaking or dismantling electrical appliances. To prevent disasters like experimenting with cleaning supplies and shaving foam, their last resort was to build a wooden fence between the top and bottom of my bunk bed. I was locked in there every evening at 7 o'clock as my dad wanted the house to be silent. He learned this from his father who locked him and his siblings in the attic when they were kids. They felt it was safe for me and I knew, it felt safe for them. My reality developed behind those bars. Looking back on it today, I know the lack of freedom had the opposite effect. I got caught in my own captivity, my own solo-experience of life, and it has influenced me ever since.

After meeting Madeleine, I became lost in the idea of being together. I didn't know how to tell her I was incredibly fascinated with her. It took me two months to write a message to her on Facebook. I was proud of asking her if she wanted to join me at a concert and waited with excitement for her reply. She couldn't make it. I withdrew and didn't make other suggestions. A few months later, I met her at a party with some common friends. She smiled at me and said 'hi' when we ran into each other. I wasn't prepared; my whole body squirmed. I wanted to tell her so many things, but I didn't get out any words. The rest of the evening, I did everything to avoid her, in fear I might say something to make her lose interest in me. I found out she worked in a store near my apartment. A few days later, I gained the courage to go to her store, pretending I was just walking by and wanted to say 'hi'. But the same thing happened. As soon as we had exchanged a few pleasantries, I left in a hurry.

I continued to think about Madeleine all the time – how I could tell her she was the woman of my dreams. I wanted to become her prince because she was my princess. This thinking process led me to a dating school where the emphasis was on me. I learned tips and tricks on how to improve myself by using respectful language, dressing better and showing more self-confidence. The tip I remember the most was called *Genuine Touch*. It was about how you could touch a girl on her knees, elbows and shoulders without it being sexual. Those respectful *safe zones* anchor rapport in a way that builds up *trust and safety*.

The struggle to become confident enough to talk with Madeleine became an obsession. I took more self-development including an intimacy course and reading books on how to build up my self-esteem. Slowly, it helped me open up. I felt more confident without drinking alcohol first. I met other women, but none compared to the devotion I felt for Madeleine... the only woman for me.

My charisma improved. During late hours on the town, I got a few kisses, some phone numbers and had my share of sexual encounters. I learned a lot about touching, erotic zones, the importance of being 'slow' to create safety. Eventually, I felt confident enough to have a conversation with Madeleine – after two years of practicing. The opportunity presented itself on a dark night at a Halloween party. We were on a farm in the countryside. It was a weekend celebration so there was no possibility to escape and nowhere to hide. It was time for me to face Madeleine and share my feelings.

After a round of dancing, I pulled her aside and said, "Madeleine, I want to have a real conversation with you." My heart was beating so hard it almost leapt out of my chest, but as soon as I started talking with her, it became quite easy. We had a conversation for four hours. I got to tell her how much I was in love with her – how much she had been on my mind since that first evening two years earlier. Her reaction was not what I had anticipated. She told me she'd felt some chemistry between us in the beginning and wanted to get to know me more. But since I never initiated anything, she stopped thinking about it. "Øivind, what you're telling me is very sweet. I really appreciate it, but it's too late now. Life has moved on. I'd like to be good friends, but nothing else."

I felt relieved and sad at the same time. I was glad I finally managed to tell Madeleine about my feelings, yet disappointed it couldn't be something more. Two years I had wasted being obsessed with her and not doing anything about it. Yet, my pursuit of the woman of my dreams had become the start of a whole new life. I learned much about myself and how to deal with my insecurities. I had worked on traumas from my childhood and came to understand that my family did what they thought was best.

Madeleine and I slept just spooning that night in the basement. I got a good-night kiss and that was it. Gradually, my obsession with her faded. Today I know there was a reason I never got to be with Madeleine. There is a saying: "What distinguishes winners from losers is that winners manage to turn their defeats into victories." I handled it quite well. Still, I often think about what might have happened if I had talked to her before it was too late. Maybe I was just in love with being in love. Maybe we wouldn't have been right for each other. I will never know. But I have learned that if you really want something, you have to go for it right away! Otherwise, it might be too late. In Love, We Trust, Live 1 Electric Life!

IGNITE ACTION STEPS

*Everybody** is affected by you coming into their field, how do you want them to feel after they met you?

*Walk out**, force a smile if you don't have one and make eye contact with people.

*Always use** sentences with "I feel", "I see" and "I experience" when talking to others.

*Own** your words.

*Put on a smile** and make people's day.

Øivind Grydeland - Norway
Marine electrical automation engineer, Electrician, Trauma Therapist, Massage Therapist, Psy-tap Therapist, Hypno Therapist with regression, EFT Therapist, Video/photographer.
www.1el.no

MARTIN DANIELS

"The Universe has your back."

Too many of us are unhappy in our current lives, numbing ourselves with drugs, alcohol, social media or TV rather than having the courage to make changes. I hope that my story will inspire you to take control of your own life and start living the life you were meant to lead. Our world is a beautiful place, you just need to embrace the infinite possibilities that are out there for you.

TO HELL AND BACK

It was mid July 2017. I could no longer silence or ignore the voices in my head or the pain in my heart. It was time for the conversation; our children were going away to summer camp for the week, it was the perfect opportunity, not that there ever can be such a thing for this kind of conversation.

Rewind three years to a Tuesday evening after a typical day in the office. I was working in the UK, renting a tiny room in a shared house, miles from my family in Croatia. I was one of the eight lost souls in that house, divorced, single, married, all looking for more love, connection and a happier life.

On the surface it looked like I had it made. I had a love of fast cars and had secured a job working for the prestigious formula auto maker, McLaren. Three times a day I scaled the spiral staircase in the McLaren Technology Centre to the ground floor, initially coming face to face with John Watson's

1981 F1 World Championship car, then walking past a plethora of other F1 hero's cars from Mika Hakkinen's to Lewis Hamilton's first F1 season car. The whole building was a playground for lovers of speed and technology. It was a dream job.

That evening I squeezed into my tiny room, barely big enough for the wardrobe and double bed it contained. I closed and locked the door and laid on the bed. It may have been tiny, but it was my space and no one else's. I was miserable. How could this be? I was in my mid 40's, had a lovely wife, great kids, was well paid, money in the bank and if you'd have measured my life by society's rules, I'd 'made it'. I'd reached the definition of success, at least on the outside, yet on the inside I felt empty. I was 1000 miles from home, doing a soulless job, earning money that I didn't need with a failing marriage and seeing very little of my children. I was an intelligent guy, or so I thought, but this was the definition of madness. I distinctly remember thinking, why have we (humans), been given all these amazing gifts? We just waste them. Worrying about so many insignificant things that somehow keep most of us enslaved in the drudgery of work, stress and fear rather than being able to enjoy the abundance of beauty in the world? I made the key decision that evening that something had to change. I had no idea what had to change, but 'it' had to change.

The three years between 2014 and 2017 had been a crazy roller-coaster ride of personal development and relationship struggles. There had been some big, big highs, and some big, big, lows. I'd grown hugely as a person, but now I was at the top of the roller-coaster, looking down the huge dip. I had no idea where it was going to take me but I knew I had the strength to handle it and I prepared myself for the fall.

My marriage had bounced along for several years; we'd discussed it wasn't working, we'd tried some things and we'd even talked about not being able to continue like this. There had been glimmers of hope and the possibility of an amazing relationship, but we'd never managed to sustain any of these ideals or dreams for very long. We both knew the relationship was over, but I knew I had to take the first step. I had to be the man in our relationship.

I'd decided three days earlier to pick the Saturday morning, the day after the kids had left for summer camp. I knew if I didn't pick a date it would continue to drift and this had drifted way too long. My body was literally screaming at me, the knots in my stomach, the pain in my heart, I had to listen and do this. There were many reasons why it had taken me so long to get to this point; some totally selfish, some for the big impact this would have on my family. Divorce for me meant losing everything I had at that time (or so I thought). We were living in Croatia, but that wasn't home for me so I'd have to move countries. Move away from my kids Oliver and Ella, to start a completely new life somewhere else in the world. New job. New home. New relationships whilst trying to maintain relationships with my kids.

I also had another daughter, Laura, from a previous life. I'd split with her mother when she was six months old and I'd spent her first 10 years in and out of court battling to see her whilst her mother did everything possible to stop this. When she was 10, I had to make one of the most difficult decisions of my life to stop seeing her as the situation was so damaging for everyone involved. We spent five years without any contact until she moved away from her mother and via the miracle of Facebook, found me and we re-kindled our relationship. What impact would divorce have on Laura when she'd already been through so much turmoil?

I was also worried about Sally. How would she cope living in Croatia with the kids and no real support network? Things had become exacerbated by our new tourism business and four rental houses that still needed lots of work.

Lastly, I was worried about me. How would I cope on my own? How had I failed to "fix" our marriage? I was worried about the impact on everyone else and my own image. I was stuck inside my head, going round and round in circles, not able to see any kind of reality, I'd lost the plot.

We went to bed together that Friday night, strangers in the same bed, a somewhat sad and familiar occurrence over the last few years. I didn't sleep much, I'd rehearsed a 1000 times in my head what to say. We both laid awake in bed that morning, not communicating as normal, when I plucked up the courage, with a very shaky voice and said, "We need to talk". Sally knew what was coming and immediately started crying. I cried too. We briefly talked, let the tears subside and then I laid there feeling numb, yet at the same time a huge sense of relief. Carrying these emotions inside of me for so long had taken a heavy burden on my psyche and this was the start of my release.

The following week was a weird mix of emotions, relief it was starting, frustration as we talked about next steps. Fear was staring at me as the next big conversation was to tell our children we were getting divorced. I felt like I was abandoning them as I wouldn't just be leaving the family home, I would be leaving the country.

Oliver and Ella returned home, and with good timing, Laura was also with us, having arrived that day in Croatia for a family holiday. We all sat around our dining table, the hub of our family life. A wedding present from my parents, it was one of the few possessions we'd transported from the UK to Croatia; the centre of meal times, fun, laughter, creativity, parties and now the place to dissolve our family life as we knew it. The kids sat in silence as we talked, not overly surprised in some ways as they knew things were not good, but the final blow is always a big shock. They headed off to their own rooms to process the news and what it meant for them. I felt relieved yet even more sad. Delivering our decision was hard, but talking about it made it even more real. This was happening.

I'd had a conference booked in Las Vegas for mid-August and decided it was best I still went, even though I was in a bad emotional state. Part of the trip was to spend a couple of days with one of my friends, Cheri, a soul sister. She was intuitive, suggesting fun and crazy activities, as I just didn't know what I needed at this stage. I had a lot of anger inside of me. She was brilliant, I ended up cancelling the conference and we did mad stuff together for the entire week like Crazy Girls Show, axe throwing, shooting guns in the desert and paragliding. All of this helped me start releasing years of frustration. She listened, was non-judgemental and created a space for me to let go. We became really close that week, more like a sister than ever. During this time in Vegas, Sally and I decided to go public on Facebook. It was a good decision. It made it easier for both of us and allowed each of us to move forward. Unfortunately for me, shortly after I posted having a great time in Vegas with Cheri it was mis-interpreted by some that she was my new girlfriend and this caused a lot of unnecessary trouble.

Two days after returning from Vegas I was packing to leave. This was one of the hardest and most horrible days of my life. I organized my life into 12 boxes and loaded them into my VW camper for the drive across Europe to the UK. I remember thinking, I'm 48, done so much in my life and now all I own is just 12 boxes of stuff. I was so stuck in my own head, still measuring success by all the wrong parameters; running so much of my life from a place of fear. I literally felt like my heart was being ripped out that day, having to leave everything behind. I'd never wanted this. I had done all that I could (or so I thought at the time) to make things work and failed. Failed myself, my wife, my kids, my mum, everyone. I was in a bad, bad place. There were some ugly scenes that day, emotional outbursts, behaviors I'll never repeat again in my life. Luckily for me, Ella, only 13 at the time had chosen to join me on the trip. We were heading back to my mum's house, so she could visit her grandparents. Having Ella as my sidekick was great, it also gave me hope for our future relationship.

Like any big decision, it is the start that is always the hardest. As we pulled out of the driveway and embarked on our 1000 mile trip, I felt a sense of relief. As the distance grew, so did my hopes. I was now on a new path. It had begun. After our two day adventure across Europe, making time for fun stops, we arrived at my mum's, feeling relieved. This started the next phase of my journey.

After some days with us, Ella was being collected by her other grandparents. I was basically treated like a leper. I'd known these two people for 18 years and whilst I understand people can take sides, I was both disgusted and very hurt. There are two sides to every story and any failed marriage has two guilty parties. Unfortunately after two years, this relationship is still broken and for no good reason.

Whilst being super appreciative that my mum had taken me in, after a few days I realized that I needed my own space to deal with the emotional turmoil inside my head. My brother's bachelor house had just become empty so I had a place of my own to get myself together. I fooled myself into thinking I was in a better emotional state and decided to throw myself into internet dating. The world had moved on a lot since I was last single and this proved to be an eye-opener, rewarding, challenging and a crazy place to be! I tried to forget the past by throwing myself into a new future, not a smart move. Take a messed-up brain and an empty heart and try to mess them up even more with new relationships. Part of it was just to feel wanted again after feeling so much rejection over the last few years.

I spent two months in the UK before returning to Croatia to visit my children. It was an emotional roller-coaster. Many people helped me during this time. Two friends helped me clear my emotional baggage and much more importantly see the reality of myself. Communication with Sally, one of the big reasons why our marriage failed, sank even lower at this time. My great friend Cheri continued her non-judgemental support from afar and allowed me to further release toxic emotions. Henrika, another great friend took the role of counsellor, asking me tough questions and making me face me. They both helped me see a new reality that I couldn't see before. So much of the anger I had inside was actually self-directed. It was easy to blame Sally for lots of things, but the reality was, everything I'd done in our marriage, I'd done voluntarily. *No one made me do anything.* This self-realization allowed me to catapult myself forward and see behaviors in myself that I was unaware of. It allowed me to free myself of the guilt I was holding and create a huge leap in my personal growth. This was an incredibly painful exercise, ironically something I don't believe I would have achieved without stepping outside our marriage and being introspective about everything.

During these two months, another key event started to unfold. Oliver had never truly settled in Croatia and was even more unhappy now that I was gone. Before I left home I'd had a few weeks to really build my relationship with Oliver and Ella and help them understand that I wasn't leaving them, but I couldn't stay. I'd made it clear that they could come with me if they wanted. Oliver had decided that he couldn't stay any longer and wanted out of Croatia. Sally and I had discussed that Oliver might finish school the following year and then move, but nothing so soon. I'd told Oliver I'd love to have him with me, but he'd have to tell his mum himself. Things were already bad enough between us and I didn't want to be accused of coercing our children back to the UK. Oliver agreed to tell his mum, but wanted my support so he'd do it when I was back.

The day came for me to fly back to Croatia to visit Oliver and Ella for the week. I was looking forward to it on one hand but quite unsure how things would be with Sally on the other. In the two months since we'd been apart, so much had happened and our relationship was worse than ever. Sally was making the most of my week with the kids by getting on with her own life. She too had gone down the internet dating route and would spend most of the week away.

That Friday, Sally collected me from the airport, a common scene from the past when I regularly travelled back and forth to the UK, only this time a very uncomfortable pickup and difficult conversations in the car. Sally was leaving early Saturday morning for a few days, so I said to Oliver that he needed to tell his mum tonight. We agreed over dinner was the right time. I was very proud of his bravery. Sally sat there and listened with no outward emotional signs or reactions. I could not believe that this seemed to have little impact on her. It saddened me. The deed was done.

Saturday came and I could relax, just me and the kids. Later that evening I received a message from Sally "Are you around tomorrow? Can we talk?" I was shocked, pleasantly shocked and said "yes". I believed Oliver's decision was a massive wakeup call for her, realizing just how disconnected she was from everyone and not just me.

The next morning I was apprehensive. Sally doesn't talk much so this was good. She arrived and we started to talk. I mean really talk. Talk like we've never talked before in our 17 years of marriage. I was shocked. She'd changed so much in just two months, but it shouldn't really be a surprise as I'd changed so much also. Our long standing connection and attraction was still there. We gave into our feelings and we made love. We talked some more. We made love again and almost got caught in the act by Oliver (who wondered what the hell was going on?) We talked more. We began envisioning a radically new future. We agreed we needed to make some massive changes and optimistically decided to start a new relationship going forward. I'd told everyone that we were 100% over, never, ever getting back together because the gap was too wide. I was wrong. I swallowed my pride, pushed my ego to one side and followed my heart instead.

Putting yourself first allows you to fully show up in the world for everybody. Make sure to look after yourself. Listen to your instincts. Trust and follow them. In doing this you honor not just the man, but the self; the truest part of you. Become the person you love and everyone else will love that person too.

Now as an accredited Life Coach, my wife and I support others in finding themselves in an authentic way. Here are some steps I took and you can take too.

IGNITE ACTION STEPS

*If you're not happy with your life, make the first decision that something has to change, without thinking about the what or the how. (That can come later.)

*Get help from friends, family and/or professional support. We all need people to help us as we cannot see our true selves.

*Get out of your head and into your heart. We are emotional beings, not intellectual. Stop trying to think your way out of emotional dilemmas.

*Tap into and follow your instincts. They are always right.

*Stop worrying about the past or the future. We're only alive today, so enjoy each and every day and live it like it might be your last. (As one day it will be!)

Martin Daniels - United Kingdom
Speaker, Coach, Author
www.reallybeingyou.com

Mike Shields

"The key to life mastery is the precision of your design,
otherwise you only have the default and noise of life."

My intention for writing this story is to share my journey of self discovery and the wisdom gained on the way. I am providing an opportunity for you to look at your own shadows, your blind spots and the way you show up in the world. How wearing a mask creates a veil of separation and only keeps you stuck, so by identifying your deepest unintegrated emotions you can bring around more energetic space for love, joy and freedom.

Awakening to Freedom: Returning to Love

I've never spent a term in a prison, although there have been occasional one-night stopovers. The sentence I put upon myself spans over four decades. It is of guilt, shame and unworthiness. I simply felt as though I never fit and that it was I who was to blame. My doubts and my apprehensions were so traumatic to me that I wore many masks to separate myself and to not allow others to see what I thought of the real me.

I have been a spiritual seeker and a personal development junkie for a long time – you could say for far too long. I have been to many places and have undertaken an enormity of various workshops, retreats, healings, attunements and plant medicines. This book is not a guide for you to follow in my footsteps, far from that indeed. To date, I have had many moments that have ignited my life. I love how the synchronicities leading up to them unfolded and how the irony and beauty of letting go of my fears and insecurities have been divinely guided. I know that without these experiences I wouldn't have had the enrichment, wisdom and depth that's been added to my life. My contribution in this book is my truth of what has unfolded for me until now. I hope there are points that resonate with you, that help you deepen your understanding or guide you to undertake further work in your own life.

A disclaimer before we start this journey... I am in no way perfect, this is a journey for me, too. The healings, inner work and reflections that came to me while writing this chapter, have been mindfully deliberated. I honor each and every word. As I weed out what has been holding me back, I plant new seeds of growth. In some ways, it feels like once my story is out there in the public domain, it no longer has a hold on me. I therefore accept and release the me I've left behind, along with my story. I am now free to be the warrior of masculinity I was destined to be, with focus, strength and clarity.

I ran away from home three times as a boy, the third time worked as I joined the army at just 16. However, I realized that wherever I have lived in the world, I am still there, I cannot escape me, my frustrations or anxieties. On top of this, to keep myself feeling safe and comforted, I turned to many addictions such as alcoholic dependencies, in order to combat my so-called sleep disorder. However, in reality this was merely to quiet down my overactive self-critique. I used 40 cigarettes a day to calm down and tried drugs to escape my reality. Gambling, as I somehow saw, was a connection between love and money.

A recent study by Duke University showed that 45% of our waking behavior is habitual. During my darker moments, it seemed like a lot more. My biggest addiction by far was keeping myself small and somehow enjoyed waking up feeling like shit each morning. The drama I created further added to my self-loathing, as did the surface addictions and the ways I played them out. Each fueled my beliefs of unworthiness. By keeping myself small and showing up in these ways, I could then go through the process of punishing myself as if this was my mistaken definition of love. I simply didn't know any other way out of these cycles and it was taking its toll on my health. Daily, I would take caffeine to keep me awake, alcohol to put me to sleep.

At the same time, I had issues and pressures with an ex-business partner. I was also having a traumatic time establishing any kind of regular access to my two daughters, after separating from their mother.

In the summer of 2010, I was at burnout. I needed to get away to recuperate, so I booked a health-retreat in Mauritius. Having awoken with a hangover on the morning of the flight, I rushed to the airport managing to squeeze in a quick breakfast at a service station enroute. This was pivotal, as by the time I changed flights in Dubai several hours later, I was badly suffering from food poisoning, which lasted the whole eight days I was away. On my return I got checked over by the doctor. After a series of tests, it transpired I had a rare blood disease.

The thing is, I still didn't take this seriously. My business was doing well. I gained a regular cycle of being with my daughters; things were moving more on my terms, however my happiness, self-worth and faith seemed flat and unfulfilling. I did stop smoking for a while as I believed that it would reduce the six weekly blood tests. In my arrogance, my underlying reasoning was, it's almost impossible to get parked at the hospital, which frustrated the hell out of me.

By 2013, I became more focused on my spiritual path, attended several retreats and workshops each year as well as getting attunements for everything under the sun and working with a whole host of healers, mediums and coaches. However, this too got tiring. Even though I had big breakthroughs, I'd return home to my isolation, drinking, smoking and more. What I discovered was, I was now addicted to chasing some kind of spiritual awakening and answers to what was missing in my life. I was doing all this seeking externally, as opposed to going to the source of my anxieties – which were and have always been, all within me.

Early on in this journey, I was at a VIP coaching day where I connected with my soul-sister Nia, a bit of a spiritual sage, with the biggest, warmest heart. We would talk for hours on the phone and meet up from time to time. Our little circle grew, and we were spiritually and emotionally raising each other's vibrations. *Awesome* was our go-to word and one day, we planned to call our meetup 'awesomeness fest', I mentioned this to my coach at the time and was told that there is already something called Awesomeness Fest and that I would be a perfect fit for it. During the drive home, my head was buzzing... I opened the door, switched on my PC and visited the Awesomeness Fest website. There were tickets for sale for an event happening in several weeks in Thailand, so I proceeded to the checkout and went through the enrolment process.

Landing in Thailand, I knew nothing of the company behind Awesomeness Fest which promotes personal development with top notch speakers. I so enjoyed seeing those who starred in the film, *The Secret*, and whilst there, I deeply experienced flow states and things synchronistically happening in my favor. I enjoyed this event so much I proceeded to attend five more and because of the deep connections with the other attendees, I went on to do other events as spin-offs; including a plant medicine retreat in Peru, a darkness retreat in India, camping in Iceland in the winter, a biohacking retreat in Austria and many more random meet-ups...

Here I was again jet setting around the world, trying to find the answers, but to no real avail. Granted, layers of issues and negative thought processes were removed, and my eyes were open to new and different ways, yet I still felt lack and unease within myself. My addictions could be dropped for a while, but then bounce back bigger and stronger at times. I felt troubled as I still had unanswered soul-searching questions keeping me awake at night, such as "What am I missing?" and "What do I need to do next?".

While in Thailand, I met Stuart and attended some of his business events near my home in the North-East of England. At my first event, I met Martin and by my third time there he disclosed that he had been on a weekend retreat just for men several weeks ago and that he was still processing the profound impact. This spoke to me deeply, as Martin was such a big-hearted and lovely man. If it could shake his world, I thought hopefully it could do the same for me. Again, I had that overwhelming moment of insight and clarity as I rushed home and booked myself straight onto it.

This new experience was called the New Warrior Training Adventure weekend run by the ManKind Project. A six-hour journey to the venue in the North of Scotland passed effortlessly with no emotional stress. Then a new reality kicked in upon arrival, I was one of 45 men attending and I was overwhelmed to see some 50 additional men there who were staffing the weekend. What I didn't mention during my spiritual retreats is that my huge group of friends were mostly all female. Now, all of a sudden, I was surrounded by men, no women in sight. I was intimidated and fearful at first. However, I witnessed many men with similar circumstances to mine, including fears, patterns, addictions and despair. I didn't feel alone anymore and despite feeling vulnerable, I also gained an overwhelming sense of inner peace and hope.

Ever since Thailand, I witnessed many females friends going off here and there on some form of self-development, goddess retreat or even priestess training. I was internally crying out, "What is there for us guys?" The answer turned out to be the Mankind Project. The model of follow-up calls, letters and an integration weekend, soon had me understanding myself more. Nowadays I don't need to wear my mask, I resonated with many journeys of the other men. They all seemed to have some form of issue deriving from childhood, some sense of shame, fear, frustration, guilt or anger. Although some of the men's emotions could be directly attributed to their parents' divorce, a death in the family, sexual abuse or other traumatic events, some like me simply became stuck, felt lack, felt alone, didn't feel or should I say, didn't allow love in. Additionally, like me, somehow our pain derived from some form of genetic or karmic issue that needed to be resolved. Resonating with my new *brothers* allowed me to dilute my own apprehensions and integrate them in a healthier and loving way. The ongoing work from the regular men's circles was an ideal way to keep diving deeper, discovering more and I particularly enjoy supporting fellow men.

Becoming a volunteer member a year later was also an eye opener. Remembering my experience with some distance, especially when we did a ceremony to evoke what we worked on during our initiation, took me to an even deeper place. Witnessing other men's reflections on their trauma felt heavy on my heart. Yet with hope, as the bi-weekly integration groups kept you coming back to yourself, which provided a safe container for me to continue showing up as who I really am.

On the last day of my second Awesomeness Fest in Dubrovnik, Croatia, Rich Litvin was on stage. When he spoke of men's circles, my ears pricked up. During that hour, he had us do an exercise in pairs. One at a time, we would begin with the words, "What I don't want you to know about me is..." We followed this with something intimate which we'd never usually share with a stranger. I loved the safety of this contained way of sharing. It was transformation for me. I felt so freed – so liberated.

A few days later, a group of us were walking along the walls of the local castle. We stopped for refreshments in the Konoba Café. Two of us went outside for a cigarette and on our return, we found the rest of the group deep in conversation. One of the women was expressing how she never spoke of the abuse she underwent in her relationship. Something bubbled up in me and I couldn't stop myself. I proceeded to use Rich's opening statement and blurted out, "What I don't want you to know about me is... I used to be an abusive person in previous relationships." This is something I never actually purged before; it felt scary saying it. I had hidden it for a long time. Our lunch that day seemed to last for hours. We all jumped on board, diving deeper into our darkness, we were all in tears at some point purging our feelings while we gathered strange looks from the waiting staff.

The way I showed up in past relationships was something I was not proud of – at all... Maybe it wasn't appropriate to share in that moment... but I felt moved to help her understand that this does go on and know that it's not her fault. I shared from my inner awareness that any man who is wounded himself is capable of doing this. Yes, it takes a weak man to hit a woman and I carry a lot of shame and guilt from this. It was such an awakening example of my unconscious definition of love playing out, my anger, fear and grief was so strong within me during those dark times, my inner child's needs not having been met and I spoke out, not with words, but with my rage and anger.

On reflection, I have hurt a lot of people physically and emotionally. I've acted out arrogantly, abusively and have even been manipulative. At times, I was flippant and have had zero empathy as I have been too self-centered on getting my own needs met. I've suffered a lot with frustration. If something wasn't going my way, I displayed rage and temper and was very judgemental and defensive. I made many assumptions and projections, causing myself further anxiety as it wasn't the truth. During all those times, I would punish myself for these behaviors, ending up being further stuck as the suppression ate away and then backfired on me. This resulted in me playing out further dramas. I have tried so very hard to numb the pain of my identity of not being enough, but these means of sedation and control always ended up further separating me from a real sense of self.

My biggest piece of work on the path to awakening has been to go within myself, to examine these ego-positions and to release their charges and triggers, then bring in forgiveness and reward myself with new beliefs about me, such as worthiness and self-assurance. I am grateful for my daughters and now my new fiancée as they give me the strength and motivation. However, this journey is ongoing. Freedom from addictions and limiting beliefs is a 'one-day-at-a-time' process. Despite who I was, I know I have a big loving heart. I cannot undo what I have done, so I still feel sad for the people I have hurt. Although, I aim to make amends as I am in service to bring Heaven onto this Earth - witnessing peace, love and tranquillity for all beings. I have undertaken an enormity of work on being me, to free myself from this self-imposed torment. Nowadays I am using these tools and wisdom for my own coaching clients and helping them become unstuck, which is both fulfilling and rewarding. Now that I am transformed, I know that I am enough, I can simply enjoy life without limits.

IGNITE ACTION STEPS

The first step is to take the time and commitment to know yourself. Stop being a junkie to YouTube clips, Facebook quotes, etc... you already have all the answers within you.

*Setting time aside, such as 30-60 minutes, sitting or lying down, **go within to meet yourself**, use the statement "I am…" and whatever phrases come up, feel into that pain.

So it could be, "I am not enough, I am bad, I am guilty etc…" Ask, "Who is at the centre of this pain?" "Who feels this pain?" "What loops and patterns appear from your childhood conditioning?"

To build on the exercise above, a thorough process could be writing down the words/phrases, (ego-positions) then separately for 8-12 minutes each, explore where these show up in your life; your relationships, as a teen, as a child. You can continue, into the womb and even past-life, until you have no more identification with this and everything is silent.

The objective of this type of inner discovery is to rid yourself of the patterns and conditioning of the false self you created and bring you back to your real-self. This in turn brings you into divine alignment and creates space for repatterning with phrases such as "I am enough", "I am worthy", "I am lovable" etc.

Another exercise, imagine you're in a bubble and it is your aura. Mentally, write all the labels you and others have given you– on post-it notes. Then go further and stick those labels, on the inside of the bubble. Now imagine a cyclone spinning around you tearing these off and clearing you of this stuck energy and imprinting. After this exercise, fill back up with self-love and positive affirmations about yourself.

With awakening, everything changes, yet everything remains the same. You arrive with a fresh perspective to life, you know yourself, you know you have and always have had the answers within. You have always been pure potential – unconditional love.

Finally there are many paths, like the Mankind Project, mens' groups, addiction recovery groups such as the 12-step program and a whole host of coaches and healers out there. My steps above are working for me and I have tried a whole lot of different ways to find my inner peace and haven. Take these steps, add to them, combine them with steps from other authors in this book, it is after all your journey, make an impact and make it beautiful. Blessings.

Mike Shields - United Kingdom
Energy Healer & Transformational Coach
www.michaelshields.co.uk

Nadim Jarjour

"I enjoy leadership the most when I lead myself into the vision I desire for myself through actions."

I wish to inspire you to have a clear vision of your future and to serve people with what you love doing.

The Two Secrets for a Great Leader

The journey of a great leader always starts by being an intelligent follower to learn from other peoples' experiences and their own.

I grew up in a small city in Lebanon where there weren't a lot of choices for activities or entertainment. I spent most of my free time with my cousins, but I valued the time with my cousin Patrick the most. We shared many experiences together and played all kinds of ball games. We taught each other what each one was good at; how to swim, how to ride a bike. We even did all the pranks for our families together. The only thing that wasn't to my liking was that Patrick was a Boy Scout and had to go to their meeting every Saturday afternoon and I ended up spending this time alone.

One day I asked Patrick if I could join them, although I had no idea about scouting. We arrived at their meeting location and found more than a hundred boy scouts in their uniforms. I was the only one wearing normal clothes. My presence was obvious to everybody and to the scout leader who we were going to talk to and ask if I could join. Without any requirements, he asked me if I will be committed and immediately accepted me when I nodded in agreement. This was a huge turning point in my life, no words can describe what this experience has done for me.

I spent five years as a Boy Scout fully engaged with the Scouts' mission. I was extremely inspired by the story of Baden Powell, the founder of the Boy Scout movement. He turned into a national hero after 217 days of a siege in Mafeking, South Africa. He helped win the war after giving serious responsibilities to youth that surprised the enemies who didn't think youth could help and make such an impact.

After the war, he wanted to start an organization to continue the mission they started during the war, an educational and international organization. What a great story and goal! One of the most influential lessons we learned from him was: "Leave the world a little better than you found it." It's a source of inspiration for so many young people from around the world.

Scouting taught me invaluable lessons and helped me acquire important skills that served me a lot. It gave me the opportunity to devote the majority of my free time doing things that inspired me to grow. It taught me the importance of continued effort on my personal development and encouraged me to always stay loyal to my country, my goals, and my fellow human beings.

Moreover, I learned how to be a good team player and deal with my team's members despite our differences and how to properly communicate with every personality. That was possible through several leadership positions I took along my journey. At scouts, we used games as learning opportunities. We had challenges to face and riddles to solve in order to win as a team. It was like personal development and team-building activities without really knowing it at the time. I only realized that when I became a leader at work. Leadership grew up within me. I had to lead adults with more serious conflicts and create a strong bond between the members despite their differences, I brought them together regardless of their temperament or their educational and social background.

Scouting helped me exit my comfort zone and learn discipline and appreciation. It helped especially during the week-long outdoor camps spent in nature sleeping in a tent, with no bed, no bathroom and no kitchen of course! I started to become aware of how grateful I should be for having a decent life. It made me think about people who don't have this privilege. Moreover, camping brought me closer to nature and taught me to respect it, appreciate it, learn from it and be responsible for protecting it.

I also built very strong friendships with like-minded people with whom I am still in contact today. They are now my best friends. We often organize gatherings and remind each other of the good and the bad moments we shared together. We support and help each other on professional and personal levels. Scouting taught me how to choose my friends wisely and know who are the ones I can count on. I believe this is possible only when you have the chance to really get to know the person, especially in tough situations. To sum up, scouting took all my interest up until the age of twenty-five and was my source of motivation. It was by far the most valuable education I received in life and the huge advantage it has is that I got to learn all these things at a young age.

From being a small team leader, I then became the whole troop's leader. I will never forget the day I was appointed. One of the seasoned chiefs told me during the ceremony, "Nadim, every leader you met so far had two lessons for you: number one, they taught you what you should do; two, they taught you what you shouldn't do. Make sure you apply their lessons to become a great leader."

What an eye-opening insight, I felt it was true. We can learn from every person we meet, even the younger ones. Whether it's from our siblings, nieces, friends or strangers we just met once; everybody has at least one lesson for us.

Nothing made me happier than the feeling of someone growing from within because of what I was able to do for them. During my five years as a leader, there were five pairs of brothers including my own brothers. I was fascinated by the fact that each individual was achieving results completely different than his brother. One was very engaged and committed to the scout activities and the other was not. So I started wondering how two persons having the same parents, the same home, the same school, the same scout leader, even the same genetic background, had two different or opposite results? That triggered a big question in my mind about how do results really happen.

I kept wondering about this question and it somehow shaped the direction of my life. After I graduated from college, I studied computer science. I loved this field and I was very motivated to graduate and start working and develop better software. I worked in different companies and each one of them had an added value to my career path. However, I had a feeling that what I was doing wasn't enough for my growth and I always strived for more. I didn't commit for more than one year at a time for the first three companies I worked with. The moment my growth reached a plateau I resigned to find another company that promised a bigger growth opportunity.

During my last employment, I was the Vice President of an IT

Consulting company helping our corporate clients improve their productivity and collaboration. I worked on re-engineering their work processes, the applications, and their methodologies, all to create an impact on the bottom line of their company. We were doing an excellent job in everything we promised our clients to do, but the overall productivity and efficiency didn't improve and I had no clue why. All the frameworks, applications and methodologies we used for our clients were the best of the best. Those methodologies were the reason why some big companies like Google, Facebook, Microsoft, etc. succeeded. Within my own team, I faced the same challenges and I didn't know how to go forward.

I started noticing that for the change in results to be real and permanent on the outside, it had to start from within the employees. My curiosity about human behavior increased dramatically. Why do people do what they do and why are the majority of employees not engaged and unhappy with the work they do?

They say, "When the student is ready, the teacher will appear." That's when I decided to grow my knowledge and I started to read books on personal development and human behavior. But I still felt the answer was missing to my questions.

Then one day, on a business flight, I noticed the man sitting next to me was absorbed in a book he was reading. I always enjoy having discussions with book readers so, I initiated the conversation and I became excited by his enthusiasm about his book. We started talking about personal development and leaders who had big impacts on people's lives around the world. At the end of the conversation, he advised me to read about a person named Bob Proctor. I had never heard about this person before, but I was excited to find out more.

The moment I got home I did a quick search about Bob Proctor. I read about him, his books, the programs he taught, and his students' comments about how the information he taught them changed their lives. I was more motivated to dive into this philosophy so I filled out a form I found on his website.

A few days later, I received a call from a lady who worked with Bob Proctor offering me to enroll in an educational program which was the outcome of 58 years he devoted to studying and teaching about human potential. I hesitated at first because everything was happening so fast and the required financial investment was very big. Thoughts were rushing through my mind, but something strong inside of me was pushing me to take this step and I took it! Honestly, after I hung up with her, it didn't feel like Nadim made the decision. Something inside of me made the decision on my behalf. Maybe my burning desire to gain a deeper understanding of human behaviors and results.

As I started seriously studying the material, and committing to the actions Bob asked me to take, I began reading the books he recommended. My interest in this information grew more than ever. After I went through the entire program, I wanted to have a conversation with Bob and thank him for all the efforts he put into creating a program covering what every human being must know about human potential and success. His teachings answered all the questions I had and completed the picture in my mind I had been searching for all this time.

Bob gave me answers to many questions:
- How do results happen?
- Why some genius people are broke in life?
- Why people do what they do?
- How does our mind work?
- Why the majority of people are not happy?
- How to implement permanent changes in our results?
- What is success, and how can we reach it?

I called the lady from Bob's office and asked her if she could put me in contact with Bob so I could have a quick conversation with him. I knew that it might never happen because I imagine how busy Bob must be. But still, I felt like I had to give it a try. To my surprise, she promised to share my request with Bob and said she would get back to me. A few moments later, I got a call back from her saying, "Bob is waiting for you on the line. Do you want me to connect you?" I couldn't believe it was happening after only a few hours from my request. He agreed to call me without even knowing who I was. When I answered and heard Bob's voice, I was speechless. At eighty-five-year-old, Bob was so down to earth, so genuine, so sincere.

I shared my appreciation and how grateful I was for the opportunity I had to learn his invaluable information. He told me, "Thank you Nadim for your message. I have heard a lot about you and I am happy that you want to have a conversation with me. I have an opportunity for you. Since you are a serious student and applied my teachings into your life and witnessed its powerful impact on your results, why don't you become my consultant? You can help me in spreading the right education in your region and help people achieve their goals."

There was a silent moment for ten seconds, I was still speechless. My intention was to simply thank him, and here he was, offering me an opportunity that never ever crossed my mind; I had no clue where it might lead me. However, deep down, I knew this could be the path I've had been looking for; a golden opportunity that would allow me to serve people around me in developing their potential and achieve their desired results. I was skeptical at first because I had a decent salary, position and job satisfaction. But at the same time, I had a burning desire to serve the people of my country and share with them the invaluable education I have received.

A few days after I asked for God's direction, it was obvious I should make the decision to go for it...and I made it because I believe everything happens for a reason and I must trust my intuition. I traveled to Toronto, Canada from Beirut, Lebanon to meet Bob and study with him for a full week! It was an incredible experience. The more I studied, the more emotionally involved I became with what Bob was teaching me.

Months after I made the decision...I resigned from my position, made a commitment to devote my life to my passion - helping others achieve greatness. I went back to my country after living for many years abroad and founded my own company, *Mentalthon*. Honestly speaking, it was a huge and scary decision. I was highly paid with lots of benefits, traveling the world, leading a team of consultants and project managers, managing huge responsibilities but all of these promises were tiny compared to the psychological reward I am getting now while serving humanity.

I sent my resignation letter to the CEO. That initiated serious negotiations that went on for weeks offering me so many perks, including a substantial raise and significant shares in the company. This made the situation even more challenging to continue with my decision. I protected and honored my dreams from the huge financial and material rewards and temptations. I made my decision with no looking back.

My education and huge interest in personal development kept growing with time. I read books from all the well-known people who worked in this field like Bruce Lipton, Joe Dispenza, Earl Nightingale, Jim Rohn, Napoléon Hill. Their approach was sometimes different but always enriching. I had a burning desire to serve people and I wanted to do what I love, so I started my own company. I chose Mentalthon as a name: "Mental" because everything starts and ends in the mind. It is difficult to achieve success and enjoy a great quality of life without a proper understanding of how the mind functions and how to use it to our liking... and "thon" from the word marathon to show the importance of continuous education just like the athlete who needs to train in a consistent way to achieve great results.

Life is full of abundance for everyone, there's no need to compete. We just need to discover what we love doing and how we love serving others. Become aware of the infinite and dormant potential within you and make a decision to go after it. I wish you to see yourself as I see you, a person with an infinite potential that you can achieve whatever your mind can conceive. Just believe in yourself and make sure you commit to the following action steps below!

IGNITE ACTION STEPS

*Decide what you want. Rediscover what you love doing. If it's challenging for you to uncover that, the following two questions can help:

- What you do not want to happen in your life? Start from the opposite.
- What's the thing that time flies while doing it?

*Make it a goal with a date. Write it on a piece of paper in the present tense and carry it wherever you go. (This is your goal card).

*Read it at least twice a day.

*Write it down when you wake up. Visualize yourself as the person who already achieved the written goal. There's a science behind that, if you are skeptical, do it anyway.

*Take daily actions on your goal. No matter how small the action is, take it. Success is to progressively move towards your desired destination or your goal. You become successful when you take daily actions, not when you achieve your goal.

Nadim Jarjour - Lebanon
Human Performance Expert
www.mentalthon.com

JUAN PABLO BARAHONA

*"Every challenge and weakness is an opportunity
to awaken your full potential."*

I invite you to go deeper, to constantly look at your blind spots and keep releasing the most subtle layers that still hold you back from your Greatness.

EMBODYING THE INNER MASTER INSIDE OF ME

I felt a deep sense of worry from a young age. All the masculine figures in my life had fallen apart. My father left our house when I was two years old and my older brother almost died when I was nine. His aggressive epilepsy was killing him. The doctors said he would not last more than one or two years. We took him to many healers and shamans to improve his condition. These new modalities and ways of thinking started my journey in breaking free from limiting beliefs.

Wanting to help my brother so much led me into the healer's path, fascinated by these subjects at just 12 years old. The inner healer in me emerged, along with my sincere passion for helping others. It wasn't a straight line to the beautiful life I live today, but it certainly helped me to understand that embracing emotions was essential to human beings. My brother, my best friend, was everything to me. When I had to accept he was never going to be truly healthy, my own inner gifts came out. Sometimes, the most emotionally painful experiences are the ones which guide us to our purpose and happiness. They are opportunities to wake up from within. A person can drop into a victim complex or become their own superhero depending on their mindset.

Emotions are the doorways to the core of all our negative beliefs, disconnection, and fears. Emotions are a sign that something inside needs work. They are like stored energy in our system that hasn't been expressed or used. In order to activate their full potential, we have to let ourselves feel. Feel to heal, I often say. For a man, this can be uncomfortable and feel somewhat odd due to society's customs. But the moment one releases all judgment, emotions help achieve a fulfilled and soulful existence.

This can be an arduous and triggering process. I used to numb my emotions because during my childhood others had said I was too emotional. I even stopped laughing. I was scared I would be told I was too loud or sounded stupid. I didn't act when I felt a surge of inspiration because others had criticized the way I sounded. I kept my anger in because I knew it wasn't an "appropriate" emotion. My appearance had also been criticized and I almost killed myself trying to fix that unfixable aspect of me.

The way we are taught to keep our emotions in goes further than the criticism we receive from other people. I learned early on I wasn't supposed to cry. "Only girls do that." As a result, I built armor around who I was and projected an image that wasn't me. I did what I thought would make others love and accept me. I stopped dancing creatively because people said I looked "gay." I quit theater club and the school band to avoid activities that were associated with 'nerds'. I wanted to be part of the cool crowd. There was always a structure I wanted to fit into. I wanted to be accepted into groups so I created images I unconsciously held to be loved and accepted. On a sadder note, I stopped expressing overall what I felt because it would 'hurt' the people I loved. I didn't want to create pain for anyone. I didn't want to feel guilty. I especially didn't want to feel rejection from my family and from my community. From early on in my childhood, I was made fun of, since I hadn't been raised to be 'tough.' Every time that happened, I hardened and became a little bit more estranged from who I really was. I was building walls all around me so that people couldn't see me, and every time I felt hurt, I would add a brick to my wall; accepting the limiting beliefs and restrictions.

We all want to feel safe, loved, accepted and, most of all, we want to feel a sense of belonging, of being "part of". We feel that sacrificing our uniqueness and what is natural to us will allow us to fit in. We forget we were trying to fit into was a cage. More often than not, that cage makes us into someone that only adapts to the social norms.

I wanted my family to be proud of me, especially since so much of our home life revolved around my brother's disease. I felt that I was the one who had to "fix" this and balance out the situation. It was no one's fault but I became the 'superhero'. I repressed all of my negative emotions becoming completely detached and disconnected.

This inner death took me to a point where I literally wanted to kill myself. I suffered from depression and didn't know how to heal. I had completely forgotten how it felt "to feel". Life didn't have any meaning and I was ready to end it all. I started numbing myself with all kinds of drugs starting with sugar, then alcohol, marijuana and finally, I got lost in cocaine. I was only 17 years old, yet hungry for enlightenment, going to different spiritual communities, studying with different teachers and trying all ways possible to access the depths of my spiritual connection. They taught me how to achieve high levels of consciousness. How the material world was just an illusion and how the only thing that mattered was my devotion and surrender to God. This didn't last because deep inside I was craving the real inner work: how to transform my emotions, my wounds, my low self-esteem and how to really find my purpose in life. I remember feeling so deluded after a seven-day immersion in an ashram, far away from what they were teaching, so lonely in my path... I felt nobody understood me and there wasn't a way to achieve what I was looking for. When we finished the immersion, driving home, my friend told me he needed to do a fast errand. Arriving at the place, I felt very weird. There was something he wasn't telling me. He returned with a gram of cocaine and told me he did this sometimes as a recreation. I was totally perplexed after everything we had just talked about in the immersion, to a point that I felt very angry and judgmental towards him. He apologized while preparing himself a thick line of white powder. When I saw the expression on his face, the power and sense of well-being that emanated from him, I totally lost my mind in envy and asked him to prepare a row for me.

As the white powder entered my nose, I immediately felt the change in my mood and perspective of the world. I felt powerful, clear and focused... I felt for the first time I had really found God. Everything I was looking for manifested in a second and I didn't even need to sniff anymore. I was completely in bliss for the whole night.

The next day I felt guilty, sad, almost depressed and with no sense of meaning for life. I called a dealer friend for more white 'god-powder' to start my 'healing journey'... that is what my crazy mind thought. I didn't use it to party or get lost in the outside world. I was totally submerged in my room, writing in my journal, walking from one end to the other; 'solving' not only my problems but the whole world's problems. I released anger and rage. I would hit my pillow, shout, then open in tears and cry until I couldn't express myself anymore. I dove into the freedom of really opening up to my emotions and at the same time feeling very focused and powerful in the healing process. My honeymoon with this "artificial god" didn't last long. After three weeks on and off the stuff, my nasal passages were completely destroyed. I stopped feeling any effect after consuming it and spiraled into a deep emptiness inside. Scared in those moments, I let it go but returned, again and again, searching for the false promise I found in that first high. For three months, I played with the devil I had mistakenly called god, going from heaven to hell in an instant and feeling worse as time passed by. Depression set in. I had lost all reasoning and wanted to run away from my skin. I hated being in my body, who I was and what I was becoming. I found myself with a knife at my wrist, clear I would never find my purpose, convinced I wasn't meant to live anymore. Kneeling on the ground... with the cold knife pushing against my wrist... my heart beating at 100 km/h, my whole body shaking... my nose bleeding... my head bursting in pain... I was so close to going... until I heard an inner voice say, "Noooo... this is enough."

I suddenly saw myself from far away, like in a very clear movie. It was as if it wasn't me anymore... I shouted as loud as I could and burst into tears, letting the knife fall down to the ground. I cried for a long time, lying on the ground until I had just enough strength to get up and call my father for help. After a deep healing conversation with him, he immediately took me to a clinic where I began recovery and started opening up to my deep healing journey.

I had reached the ultimate level of suffering and was taken on an exploration of deep transformational work. I began discovering little by little who I truly was. The more I expressed everything I had suppressed in my life, the lighter I would feel. I healed wounds I had been carrying since I was a little boy. I started laughing, playing, singing, being natural, spontaneous and authentic again. I had to search deep inside for everything I had tried to hide and let go of all the frozen emotions which had never been expressed, stuck inside of me. Everything from the past was trapped in my body. I had learned to hide from my truth for years, and it took a deep commitment to release my blockages to smile again. I had to summon up the courage to melt the ice around my heart so that I could connect with the power of my vulnerability.

After this intense work with psychologists and doctors, I knew I needed more tools. I was just beginning my unwinding process. I found a spiritual men's community where they worked with addictions and other men, to find fulfillment and wholeness that nothing outward could provide. Amazing teachers helped me return to a simple lifestyle, where I could speak my truth from my heart and love myself no matter what.

As part of my healing process, I continued my spiritual work, on myself and by helping others. At the age of 20, the phoenix inside me rose up from the ashes. I became the leader in a Costa Rican community dedicating two years to help all kinds of men in their transformational journeys: from people living on the street to repressed artists, musicians, entrepreneurs, visionaries, even lawyers, doctors and professionals not living their truth. This was really where my obsession for helping others began and I focused all my energy in expanding all the tools I could learn to support myself and others in their inner transformations. After so many years, my conclusion was that we all create a "shadow purpose" to adapt to society. But very few listen to their inner guidance and follow their divine purpose. Many just adapt and numb themselves with the material world and everything that society considers acceptable... like pornography, cigarettes, alcohol, sugar, gambling, sex, buying 'things', Facebooking, texting, sexting and all the other ways we find refuge to escape our inner truth. Others, like me, 'fail' at that game, heading for the most suicidal substance we can find.

I don't judge anything or anyone. I have done it all, feeling the same emptiness after. When we continue looking for something outside ourselves to feel the joy of being alive, we continue running away from our Divine Purpose. Dislodged from our greatness, from our Wild and Authentic Being that is unique and wants to share our gifts with the world. The moment we start judging ourselves and start controlling the way we "should be" and what we "should do" in life, we start disconnecting from our essence.

I recount my experience so you can see how every obstacle becomes an opportunity to succeed and find what you may have been looking for all your life. No matter how dark and heavy things can get for you, know you can find a state where you can live in accordance with your inner freedom, and a sense of self-love.

After many years of breakthroughs and awakenings in many different disciplines, I have come to understand every single individual is capable of that miracle. We can all learn to cultivate high energy, a healthy body, a clear mind, focused awareness, balanced emotions, empowerment, determination, abundance, intuition, confidence, inner peace and joy. This isn't a dream reserved for a few. It is a deep process that requires a strong conviction that we give our all to it.

Feeling your emotions isn't a luxury you get around to when you decide you have time. It is a requirement to liberate yourself and live the life you truly want. When we become grounded physically and emotionally we start feeling on the deepest level who we truly are. After that, we can move to tackle our greatest ally and most serious enemy: the mind.

Over time, I began to feel the balance between feeling powerful, confident and centered in my body and at the same time feeling all emotions were accessible to me. I saw how I could use energy-in-motion to manifest the life of my dreams. I completely opened up into what I call *Surrendered Manifestation*: a beautiful harmonious process of listening to your inner voice, being available for your intuition to speak, accepting your inner knowing and being successful in life. This empowers you to manifest and achieve from a place of ease, grace and flow. The more I surrendered, the more I opened up to gifts and possibilities in my life. The more I embodied it, the more I awakened the highest version of myself; the more amazing the synchronicities which showed up, matching my vibration and the energy I was emanating. I began traveling the world teaching what I loved, living the life of my dreams, from a space of vulnerability and surrender. From a space of listening, trusting and acting from that inner voice that was now awake. Guiding me and showing men the way. From that same space, I manifested the relationship of my dreams, attracting a partner who would match my vibration without feeling dimmed by my fire, and empowering each other to even higher versions of ourselves.

This was the moment when I can say I really started living...

After doing deep internal work of release and transformation, I can laugh like a child without shame. I flow naturally with whatever feels good to do without trying to be approved or loved. What I once denied, I now use to help people come back to their natural state of bliss, creativity, and flow. I work with all kinds of mind-sets, heart-sets, and core-sets to help men accept who they are and start shining from their core and their inner gifts. My vulnerability has become my most powerful tool.

No matter how deep the emptiness feels inside, we always have the choice to release whatever is dimming our light and remember who we really are... We always have the choice to expand and grow, burning any sense of domestication and limiting belief that is holding back our deepest truth from shining through. Every experience, every choice we made, every pain we have felt is a stepping stone to open up more space inside so we can receive, feel, and be more. It is all available to us right now...Yes, the moment can be now! You just have to say yes and the whole Universe will support you.

IGNITE ACTION STEPS

* **Be raw** and real with where you are in every area of your life. Are you listening to your deepest desires or conforming yourself to mediocrity? Do you feel completely fulfilled with who you are, your relationships and what you are doing in the world?

* **Commit** to releasing in every way possible everything that is holding you back. Observe masks you have used to show something to the world that is not true, any emotions you have never expressed and felt ashamed of, hiding them from the world so they don't judge you. Let go of the persona that wants to appear in a certain way, that part of you that wants to feel loved, admired and accepted. Know yourself and all the habits that take you away from being focused and centered in manifesting the life of your dreams.

* **Show up** as the highest version of yourself. How do you walk, breathe, move, think and act even when no one is watching? How do you show up in the world? How do you relate to people? What do you talk about? What are you tolerating in yourself and others? How present are you in your family and your community? Remember it's all interrelated and how we do one small thing is how we do everything. Radiate your Greatness into the world. Let your inner magnetism shine. Be focused on your vision. Love yourself no matter what, knowing the more you contribute to the world with your gifts, the more abundance you will live in your life. **Just be authentically you.**

Juan Pablo Barahona - Costa Rica
Transformational Speaker, Author, Coach, and Healer
juanpablobarahona.com & consciouslivingschool.com

Rawle James

"My life is a beautiful balance of light and dark
for without both there is no growth."

I hold no intent or expectation for the readers of the men's Ignite book but one. Love yourself. Loving yourself takes work and patience. In *My Father's Voice* is my invitation to get in touch with your own story.

In My Father's Voice

There I sat at my favorite coffee house on a Wednesday evening after a day spent uninspired at the office. I found myself holding space with about ten others as music played in the background. A man on his laptop intently pounding brilliance on his keyboard. To my left, a young woman, probably a student, researching and looking like she's writing a paper. A mother and father having a robust conversation while their little boy is fixated by what's on his screen. One barista busily putting away just delivered baked goods as another scrambled to serve a customer. And me. I'm trying to trust the pen as it attempts to flow across the paper, capturing from my memory banks the suspended moment that ignited my awakening.

I am a grown man in the last days of my 57th rotation around the sun, still having moments of doubt about being a good writer. Countless times my friends and colleagues have told me, "You have a way with words." But in those moments of praise, my default takes me back to being a 12-year-old boy. Why 12, you may ask? Well I hold a memory of my Pops showing up for my 12th birthday. His gift of 25 cents and a brief decree of, "I hope you are doing your best," followed by his quick exit. When this 12-year-old boy appears in my mind, he is always accompanied by his father's voice — the original farmer who planted seeds of, "You are too fat", "Too lazy", "You'll never amount to anything," into the fertile soil of me and my brothers' minds. All we were trying to figure out was how to get our Pop's approval.

As a boy, I just loved drawing. I was really good at it! When I wasn't outside playing football or on my bed flipping through an encyclopedia, I was drawing — always tracing characters from the TV guide or doodling from my imagination. And singing! It was right up there with drawing. There was always a tune or melody in my head. Still today, if I'm breathing, I'm humming. I remember back in grade six, auditioning for an open try-out for choir — I made it! I could not believe I got selected and furthermore, I remember the teacher saying, "Where have you been hiding?"

Truth be told, I hid in my father's voice. I honestly can't remember as a young boy, a teenager, or as a young man, a time when I was not afraid and angry. These, in my mind, were justifications for hiding my talents. Sure, I played sports. My brothers and the kids in the neighborhood lived to play sports, especially football and baseball; we played it all. These fearful and angry emotions started early as the other kids saw how good I was but I just never really allowed myself to shine. I was always thinking I wasn't good enough or that the other kids were better than me — the chubby, slow kid.

Inside, I was a great athlete — A great singer — A great dancer. Inside, I was smart and created many moments where my father's voice did not have power over me. In those moments, I was just as talented and cute as any other kid. Inside, no one ever said I wasn't good enough. Well, that's a lie — because my father's voice strangely enough, started sounding like mine.

So here I am, a month from my 58th rotation. I'm feeling strong within. Damn it, I feel groovy. I'm in the good graces of the universe as I embrace life and all my talents at this stage. Yet, as confident as I feel, in the midst of this moment, while attempting to write my Ignite Moment, I find myself fighting my father's voice that's masked as my own.

My life has been a series of suspended moments. Instants that shaped the man who powers this pen; moments lived in the time loop of my memories which houses the wisdom that guides my walk. Like all who inhabit this world, I have had many defining moments that have shaped my perception of self, life and the choices I put forth into the world. I no longer view life as good or bad, right or wrong. This applies especially to my experiences. Before my Ignite Moment, I could not understand why God would allow so much bad to be cascaded upon me. My family ended, as I knew it, when I was six – when my mother left my brothers and me to be a nanny in America. Can you imagine leaving your kids to go to another country to raise someone else's family so that your own family can have a better life?

As far as my early memories go, we had a good life. My father always wanted to realize his dreams of moving to the United States of America. The roller-coaster ride started when I was eight years old. My father, my two brothers and I left Trinidad and Tobago to join our Mom in Brooklyn, New York. Then for two years my brothers and I were taken, without our mother's permission, to live with my father's Uncle and his wife. Once again, our mother was forced from our lives. This time no Pops, no Mom and an Uncle who redefined the meaning of mean. Thank God for his wife Ms. Lucy, who did her best to make life enjoyable for us. In early 1972, we were returned to our mother and lived in Brooklyn until my departure for Toronto. As the eldest, I always had lots of questions that my father was not prepared to answer. His usual answer would be, "When you guys are older, I'll explain." I guess we never got old enough.

There are other benchmark moments in my life that I vividly recall, like the first time I came to Canada. I still remember driving up Queen Elizabeth Way and seeing the CN Tower. However, the excitement of that time was cloaked with fear as I was concerned about the negative, adversarial relationship between my stepfather and I. It seemed to be a common theme with the men in my life at that time: my Pops, step-father, and paternal uncle. As well, I felt cut off from Pops and my two brothers who were living in Hollywood, California.

Another vivid memory was the first time I made a presentation before a roomful of strangers (business people outside of colleagues) and realized, "This is what I am meant to do." And the summit of memories: the birth of my three children (especially since I never thought I would be a father) and being there to see their exits from the portal and taking their first breath of life. Literally, my heart skipped beats. I am sure I missed a few breaths as I stood in awe and amazement at the beauty and strength of their mothers. I've been blessed with many special moments; however, there is one that stands head and shoulders above even the births of my three kids.

To steal some of Churchill's thunder, December 17th, 2001 at 1:45 pm, is a moment that will live in my infamy. It altered my consciousness… my life. This happened on a snowy Monday in Toronto. I took the day off work to do what I was good at – hiding from the world when things go bump in the night. I wasn't enjoying the corporate world anymore. I'm not sure I ever really did.

My marriage had ended earlier that year and I'd moved to a neighbor across the street. I carried the illusion that a wife and kid, then two and a half, were enough to hold together what I knew was crumbling. Anger soon consumed me. I was not in a good place, inside or out. I'd become a man trapped in his victim state of mind. I remember this like it was yesterday. On that snowy Monday, we (my ex-wife and I) had a nasty fight on the phone. I violently hung up in a stage of rage. I was angry with myself, not her. I couldn't believe the vile language I used against the mother of my son. Actually yes, I could, for I had learned from the master — my father. (I still hold memories of my father's anger, words and abuse towards my Mom.) But I am not my father.

How could I have spoken to the mother of my son that way? I'd vowed I would never abuse a woman. Who was I kidding? I have spoken many times in such a manner; anger was my default. My thoughts were dark. I wanted to hurt her as she had hurt me. I wanted her to see who she'd abandoned like an animal at the side of the road. My thoughts were all over the place, with no rhyme or reason to them. My default reaction was to fall into what was familiar, "Tonight, I'm going out to get drunk and get laid."

That's when it happened! As soon as the tail end of that thought exited, I heard a voice. The voice sounded like me, but I knew it wasn't, for it wasn't angry. The voice simply stated, "Why are you going to do that?" "You know what you will get." In a heartbeat, my world stopped. I was frozen. "What was that?" Was it the burning bush or did I have a psychotic break? I remember looking around to see if I was alone. I must have snapped. But I know what I heard. It was as real as I am. I also knew the woman I needed to call –- my first spiritual guide. We had not yet met in the flesh.

I don't remember looking for her card. I do remember though, how I got it. A few weeks earlier I had run into an ex-colleague in downtown Toronto. I hadn't seen her for a while so we decided to grab a coffee to get caught up. I found myself sharing things about me I'd always kept hidden. The pain I felt; the anger that stirred within that I thought I hid so well. My friend looked at me and said, "Sounds like you are seeking." Like in a movie, she reached into her purse, drew out that business card, slid it across the table and told me, "Call this woman." That was it. We finished our coffees over small-talk.

I did call that woman soon after, introduced myself, and set up a meeting. Of course, I didn't honor said meeting and, if memory serves, there were two other times I chose to cancel as well. I always had some elaborate lie as to why I couldn't see her. "I'm sorry but…" She would reply with, "No sorries. You're just not ready to connect with it." (A phrase I still use to this day.)

That Monday afternoon, immediately after hearing 'the voice' I was preoccupied as I pulled out her card. "What had just happened?" I found myself calling her and telling her of the experience that just transpired in my kitchen. She quickly replied, "Sounds like you're ready now." "Come see me tomorrow at 10:00 AM."

The next morning, I drove an hour to meet this stranger who really wasn't a stranger. I arrived right on time and was greeted by a silver/blonde haired woman. She welcomed me. We sat across from each other in her office and she didn't speak for what seemed like an hour. I remember feeling very uncomfortable and she sensed it as well. "Why are you here?" she asked. I replied, "I don't know. You told me to be here at 10:00." She asked again, "Why are you here?" Again, I replied, "I don't know."

"You're not ready to connect with it," she says, then for the 30 minutes she performed Reiki on me. Afterwards, we proceeded to her kitchen where she made me lemon tea. We sat drinking tea and just talked. To this day I still have no idea what we spoke of. All I know is that when I departed from her home around 1:00 PM, everything and I mean everything, in my world had flipped. I felt different, like I had awoken from a dream.

In the ensuing weeks, I started doing inner work with her. An unfamiliar and unsettling feeling started to emerge and, even though my fears heightened, I kept returning. There was a new fear stirring inside that I didn't give voice to. I kept showing up and looked forward to sharing with her.

A couple of months passed before my next guide made her appearance. It was Spring of 2002 and I was at a networking event in downtown Toronto. This kind of event was filled with lots of small-talk and bullshit about life and accomplishments. These kind of gatherings always made me feel small, inadequate and the use of bullshit was baffling. I saw a woman across the room. Our eyes met and we started making our way towards each other. Fixated on her being, I extended my right hand, "Hello, I'm Rawle James."

We did the traditional exchange of rank and serial number. We had lots in common. We were both former recruiters and, in various stages of our careers, managed and assisted in the professional development of others. Very quickly into our conversation, I found myself once again sharing feelings about myself and my world, which I usually kept hidden. I'm not sure how it came about, but she simply said, "I would love to work with you," meaning personal self-mastery work. But as usual, my finances were strained and not in order. I thanked her, saying, "Maybe in the future." We exchanged business cards and that was that; or so I thought!

She called me the very next morning asking to meet. I once again stated that I was not in a financial position to partake of her services. She repeated her request and I finally agreed to meet at her home after work that day. When I arrived she greeted me with a big warm smile and guided me towards her living room where she had tea waiting for us. As she slowly and attentively served what she had prepared, she told me a story: "After we parted yesterday, I came home and settled into my evening. Later as I slept, I dreamed that Yeshua (Jesus) appeared and commanded me, "You have to work with this man; he has important work to do. You must give him the gift of your time.""

There I was, in this stranger's home, dumbfounded by what I just heard. Yet, it felt right. She asked, "Will you accept this gift?" Without hesitation, I said, "Yes." You see, I had asked the universe for help and, once again, I was provided the teacher. We agreed to meet Mondays from 11:00 AM to 3:00 PM for 12 weeks.

So, it began. We worked with endless streams of consciousness writing, meditating, chanting, talking about my life (childhood, parents, siblings) and sexual and physical abuse. My understanding of pain, suffering, trauma, forgiveness, surrendering and rebirth shifted. It felt like the old Rawle had died and after 12 weeks a new me emerged. The victim that was Rawle relinquished to allow the victor to walk. My Ignite Moment just provided the spark. The gifts of those two earth angels who answered the call I placed to the universe, guided me through an awakening that I didn't think was possible. They gently and lovingly opened me up inside to the wonders and magic of the universe. I became comfortable with loving me and the more comfortable I got with my worthiness, the stronger I felt within.

My truth is: I am not here to have a spiritual experience, for I am spirit. I am here to master this human journey where all my experiences are of value. In this new evolution of me, I began seeing my parents differently and understanding the soul contract I'd made with them so long ago. I made my peace with them both, as I realized that there is nothing to forgive them for; they did their best.

Today, I embrace my father's voice. I have learned so much about life and people from that man. The man whom I say proudly taught me about being a man in his way and from his love. Through the practice of forgiving myself, I've let go of the burden I carried and hid so well. In learning how to love myself and feel my worthiness, I got right with the Universe/God/ Source. I am not on a path that's less travelled because from the moment of my arrival on Earth, I was on the path. I was never broken nor needing fixing. I am evolution - so I am always evolving. I trust it will work out. To date, it continues...

IGNITE ACTION STEPS

*The power of choice resides in you. You are the creator of your reality.

*Stay open to the teachers that appear, because they will show up. In those moments, as much as it may be foreign to you, trust your intuition.

*Become a researcher in your past for it is a vault of wisdom to map your future.

*Before you can 'let go of it' you must first be willing to go within to understand it.

*We are here to have all experiences. Light cannot exist without Dark.

*All that you desire and want in life lies on the other side of what you fear.

*Be an example to others by knowing how to love yourself. (For me this is emulated by Gandhi saying, "It takes a lit candle to light another."

*Seek first to understand, then be understood. The practice of empathy.

Rawle Iam James - Canada
Inspirational Speaker/Poet
www.rawlejames.ca

SANTIAGO RAFAEL PASCUAL

"You will know the truth of your ego,
and the truth you emanate will set you free."

**The main purpose of my story is liberation of our true being. In my ex-
periences, I've learned how miserable I could be with the blinders of my
ego. What we cannot see is the most dangerous enemy of our freedom;
an invisible prison. I share with you ways out of it and the journey that
reshaped my reality and identity.**

LIBERATION FROM INVISIBLE PRISONS

I was raised as a prince. As a child, my father called me 'my little prince'.
He would bring me gifts and do his best to provide optimal conditions. I
remember playing polo with the prince of Malaysia when I was 11. Being
treated as and placed in the elite wherever I went, became a way of being. I
just followed the inertia of the Royal Chariot.

By the age of 22, I had studied seven years of business administration
since I had to uphold the 'legacy of the kingdom'. I worked with my father in
'first-need' politics that consisted of delivering 'food' to people in need. One
day, picking up one kilogram of sugar, my body was paralyzed by pain. My
lower back and legs felt like having smashed glass inside. This sensation had
been getting worse over the past few years, but at this moment, I couldn't bear

it. I could not tolerate being in my body. During the nights, I couldn't sleep due to the discomfort and suffering. If someone offered me to chop my legs off I would have accepted. In addition to this, my work environment was full of attitudes tainted by envy and resentment. University was dull and tedious. These were huge drains on my life energy. I felt exhausted all the time. I begged for willpower.

My life at that moment was unbearable. I had to keep myself numbed with food, video games and alcohol. Parties, addictions and 'friends' were my pseudo companions of loneliness. I weighed 104 kilograms (229 pounds), with arthritis, depression and all my addictions. This is where the inertia of life took me. Until one night I saw a dancer.

I was at a hip-hop party and a rare connection inside myself happened-- distinct brain synapses between senses I had never felt before. The dancer's movement revealed a sound I was not hearing. It felt like magic. A strong force inside compelled me to follow this dancer. He was a person with special effects that defied reality. I had to learn from him, so I went to his classes. The bouncing movements felt like glass cutting from inside my knees and my extra 25 kilograms pressuring against them. I danced through the pain. Painkillers and muscle relaxers now had a purpose: to be able to dance.

The mix of having a purpose and overcoming the unbearable pain of my existence fueled me to grow exponentially in the dancing environment. In one year, I went to represent my country at the Hip-Hop world championship and the second year I attended, I returned as Ambassador of World of Dance in South America. Now I had a big responsibility: Dance had saved me and I had to save Dance.

Dancing gave me a tribe of people with graceful charisma that awakened my sense of belonging and feeling alive again. In this new world, I met highly sensitive persons, more connected with spirituality. I started taking off my blinders and numbness while bending the direction of my own inertia. Still, I was in between worlds. I was corrupting the new world I got into by getting other dancers into drinking, video games and unhealthy substances. I was influential and I was not using my power correctly.

Two years later, at a dancers' party, I met my dance teacher sister, who had just come from India. There was a great magnetism, mystical sparks and a sense of transcendence in the field between us. We locked looks, leaned into conversation. She invited me for a session; I felt a calling. I went.

Her therapy changed my life. With my eyes closed, I suddenly started watching a sequence of memories, scenes, symbols and first-person experiences. Inner worlds and direct access to the most magnificent places

I've never imagined. (Not even the craziest video game could compare to what was shown. The sense of light-speed remembrance felt like when Neo gets programmed in The Matrix.)

From this moment on I never saw darkness with my eyes closed again. I always see lights, shapes, beings and scenes. This may sound like a superpower but it had a sharp double edge. I couldn't control it. Imagine how maddening it was to suddenly blink and see a dragon coming to your face, or watching multiple faces emerge from one person. This was hard to process and adapt to. I needed to understand it for my own survival.

To mingle with my normal life, I studied and gathered all the mentors and resources I could find. Watching therapists and channelers who knew how to handle this was useful. Healing, meditation and channeling practices came to me organically. I dived deeply into psychology, secret ancestral knowledge and ontology to understand and deal with my transformation. I applied these learnings to change my behavior, my way of being. I empowered myself and became ready to exercise my new powers.

This same year, I created Life Artists Formation Associated in Manifestation (LAFAM) as a movement to promote artists. Remember I had the mission of saving Dance?

The first event of LAFAM was huge: 600 persons, 3 days, 2 parties, with international judges and participants in our artistic performances. The purpose was noble: bringing together the values of Peace, Love, Unity and Having Fun. This was heroic and uplifted faith in everyone. But these showy lights were a big ship burning… my immolation.

I was blinded by my omnipotence and trapped in the fantasy of, single-handedly, saving Dance, saving Art... What a delusion! I took for granted that everyone's intentions were noble and only helpful. I learned there was a dissociation between my vision, the dream I projected, and others' interests, understanding and actions. The lack of clarity, excess of chaos and the weight that entails setting up something of this magnitude, burned me in all areas: economically, physically, emotionally and spiritually. I even almost lost my "dream girlfriend" for having 'tunnel vision' in this mission. This proved the quality of commitments I had. These were many low blows all at once. I was broke, not only financially, but of trust (of me in myself, of me in others and of others in me). This intense experience shook me. It took me many days in solitude to integrate and reassemble myself. From rock bottom, after feeling broken and disappointed about my capacities and dreams, I started my reconstruction.

I internalized self-empowering habits and spiritual practices even more. I quit meat. This was annoying for my father who kept the tradition of Sunday's asados (Argentinian barbecue). My grandfather couldn't understand why I didn't eat fish. He even tried to convince me, "But they are the fruit of the sea!" Clearly, my life philosophy altered the family table and I was vilified for "being a delusional failure," like when I did a big event and they had to save me. A dynamic of guilt and debt was a constant erosion over everything I tried to do. I acknowledge, it was scary and traumatic for them too, but after many months, I couldn't tolerate it anymore. The projections of their fears and distrust were damaging my self-esteem and growth. I needed to liberate myself from these hooks that were bringing me down. The internal and external war was non-stop.

If I meditated, I was idle, lost in the dream world. All spirituality, self-help and personal development were useless, crazy ideas in their eyes. Except for my grandmother, who gave me a book that changed my life, *The Four Agreements*. By Don Miguel Ruiz. His philosophy and deep wisdom reshaped my perception of reality. As an artist of life, I became resourceful and empowered to sculpt my masterpiece of life. This was a leverage point in the war to be me. Their stories no longer had power over my life-script.

During this time, I learned many healing techniques, state management and reality sculpting tools. I detected and deactivated many viruses in my system, my communication and relationships. Power struggles, domination, manipulation and toxic dynamics were cleared in this process. I changed so much that my family and friends couldn't recognize me. They lost me. (They lost their projection of me).

I still wanted to unite my family. I had to be congruent since LAFAM was born through the impulse of reconnecting my family. I was really committed but the layers between us were too many. We were in different worlds, in different vibrations.

I adopted a cat. They kicked me out. I had to leave the home where I lived for most of my life. I lived alone, my cat for company, figuring myself out and still healing from the traumatic experience of the event, plus the constant wars I was having in many dimensions. I returned my car and credit card to my father so his dominance and scolding entitlement would stop. This triggered him. Meanwhile, I was teaching dance classes that didn't even pay the rent and I had to take the assistance food that I used to deliver before (that I knew was poison). I felt the indignity. This was my breaking point.

My father was running his political campaign. I saw his public profile highlighting "family father." He was gaining many enemies in the political disputes and I was feeling exposed, vulnerable and an easy target to bring him down. At that moment my reasoning was: "He is going to spend a lot of money in the campaign and I'm the weakest link. He is not fathering me properly. He is blinded and cannot care less." If I spoke to the media, sharing my say and feelings, his chances of winning would be gone. So why even bother spending the campaign money? Instead, I suggested he give it to me so I could sustain, support and protect myself. This is what I proposed, and yes, it was a kind of blackmail. I'll admit it was my lowest moral point. He tried to diminish me with psychological manipulation, "You think the press will believe You?" This was a declaration of war. I'd never had my father as an enemy before and I never wanted to.

That same week my house was robbed, gone were most of my clothes and musical instruments. I felt so vulnerable that I went back to my mother's house. My father got 'a friend of his', a psychiatrist to check on me. With my intentions of peacemaking, I agreed to receive his visits. He came twice. Shortly after, my father came to propose an overnight family trip. I was filled with hope and gladly accepted. I really wanted to spend quality time, unite the family and to be understood.

Betrayal came in a way I never expected. I was kidnapped. I felt sleepy after our lunch and woke up inside a mental asylum. In there, they forced me to sign that I was entering at my own will. My say didn't matter at this point. I signed with the condition of not being drugged. The first thing they did was inject me. This was the highest treason. I announced to my father: "You haven't earned an enemy, you have lost a son."

"You are resourceful internally, you will get out of this while helping many others." my mother told me while crying helplessly. Her words uplifted my faith and I knew this was the hardest challenge I had to go through… my crucifixion.

I could write a whole book of my experiences there. I learned this place was full of sensitive, hurt and misunderstood persons. They were a burden to their families so it was better to have them locked down and numbed. Inside, I sang to the point of bringing tears of emotion to the ones there. I realized I was needed there, too. I naturally kept helping and teaching people how to heal through art, creativity and the connection with themselves. Even in my worst moments, no one could take away who I truly am.

After five weeks, I got out; many had heard nothing of me during this time. Others heard the pitiful version that was told about me. I felt my reputation, my voice and my will were lost while in that prison. The prison was not only the physical walls and the drugs enforced on me. Deceit and illusion were really what took my trust and freedom.

Depression and addictions came back strongly along with being overweight. These were side effects of how I felt inside. Still feeling deep sadness and traumatized from this experience, I had to climb back. In doing so, I realized this was a purge of persons and the environment I had. An opportunity to rebuild myself. This disrupted the inertia that I was not able to see before. I evolved so fast that all my old reality had to collapse abruptly. I already knew the way out of hell; aligning my truth, inner peace and virtues.

Within six months, I was off the enforced drugs and I recovered my independence. Returned to my study routines and habits of power. Connected with new people, established new relationships and started traveling, healing myself and everyone around me. Now I value my willpower, my freedom and my lucidity more than ever. Having lived in the internal hell, I learned how to cultivate and build the inner heaven.

There were layers of my ego and pain that I was not able to work on alone. Having an Akashic Records reading was the most liberating and clarifying experience. This gave me such peace and alignment that I could finally embody my purpose.

In the past three years, I've connected with and guided thousands of people from more than forty countries to higher guidance and health. I attained mastery in Akashic Records, which is my main way of reconnecting to alignment, healing and empowering. The feedback I get from the people that received therapies and training from me is the reflection of the graceful fulfilling reality I'm manifesting.

Through these experiences, my whole family became stronger. We improved our relationships with more understanding and harmony. I forgave my father and we are at peace now. He is proud that I found my way and I'm happy and fulfilled with what I do.

LAFAM is the lighthouse from where transformational resources and opportunities are provided and beamed into the world. We connect soul family with healthy dynamics and honorability codes to keep aligned to our true selves. With our formations, we empower and enable synergies between artists of life to manifest masterpieces with our lives.

Ignite Action Steps

Making the invisible, visible: Truth and Discernment - Discernment is essential for identifying Truth. Clear definitions are foundations of discernment. The invisible prison, the ego and its dynamics can be disrupted. For this:

*Study and identify Cognitive Biases. (Psychological Blinders)

*Learn about your pain body and triggers. (*A New Earth- Eckhart Tolle*)

*Work on the definitions of your Hell, Heaven and Shadow. (Dr. Jordan Peterson, great for personal development and morals. Dive in his wisdom.)

*Define yourself, your heart Values and priorities with Clarity. (Yoram Baltinester, an author in this book, has helped me greatly on this. Honor and gratitude to him.)

*Learn about assertive communication and healthy relationship codes. These are vital for symbiotic relationships. (Free resources provided at LAFAM.org)

*Practice detecting, in yourself and others, the biases, pain bodies and invitations to your Hell/Heaven. Just be aware, the exercise here is to not react.

Inner Peace and Virtues Cultivation - Peace, Pax from Latin, literally means pact. Being inside a pact with ourselves enables us to be in our personal power and integrity. It is our vehicle out of misery. For this:

*Declare who you are, the agreements with yourself that are non-negotiable. What are core parts of your being that you won't let anybody sabotage? Not even yourself. By not reacting and staying in your power, you can choose to safeguard your peace.

*Exercise your spiritual fitness and willpower. Virtues are muscles of your being and protectors of your Peace. Each decision, reaction and behavior is an opportunity to grow stronger or make yourself weaker. Humbleness melts egos and helps us learn. Compassion enables us to re-channel pain into wisdom. Gratitude brings our heaven closer. (Try the *Six Phase Meditation*- Vishen Lakhiani)

*Read *The Four Agreements*- Don Miguel Ruiz.

Self Awareness and Emanation - Self-awareness and proper feedback from our surroundings allow us to evolve.

*Play the 'states of awareness game' by listening to yourself. You are always in a state. This is 'from where you are being' and from all your thoughts, emotions and possibilities can happen. Listening to the inner narratives while connecting to your breathing allows you to control and redirect your state. Your state is a big part of your emanation.

*Have trustworthy persons that remind you of the best of you and help you keep aligned to your true self.

Santiago Rafael Pascual - Argentina
LAFAM Founder, Master in Akashic Records
www.lafam.org

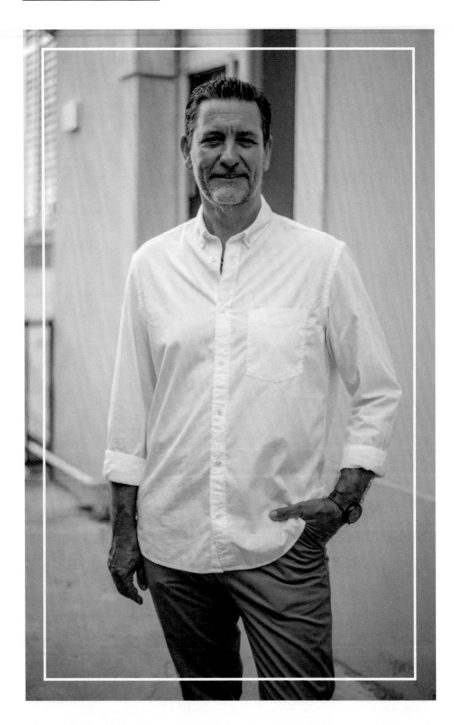

TODD MURRAY

"Get out of your own way. Be humble. Stay open and receive even
when it's scary. That's when the magic happens."

**I seek to make a lasting impact, no matter how big or small; hoping to
make the world a better place. It is my intention that my story inspires
you to connect. To share and inspire by making the most of the resources
you have both internally and externally.**

GENETICS SET ME UP FOR ESCAPE

I grew up as a typical upper-middle-class white kid in San Diego,
California. I went to high school at a private prep school in La Jolla with
mostly prestigious misfits all trying to make our way through the boxes
we were being placed into. I wasn't cut out for the Ivy League future and
was therefore guided condescendingly to an 'appropriate' university for my
skillset – University of Southern California (USC).

In 1990 I graduated from USC which is also known as an ultra-
conservative school and the University for Spoiled Children as I recently
learned from one of the other authors in this book.

After living the 'American Dream' of typical southern California lifestyle
and university fraternity boy experience, I decided to travel. Unlike the other
USC grads, rather than interviewing for internships with accounting firms
and corporate real estate offices, I bought a one-way ticket to Cabo San
Lucas, Mexico. I was looking for purpose and any reason or chance to avoid

participating in the 'real world'.

My genetics can be traced to a long line of escape artists who leave home, start businesses, run away to other places, countries, and even sailboats. I found a job on the beach and eventually ended up running the social program at the largest hotel in Cabo. My college sweetheart quit her corporate job soon after and joined me there despite our uncertain futures. The family guilt trip eventually ensnared me and I returned to San Diego to start a career in the car business. My girlfriend protested strongly, saying, "You don't want to go back there." Ultimately she was right.

My career progressed through various forms of sales. I went from selling cars to sales training to selling pharmaceuticals to doctors and hospitals. This is where I burned out quickly in 1994. I couldn't do it anymore; I couldn't make empty promises about products I didn't believe in. I was living a lie trying to be a corporate clone. My burnout took various forms from showing up late, poor relationships, gaining weight, to spending money I didn't have.

A year later, my college sweetheart, Gina, and I got married. We bought one-way tickets to Europe for a honeymoon...do you see any patterns here? We left corporate America behind us and set off with a limited budget for adventure in Europe. We had a rough plan to end up working and living in Barcelona. We ate bread and cheese for a year and free happy hour tapas wherever we could find them. We never found jobs and eventually, the money ran out. We came back to the United States broke and unemployed. The pressure from home to "get a real job" won again. There were lots of, "We told you so" naysayers.

The year 1996 was not a strong year in our early married life. Because we did not find employment in Europe as planned, our dreams and expectations came crashing down. Yet, we couldn't let go. There was no scenario where we were going to succumb to society and "go quietly into the night." We were rebels at heart although we never really admitted it. Our actions proved differently --we persisted. This wasn't the way I saw things unfolding but the fire only grew stronger. People say "selling begins when the customer says 'no.'" The Universe was just getting started, as this was all part of a journey in learning.

I had an inside lead with a great job with Mercedes Benz and they asked me to an interview. I was sure to get a job as a sales trainer. No questions asked. I knew how to sell. They flew me to New Jersey for the interview and treated me well. It was an epic failure. I didn't get the job and I was crushed. I couldn't digest it. I was lower than I had ever been. Newly married, broke, ashamed, living at home. It felt like the walls were closing in on me and I could see no way out.

One day when my wife picked up the newspaper she saw a job fair in San Francisco. Why not? We had nothing to lose and we could sleep in the guest room of her friend in Berkeley. We packed up two suitcases and the cat in our economy car and set off again into the unknown. We went to the job fair and handed out resumes. My wife got a job with AMEX travel in the city and I got a job selling pagers in the East Bay. We rented a tiny one-bedroom apartment in the East Bay and started over. We frequently ate $1 happy hour food at TGIFridays for date night and struggled to pay many bills. We found ourselves more than $50,000 in debt with nothing to show for it. Creditors were calling and we were trying to hold things together.

Still, we were determined to do whatever it took to return to Europe. We read books about Europe, we watched Rick Steves' videos, listened to music, went to European cafes, anything that was European. To this day, the song "La vie en rose" reminds us of the cafe where we would dream of a life in Europe. We would fantasize about French cafes and what we would eat. We described the scenery as if it was right in front of us. We could almost reach out and touch it, although, in reality, we were sitting in a strip mall somewhere in Northern California.

One day at work I was cold calling dead leads from the 'dead file' box. These leads were considered dead and not worth your time. I would spend hours on the phone, constantly hearing people say "no" all day long. I began to believe there was no end in sight. Each day became harder and harder to pick up the phone and try to sell something nobody wanted. I would stare at the phone on the desk like an enemy and then gain the courage to attack it. I sat in a cubicle in a sea of similar layouts. I began doubting myself and struggled to find the courage to face another day.

The drive to work seemed to be longer every day. I would sit in traffic with my mind wandering to faraway places. I would look around at the people in the surrounding cars and see the same lifeless expressions on the faces of all the other commuters fighting to get into the city on the expressway. There had to be an answer. There had to be another way. There is no way this would be what I was going to do for a living. Not here, no way.

Then I saw a name somebody told me about. It was a new and upcoming software company called PeopleSoft. I searched their website for an office in Europe. Yes, the Europe headquarters were in Amsterdam. That will do. I pulled the card from the file so nobody else would call them. I treasured it like a secret in my pocket. I knew there was a one in a million chance of them saying yes...but that one in a million could be me. I made it my mission to get a job there and wouldn't stop until I did. I asked everyone I met if they ever heard of them. I looked for information about them in the news.

I called them and called some more. I was told "no" again and again by the communications manager. Eventually, I connected with someone who gave me hope. I started a daily conversation with the purchasing department contact. On my calls every chance I could say "did I mention", "have I told you about" we both got to the point of my daily call became a joke and we started joking around on the calls. I was building rapport, I knew this.

Step by step, call by call. I had to get a foot in the door if I was going to have a remote chance of convincing them after enough years of service they could send me to Europe. I brought bagels, donuts, and some free pagers to just to get in the door, anything for a conversation and face to face contact. I sold value, persistence, commitment, and capability. The pagers were the wedge to get a conversation going. If I could just get the conversation started, then I could probe and uncover objections to overcome. I just had to get in the door. First sell the customer, next show them how awesome your customer service is, next convince them you were meant to work for them, get an interview, get a job, get experience, get transferred to Europe. The road ahead was long but it all started with a single step. One phone call.

First, I sold them five pagers, then 15, then eventually converted the entire corporate account of 5000 over six months. I busted my butt to provide unbelievable customer service. The sale was the first step.

I had work to do now, loads of it. I learned what email they used then went to the book store and bought the Dummies Guide for every office application I knew they used. Same for SQL, Client Server, and database 101. I sold pagers during the day and learned everything I could teach myself at night. Next, I studied their press releases, news, financial reports, technology, anything, and everything. They knew I wasn't going away. With unwavering determination, slowly I worked my way in the door winning an interview.

After an interview period that lasted a couple of long, sleepless months, an offer came and I nearly passed out. We laughed, we cried, we panicked. I was being hired directly into Amsterdam HQ in the consulting division. We were being relocated as local Dutch employees. They put me through IT boot camp and taught me everything I needed to survive day one. The rest was up to me. It wasn't glorious but we didn't care. It was the biggest success of my life. We were going back to Europe with a job! Through hard work, commitment, persistence, and sheer laser-focused intention, in 1997 I was finally employed by PeopleSoft Europe. Once I was on the inside, the drive and learning accelerated--I researched anything I could find. I devoured every assignment, technology changes, and opportunity. I volunteered for everything then figured it out once I started.

My rebel past was not done yet. I loved my job and how I earned it. I loved the experience and living in Europe. I was grateful. However, something inside me was burning and I couldn't figure it out. I wasn't the greatest employee. Even though I held the dream job I thought I always wanted, there was something inside enticing me to do my own thing. I didn't know what it was until one day I was working next to an independent contractor doing the same job as me charging three times the price. Click. Click. Boom! I now had a new target to shoot for. I needed to be my own boss with the experience and knowledge I had. This was another step in my journey; now I felt I was really getting started.

Three years later I left PeopleSoft to start my own practice. That set off an IT Consulting career spanning over 20 years which has flourished into an IT Service Delivery company that generates good income, allowed us to raise three children in Italy, and initiate a non-profit organization supporting refugees globally. We are still doing life our way, challenging the system, whatever that means for us at the moment.

Back in 1996, I was at the lowest point in my life with no viable way out. I can't explain why I just knew following the crowd wasn't my thing. We challenged the "rules" that were "normal". We bought tickets without plans, we leaped into new experiences spontaneously, we raised kids in Europe, we moved to countries not knowing the languages, we fought with stereotypes and expectations, we challenged "best practices" and more. We did it our way and didn't give up.

We are still doing it our way. We still challenge the system, whatever that means. I don't work in an office, my clients must allow me to work remotely. Our children have been World Schooling for over seven years without a formal education plan. The children's education has skyrocketed. We routinely travel to more than thirty countries each year while I continue to maintain a full consulting practice and volunteer whenever possible. We travel to countries that are on the "not recommended travel" advisory and we have wonderful experiences with locals. We are doing the things that are supposed to cause adverse reactions and risk/danger in our lives yet the opposite has happened. My business flourishes and grows each year. The children excel in education and give back. Our relationships deepen and apparently, we have more fun than we are supposed to at our age.

Trust the process. Make a plan and execute relentlessly. Trust your intuition. Make it your own. The path will be put in front of you clearly when you are working in the right direction. Just because someone says it's a 'dead lead', make the call and see for yourself.

I didn't trust myself early enough. I lacked self-confidence in my own decisions and followed others by default. The "Brules"--better rules-- in my head were constantly reinforced by family and friends. The "Brules" make everyone else feel better about their situation. "If you are like me then I feel justified; I am doing the right thing. If you are living your dreams, I don't want to see it because I am not brave like you." I let them win too often. My head became a battleground for "shoulds". It didn't have to be this hard if I had had a better sense of what life offered outside the "Brules."

My life changed me. I didn't change my life. It sounds backward but that's what happened to me. Travel changed me. Travel, by definition, forces you out of your comfort zone by. You try to bring your "comforts" with you when you travel, however, the beauty lies in the unknown. I pushed boundaries that were uncomfortable. This situation still happens on occasion. Feel the fear and do it anyway. You are braver than you know.

I didn't put my finger on it until I was 50 years old. I didn't see the "Brules" clearly. The things I was "supposed" to do were always getting in the way. The education I was supposed to have. The work experience I was supposed to have. I was supposed to be articulate and conversational with debating skills and wit. All these things were stuck in my head and made me feel I was less than average. This wasn't the case and I didn't realize it until later in life. I am more than good enough.

We have challenged traditional education and are constantly critiqued for our style of learning. Yet, the kids excel above all "standards". My marriage has survived the worst of times, and 25 years later, growing stronger every day. My career should have been a disaster, yet it just keeps growing. And me... well, the story isn't over, not even close. I know there is so much to learn, love, laugh, and live. I don't know how this will play out, however, there are a few common themes I have come to respect in my "unplanned", "unorthodox" life.

IGNITE ACTION STEPS

* **I don't** have the answers yet. "I don't know" is a phrase I am comfortable with. What I do know, is that 99% comes from inside me. Searching externally without having searched first internally is key.

* **Act** from a place of giving and contribution. When I am focused only

on myself, my results are shallow and fleeting. Approaching life with a spirit of contribution to a larger purpose is key for me. It has literally transformed me. I contribute to my family and humanity. I contribute to the betterment of the environment, even in the smallest ways.

* **Live** life on your terms. My life, wife, kids, and career were not supposed to "turn out" as great as they are based on the "path" we took.

* **Let** your life be an example of contribution, learning, and giving back.

* **Get** out of your own way. Be humble. Stay open and receive even when it's scary. That's when the magic happens.

I will continue practicing ease with not knowing how my life will play out. I am okay with that. How much uncertainty can you handle?

Todd Murray - Greece
Founder/Director Snowgoose, Inc.
https://snowgoose.io

Warren
Falkenstein

"When you find the purpose of pain, which we all experience in one way or another, grab hold, look within and find the hero inside you."

My intention is that in reading my story, you will choose to take the journey within to find your inner strength just waiting to be discovered. Then you will truly learn to know your roots and not just your leaves.

The Day I Met My Hero

We live, we breathe, we laugh, we cry.... C'est la vie... or is it?

Choosing to live a life of service to others, I believe each and every one of us are purposefully placed on this beautiful planet for many different reasons. Some may venture on the journey of unraveling their personal calling, searching for their purpose of being in one given lifetime. Others may just decide to coast through life and not discover their path of awareness at all.

There is no right or wrong choice when it comes to choosing to live a life of purpose. Nor is there a right or wrong identification as to what that purpose is. I wasn't exactly born with an instruction manual and I am pretty sure you weren't either. Unless we merit hearing a voice from above telling us exactly what it is we must do in this world. At the end of the day, our purpose in life is what we choose it to be.

During our lifetime, we will have experiences that define us in more ways than one – moments of joy, learning, tragedy, sorrow, pain, miracles and blessings. A strong mindset and connection to the higher universal cosmic forces, along with our connection to the inner spark of creation within us act as two of our greatest assets when navigating through this physical plane.

That inner strength, that ever-glowing spark of creation, that voice within, that sweet soul of mine. The hero within... How do we attain that level of connection? How do we connect with that hero inside? How long will it take? What steps must I make? How do I call upon that power when I need it the most? That moment, I now know, can only be described as a connection to the above that triggers a powerful connection within that unites the two.

That connection happened for me on October 31st, 2018, in an eastern Canadian hospital. That was the day that ignited a shift in consciousness that literally changed my state of being. I had just left a doctor's office, after having a not-so-positive experience. After months of the same conversation about the inevitable, it was time to make a decision to book a surgery I had delayed for years. I could barely speak or move as I chose the date.

First, I called one of my mentors to check for any scheduling conflicts. Surgery had to take second place to what was most important in my healing process. I'd been nominated to present an initiative, on stage in front of a massively large audience. My assignment, bigger than anything I could imagine and dear to my heart, was to identify a local problem and present a solution with the goal to take it globally – a commitment which required a scary leap of faith. I wasn't prepared to give that up despite what the doctors suggested. I was dedicated to creating a solution to an epidemic for people suffering from chronic illnesses, to the extent they spend most of their days either in bed, suffering or going to doctors. Some can barely work or make a living and therefore, cannot pay for alternative medicine treatments, which have the potential to raise their cellular energy levels, which makes it possible for them to contribute more to society. The intention of my initiative "FundTheTreatment.org" is to provide support and funding to patients with chronic illnesses for alternative medicine treatments and protocols. Good thing something made me check on the presentation date because I needed to speak at the 2018 Global Changemaker Series on the day I had just scheduled surgery.

I slowly walked down the hallway to the busy hospital lobby... Do you know that feeling when you finally made a decision without fully knowing the end result? The surgeon made it clear that the outcome is undefined, yet something needed to be done.

I stood there in the lobby leaning on my crutches – for a moment, time came to a halt...

I looked up to the heavens as I felt a tear rolling down my cheek. There were doctors flying past me with their coffee in one hand and a cell phone in the other. Stretchers and wheelchairs were speeding by. There were people dressed as clowns for Halloween, which added to the irony of it all. I caught myself thinking, "They should either put street lights or have traffic cops in this lobby. It felt like a 'danger zone'!

Growing up with a chronic illness, I heard doctors' hopeless one-minded opinions my whole life. I saw people suffering in waiting rooms and hallways. I needed to find something bigger that would support me on my journey. That evolved into a mindset, a belief that I am the creator of my circumstances, therefore, I am responsible for what I have attracted into my life. My thoughts, actions and feelings are constantly sending out a frequency that affects the outcome of the next moment in my journey. Allocating energy towards anger, resentment and blame does not serve my higher purpose.

Standing there in that hospital lobby, I knew I was going to get through this. I just didn't know how. I was in a test of my beliefs, to either let my fear override or let the Light in to guide me through the process, walk my talk and allow for the bigger picture, guidance and solutions to reveal themselves through grace instead of resistance.

I want you to understand something; it wasn't just the surgery I was afraid of. For my entire life, I've had to navigate the medical system and I am grateful for all the support. Still, deciding to go ahead with this operation was very difficult. I have lived with a chronic degenerative illness and physical disability for over 34 years. I have spent most of my life in a wheelchair, have had many upon many hospital scares, have lost functionality and parts of many of my fingers. The list goes on. Yes, there was the fear of the unknown, yet that was not what I was entirely concerned about.

It felt to me as if sharp, medieval arrows were firing at me from every direction. It was the feeling of reaching my limits, there was no room to handle anything more, unless I had a bigger vessel... within. This surgery felt daunting because it was 'another thing to deal with' on top of everything else on my plate. Plus the additional '*do-everything-preneur*' mentality I had chosen to create, pursue and deal with in my life.

Emails and texts were flying in, my phone was ringing and my to-do list was overflowing. I was dealing with a physical flare-up and I was already three weeks behind in an intense training program. Running to... oh wait, I mean, hopping on crutches in and out of so many hospitals and clinics, takes up a lot of time. I had seriously fallen behind on many commitments I had given my word to. My integrity in all areas of my life had been lost... so I felt...

My word to myself, to others and my integrity is important and meaningful to me, I did not feel complete and whole. I felt as if I hit a wall. This was just too much...

Yet, I didn't blame nor did I choose at that moment to become a victim of circumstances, which in some other people's eyes or minds they would say that I had *Every* reason to. Instead, I choose to live a life of purpose... a life of purpose over pain... together with faith and certainty knowing I am not alone. I am fully aware of other souls dealing with worse situations. But, how you may wonder? How did I navigate through such distress?

I honestly believe I am only given what I can handle in life, whatever that may be. However, I am fully aware that some situations will feel so extreme and terrifying. They may trigger doubts and uncertainty that in turn can result in such fear and hopelessness that no words can describe what an individual may be experiencing. My heart goes out to people in such scenarios because I've been there. However, as long as I am still present and breathing, I believe I am still needed in this world.

I just wanted to know how? How am I able to take on more? How am I able to mentally, physically, emotionally handle more on top of all I was already dealing with *and* living a purposeful life? My cup was overflowing.

I took a big breath, looked up to the ceiling ... and called out to the heavens .... "I am not blaming, I am here... Just show me how... just show me how... that is all I ask."

I surrendered. I let go. I truly requested assistance from a higher source with all my heart and soul. In an instant, something ignited in me that was one of the most beautifully profound moments that I am grateful to have ever experienced.

It was as if I was watching and rewinding a movie. I was in complete observer state. I have never felt so grounded and present in my life. I watched through my mind's eye, like a movie stuck on fast forward, scenes of my struggles, pain, suffering and challenges – plus my attitude and state of being throughout them all. I saw myself through the eyes of another and I learned about me.

In the past few years, I cannot even begin to count how many times I have been called an inspiration, a leader, an example, a warrior, a peaceful warrior and a hero. To be honest, sometimes it feels like a "Happy New Year" or "Happy Birthday" type of greeting. Without question, I am beyond grateful for the gifts and merit I have to move, touch and inspire so many souls. I never actually plan or take into account the amount of influence I project and give to my environments. I just go. Move on. Deal with the situation in the most positive and proactive way possible. I smile and move forward.

That October day in the hospital was the first time I saw from the outside and felt on the inside how strong I truly was, and wow, was I impressed! It's one thing for people to tell you how strong and courageous you are but to actually feel it for yourself is a whole new reality. It was my paradigm shift.

I saw what I needed to see, and it ignited a power and strength within me that I did not know was even there. I had never acknowledged myself for what I have gone through in my physical challenges. I finally realized how much I had accomplished despite my disability on top of all the daily health challenges I had to deal with.

Tears were rolling down my cheeks. I felt tremendous strength, courage and an energy like I have never felt before. I received that bigger vessel from within and I was able to and ready to handle more. I carefully made my way sideways through the crowd and walked into the restroom. I looked up at the wall only to see a marketing campaign that said: "Where Impossible Becomes I'm Possible" … I was done.

As I returned home, about to settle down, still in shock and inner awe, my phone rang. It was my dad, "Warren, what happened today at the hospital?" he asked me. I started to tremble - doing my best not to cry. "Dad…" I said… "Dad… today is the day I learned how strong I truly am."

Since then, together with all my previous work in the spiritual, self-development field, I walked a path of higher courage, strength and certainty. Like the *Lion* I truly am. You see, each and every one of us has our life story to go through, our challenges and victories. Life is a series of paradoxes and miracles. It takes a lot of courage and strength to do what we do, to survive, to cope, to live, to laugh and to love.

There are going to be moments in our lifetime when we will see ourselves from the eyes of an observer, from the eyes of love…. From the eyes of our soul… this, my friends, is what self-love is all about… in order to love, serve and truly help another… we must go through what we need to.

Each of us are on our own journey and can only handle the amount of pressure our inner vessel is able to contain. Many people have mentioned to me that they feel they cannot "complain" to me about their struggle or pain. Comparing our pain to another may inspire us to keep going and get through our current circumstance. However, it is the way the person deals with the situation you are comparing yourself to, that will inspire a shift in nature. Are they angry or peaceful? Are they driven or remaining positive despite the circumstance? You see, we inspire others to thrive through our state of being. What we do need from each other is the love, support and motivation to not only get through, but to focus on the bigger picture and the greatest possible outcome.

We all go through our own journey of life. Each of us will take the time we are meant to in order to be ready for the next chapter. It took me a long time to receive my driver's license, but hey, I did it! I am glad I kept trying!

The challenges we face are what will encourage our inner vessel to grow and develop a higher tolerance for what we can handle, whether it be pain, a challenge or even a victory! Always a good idea to check in with yourself on how you react to all different types of situations. Once, our vessel expands we become stronger, mentally, physically and emotionally.

I'm not asking you to believe me... **I'm asking you to believe in yourself...** and acknowledge that you were divinely created to be in this world, for the light you hold within – is your gift to shine and bring light to all humanity... forevermore.

IGNITE ACTION STEPS

Below you will find a few guidelines you can apply in order to create new habits which will be useful when the time comes for you to "Let the Light in" and transform your current perspective during any given situation.

*Pay attention to your reactions in every given situation. Have you ever been driving and there is a really nice fellow wildly beeping his horn and speeding up frantically, while shouting at all the other cars on the road at their stupidity? What usually happens next for me is that we both end up at the red light at the same time. Our destinations were the same, we were both on the same road, yet our actions and reactions were different.

I always ask, "Was it worth it?" to get all uptight and angry, only to end up at the street light at the same time as the other drivers you were scolding? Our emotional state affects our health, mind and our environment. It sends out a magnetizing frequency into the universe which in turn acts as a request. By monitoring your reactions, you will begin to create an awareness around them, learn about yourself and enjoy the process of becoming a creator and observer of your own life.

Inner hero development training. As with everything in life, practice, consistency and training is needed for any self-improvement to take place. Most of all, it's being open to guidance and possibilities. Begin to identify your external and internal triggers. What are your buttons that other people tend to constantly push? What are the things about yourself that bother you the most? I encourage you to take note of all that in a journal. Once, it is written on paper you can begin to see yourself as an observer. For each flaw you find within and each button trigger you identify – ask yourself three times "Why does this bother me?" and list the answers for each. The goal is for you to see yourself from the outside and realize there is no meaning or need for these discomforts at all!

Have faith. In whatever form that means to you. You were gifted this life for a reason and each stage of your journey will have its ups and downs. There are many stories of failure to victory out there, from Michael Jordan to J.K Rowling. I believe every breath we take and each new day, is verification we are needed in this world. I encourage you to take time daily, to connect to something greater than yourself in order to connect to that greatness within at the deepest level.

Make a list of all you have gone through. What are you grateful for? What you have accomplished? How amazing it is that you are able to achieve all that you have and continue to do? When a new challenge arises, look for the bigger picture and not what you think is so important right then. Sometimes in life, it is what we don't know that results in something even better than what we hoped for down the line.

Ask for support. Ask from the right place, you will receive it. Yet, you must be open to accepting Light and be sending out positive frequencies to receive it as well.

Warren Falkenstein - Canada
Award winning inspirational speaker, mindset coach,
spiritual thought leader and teacher.
www.WalkwithWarren.com

Parth Nilawar

"Who you are as a man and how you relate to the world is highly dependent on the relationship you had with your father."

The power of procreation is completely different than the power of raising those creations. My intention is to create a global movement to empower fathers to become conscious of this difference. I envision a world where fathers don't perceive themselves as providers for the household but humans with strong bonds with each and every person in the family and raising the quality of life for everyone involved.

Fire and Freedom

I arrived home for my father's funeral, not expecting a crowd of hundreds, but it was representative of how social he was despite his fiery facade. Obviously, many saw beyond that and knew he was kind-hearted and meant well for everyone. Although that's not what you experienced interacting with him, you'd realize it with time; whatever he did was earnestly wanting to push you forward.

But he could not push himself forward and wait until my arrival so I could see him in person one last time. I was based in Germany and booked my tickets to India, to spend a month with him when I heard his lung fibrosis had worsened, making him rely on external oxygen supply 24x7. Though meek and bed ridden, everyone around him including his doctor in the last days in the hospital spoke about his alertness and feistiness. He could not speak much by then, but was interacting with almost everyone in his extended social circles by messaging through his smartphone. He had adapted quite fast to that bit of technology. People who were not as close in the family, could not have imagined his physical decline. Dad even got everyone's tax returns filed through phone in his last week and the tax consultant was completely unaware of his ill health.

As I stood, a Hindu son, in front of his body lying on wood, waiting to light the fire ('Agni' in Sanskrit) for his cremation, our years together flashed in front of my eyes. According to Hindu traditions, the eldest son becomes responsible for the family in the absence of the father and is expected to lead the rituals. Cremation symbolises freeing the soul from the physical body by offering the body to the Agni. As I stood there with the fire in my hand, to free my father's spirit, the biggest moment of our lives from 20 years ago came rushing up in my memory. It was when he had freed my spirit.

Like most fathers, he had big aspirations for me. They were actually his aspirations for himself, which he had carried till being weighed down by responsibilities put on him by the earlier generations in our family. But he had stood his ground well amongst all the chaos around him, while building his life with my Mom. We had humble beginnings; he started as a clerk in the bank, making his way up to becoming the Manager a few years before his retirement. My Mom, an artist and teacher, supported the household which included my grandparents. She was the main caregiver, as they had health issues, but still managed to grow her work as an artist with support from my father.

Dad was supportive of everyone around him to do their best. Even when the others did not see their own potential, he would stay persistent with his encouragement. He was very meticulous in his observations capturing any deviation from the norm in a glance; whether it is text in any documentation or stuff in the house. He was honest, very responsible, straightforward in his communication and bit too fastidious.

Before my younger sister arrived, I was lucky enough, as their firstborn, to receive four years of undivided attention from them. It gave me a strong foundation for life. I remember Dad spending hours with me during school years, making sure that I understood all the concepts of mathematics, science and English grammar. From Mom, I received creative influence, as her art classes took place on our premises as she was always on double duty at home even while teaching art.

Because of the exposures my parents gave me, I always excelled in school. Academic performance was a great source of admiration in our family and I was always revered in that regard in our community. As a student, I had a sense that my parents were foregoing luxuries, to make it happen. One such choice my dad made is still recounted after many years. He opted to *not* buy a TV, which was commonly seen in a typical middle class Indian home of the '90s. A few situations arose where a family member was going to be on TV; we had to visit neighbours to experience that! When I was 15, he bought us an expensive set of World Book Encyclopedias. Then I knew, it wasn't a matter of finances but of choice. Years after, when I bought a TV for my parents and I saw how much he liked it, I felt more grateful for his sacrifices.

Tight budgeting made it possible for us to go on school trips. The biggest sacrifice was, Dad chose to pass on promotions for several years as accepting them meant he could be posted anywhere in the country, including remote villages. He made it his priority to be there to support our scholarly pursuits along with the exposures available in the city and keep us together as a family. All these sacrifices on his part put pressure on us to live up to his expectations. It was unintentional, but it was there.

I do not recall him buying anything for me unless I won it with a scholastic achievement. Though I had got used to it over the years, I started to feel the real intensity of that pressure in tenth grade. Board exams for tenth and twelfth are the biggest stepping stones in Indian culture towards creating your professional path and hence life. My father had missed being on the merit list just by few marks during his time and he desperately wanted me to fulfill his dream. I was in no way against it and would have loved it myself. But Dad was a well-known micro-manager. His good intentions could not be perceived by others interacting with him. People would jokingly comment about our grit to be around him all the time. His trust issues started surfacing more, as he started feeling restless with whatever I did those months. He was reminding me at every opportunity, "It's not easy. Don't take it lightly. It can make or break your life. I don't want you to feel the same as I have felt all my life for missing out by a whisker."

He was not open to the sincerity of my efforts, I felt. At the beginning of the year, I had meticulously planned, considering my strengths and weaknesses, how I could be on the Merit list of the district (potentially even the state!). Being in India it meant, being in the top 100 amongst millions of students. Calibrating for a goal to set my sights on was tricky as every year's results varied. To establish a benchmark, I approached one of my teacher's sons who had stood second in the divisional list a year prior, with 675 marks out of 750. After discussion about his preparations, I set a goal of 680 for myself which I thought gave me good chances of being in the top 10 at least. I calculated how much I would need to score in each subject to get to 680. It seemed doable if I took enough efforts. I felt comfortable with the way things were going. I had spent months changing my handwriting to make an impression at a glance. Discovering that languages (I had 4 of them!) would give me the biggest leap ahead of the crowd, I focused my energy on upgrading my linguistic skills in English, Hindi, Marathi and Sanskrit.

I was balancing my time and energy for a goal that was not too easy nor too difficult. Dad seemed okay with my thought process around the goal setting when I shared with him. But his fears from his own past experiences started playing into our conversations at the onset of tenth grade. A few months in, at family dinner table, when he repeated the same point about not leaving any stone unturned to be on the merit list, I snapped. That was very unusual of me. I had not seen anyone who knew my father, confront him, not even his own father. I said to my Dad very confidently and assertively, "Dad, I know what I am doing. But *you* are not realising what you are doing. I have shared with you my goal of 680 and you are okay with it. I am comfortable with my efforts towards achieving it, but if you are not, don't pass it on to me. I want to be on the merit list as much as you do, but your energy is not helping me at all." I could have stopped there. I do not know what got into the 16-year-old me that night. I continued "I don't want you to talk to me about my preparations or exams or anything on the topic until we see the results. If I end up scoring 680, being on the merit list like we all want, I expect independence to make my own decisions FOREVER. If, like you, I am not successful and fail to be on the list, I'll listen to everything you have to say for the rest of my life." Silence filled the room – no one was expecting that, not even me! My normal reaction would have been to take it back out of respect but something was stopping me. Something I had never experienced before. When everyone realised that I was not going to take it back, they waited for Dad's reaction. After a brief pause, all he said was "Okay" and continued with dinner. I was not sure from his reaction, if he realised the gravity of what I meant. But at that time, all I wanted was the tension in the room to ease, which he had allowed. I let it go as well.

That conversation floated in my head for a few days before fading. Mom caught me alone the next day, trying to support both sides."I know you will succeed. It will mean a lot to your father and me as well. You will make us proud." It felt good as it allowed me to focus on my efforts. I dove into all the preparation. The exams went well, but there was always uncertainty.

Meanwhile, there were future plans to be made but everything depended on the results. I took an intense 500 questions personality test that would recommend the best career options for me. Interestingly, the test also had 50 questions to be answered by parents. One question stood out: 'On your routine commute to work, would you choose: A: the fastest route everyday; B: the longer but scenic route everyday; or C: depending on how you feel that day?' While choosing 'C' for myself, I knew Dad would choose 'A', which I would never choose. Out of curiosity, I checked with Dad, who declared, "I don't understand. Why would anyone choose other than 'A', when all you have to do is reach work?" That shed a strong light on differences in our personalities.

The week of the tenth grade results approached. Tension was growing, not only in our family but also our social circles. The school I attended had far and few merit-listers over the years. But everyone had high hopes for me. I sensed something big coming my way. I just could not tell if it was good or bad. Although millions of students get their marksheets on the same day, I thought, I would find out a day or two in advance if it was a worthy result. My anticipation started building days ahead. But well into the evening before the results would be declared, I hadn't heard anything. Most probable was through the phone, so my ears were super alert for its ring.

The tenth results were a big event back then. The media and press conducted interviews with merit list holders. If I was in the top five, they'd definitely contact us sometime in advance. But not having heard anything till a day prior, started to create a bad feeling inside me. That morning, as I prepared to leave for school, I was trying to collect every bit of optimism I could. Dad had already reached work and just when I was about to leave, the phone rang. Mom grabbed it before I could. It was Dad. I heard his "Congratulations!" and her "To you too!". Teary eyed, she passed the phone to me. Dad's voice was wavering as he repeated, "Congratulations, my son!"

He had found a way to reach one of the newspapers through his acquaintances. It was confirmed that I was on the list. I stood 17th in the division, not as high a rank as I had expected but being on the list had delighted them. I felt good but not enough. 17th did not tell me what I needed to know.

I reached school to a very unexpectedly gracious welcome. 17th was the highest rank in our school's entire history. The joy shared by everyone cheered me up a bit. The school was buzzing as it had four students on the list that year, which had never happened before. We all got together in our classrooms for marklist distribution. Because I had planned my scores in every subject, I was very curious about every detail. That I had stood 17th among a few million and made my parents proud, had still not weighed in. The mark-sheets were being distributed as per our alphabetical roll-call. Finally my name was called; the whole class started clapping and cheering. I thought as I walked to the front, "This is what walking on the red carpet might feel like." The teacher handed me my mark-list, as I scanned it, key details like '17th in the Divisional Board', 'Passed with Distinction' caught my eye. But then one number broke everything that was built up inside – I started crying. My teacher cheered me, "It's true! You should celebrate!!!"

My total read **680**. Exactly 680 – not one plus or minus with all the probabilities of individual scores in each of the questions in each of the subjects…it still summed up to be 680. For the very first time, I felt something greater beyond having my back. I knew the details did not matter to anyone else except me.

The whole world changed the next day. I felt a new-found respect in everyone's greetings. But most importantly, I felt a strong change in my father – it stayed throughout his life. Although in the past, he invited opinions from all on decisions that affected everyone, like where to go on vacation or which product to buy for the home, suddenly the worth of my opinion shifted to a more important degree. He also loosened up on me considerably. It was as if getting on that list marked my rite of passage into manhood - in a modern way. There are many ceremonial rites of passage in a lot of traditions representing the stepping of males from boyhood to manhood, but mine was an unplanned real life experience. That opened a big thought process for me about what I would do in the role of a father. How would I keep my children free from my expectations?

Not having found my answer to that question after many years, I opted for a course on conscious parenting when we were pregnant; it helped more than I had expected. Even my parents had willingly joined the course with me and my wife when I asked them. It was something pretty uncommon for most Indian parents, (forget grandparents!), to actually invest in upgrading their parenting. What we learned had a huge impact on our lives. I feel more parents need to open up to something like this to prepare themselves for raising children. It inspired me to found *WonderLives Organisation*, a community for parents, to seek expert support on parenting challenges.

It has become my life's mission to spread awareness about conscious parenting. What drives me now is to inspire people to seek mentoring for their role as parents, just like they do for any other profession. To make it accessible to as many people as possible, we began offering these courses online. When we started running the pilot batches, Dad was already bedridden because of his oxygen needs. I would send him the invites for our group calls just for him to relax and get exposed to something positive. He attended them very diligently. I could feel in his messages to me, (his preferred mode of communication in the last few months), that he was really proud of what I was doing. We had come a long way from that night when I confronted him at the dinner table. It was the biggest praise and acceptance I had ever felt from him.

Standing at the pyre, I realized it was his 'fire' that I seeked freedom from at 16. Yet, now it was fire in my hand that I had to ignite and ultimately free his soul from this world!

IGNITE ACTION STEPS

*Reflect on your relationship with your father and how it has affected you. If you are a parent, definitely take a deep look at how it's impacted you and how it may also be affecting your children. Don't hesitate to meet a counselor or a healer if you have the slightest doubt.

*Communicate. Don't underestimate the reparation you can do at any stage of life. Talk to your father about the old times. And definitely gift good memories to your children.

*Find a parenting mentor. Make sure you are not passing *your* baggage to your children. With the help of experts, you can find a way to provide a launchpad for your children towards happy and fulfilling lives.

*Find your 680 magic. Find a way to connect with your higher self. Make it a priority to allocate time to hear the voice inside of you and give it space in a journal.

Parth Nilawar - Germany
Co-founder of WonderLives Organisation, Motivational Speaker,
Conscious Parenting Evangelist
www.wonderlives.org

YORAM
BALTINESTER

"When you do your part, you fill in a spot in the great puzzle of Life. When you do not do your part, you leave a hole. Do your part."

Inspiration does not arrive by invitation. Yet many, when inspired, feel the idea is 'too big' for them. My intention in this story is to move you to step up and do your part. However small or insignificant – start it. Do it. For the small part that you do may well be the linchpin of *Life* itself.

DO YOUR PART

The number sent a shockwave throughout the room. $160,000?! Some people were obviously, and understandably, skeptical. The speaker was unphased. "This is the third and last time we are having the Wealthy Visionary Conference," she said, "This year, let's come together and raise more than we raised in all three years we've had it combined!" With that and her smile, we were off for the break. Well, not all of us. I stayed in my seat, considering what to do. I was disappointed, frustrated, and tired.

It started a year earlier. At the same conference, and to be exact, in the same fundraising part of it. I liked the cause which was being presented. I love education and bringing it to places where children are deprived. For example, Africa is well worth the support. At the time, my wife and I were in debt and making a donation was out of the question. I guess I had that "maybe we can help after all?" kind of look on my face because as I peeked over at my wife Shifra, she signaled a definite "No, not this time." I felt torn between a vision that captured my heart and the harsh reality of the six-figure debt we were carrying. Yet, I knew giving to others is foundational to success. It felt as if my head was watching my heart as I put my hand into my pocket. I snuck out a $20 dollar bill and handed it over those collecting funds. Not wanting any argument, I never told Shifra.

This year things were different. We were still in debt just like before. But something had changed and I felt even more conflicted than in the previous year. Three months earlier I had created a crazy, ambitious goal of my own. I decided to earn $100,000 in 90 days. Ambitious, because I had only made $34,000 in the preceding 12 months. Marcia, my business mentor, guided me to plan out the 90 days on my calendar. When I did, to my pleasant surprise I noticed the 90-day period ended up exactly on the day when I would attend her live event: the Wealthy Visionary Conference! I don't know about you, but I get excited when things come together like this. A rush of energy went through my body. How amazing would it be if I could achieve my financial goal and celebrate it at the conference, on the same date as her banner event!

No longer focused on the impossibility of the too-big-for-little-me challenge, my mind shifted into gear and started making plans. I made a pact with myself. If I was successful in earning the $100,000 within these 90 days, I'd donate the sale that got me across the finish-line to a charitable cause. How convenient that this conference supported a charity which I liked so much! Heck, yeah, I thought! Let the games begin!

It may have been that I made that pact with God, not myself...who knows? It was a stretch goal. Maybe God inspired me to plant the seeds of opportunity and growth in my own path. It was a formidable challenge with lots to learn and practice. If I were to grow up this quickly, I had to align my mindset and skills with my actions and energy. I went to work.

I was an entrepreneur and making sales was the only way to reach my goal. The beginning was slow. In the first week, I made no sales at all. In the second week, I also made no sales. In the third week, I made no sales--again! It wasn't until the fourth week that I started seeing results. In the first 30 days, I only made $5,000. I questioned myself. "Am I going to make it?" The next month, I gained momentum: $25,000 for month number two, equalling $30,000 in total. These were great months, but still not promising when I looked at my goal. "It's a sprint" I coached myself, "don't judge partial results." I accelerated my efforts. The third month saw more sales. The stream of income accelerated like it never had before. I poured even more energy into a flurry of events and activities, phone calls, posts, emails and meetings. The flow took over. I became so focused on the goal, I almost forgot about the conference.

As I made my way to Los Angeles to attend the Wealthy Visionary Conference, I was not in a good mood. You see, on the third month I made $63,000! It was the best income month of my life, but my total income for the 90 days was $93,000. I had failed to reach my goal.

Don't get me wrong. Being sad having made that amount of money in just 90 days was a stretch. I was grateful. I was relieved and hopeful for a future without the suffocating frustration of endless bills and necessities which could not be paid. Maybe, I felt, now we can replace that carpet or fly the kids to see grandma. Nevertheless, that little voice in my head was taunting me about how close I got and told me I was a loser for missing my goal by such a small amount.

As the day passed my frustration grew. There will be no celebration for me today. I was down, I was defeated and I lost interest in the conference. At lunchtime, I wasn't hungry. I stayed in my seat as people left for the break. Instead of worrying about food, I scrolled aimlessly through my Facebook feed, emails, and texts. Secretly, I hoped for some emergency to save me by forcing me to leave.

I scanned my email inbox…. *From: Glenn. Subject: your proposal.*

My heart stopped. My hands were shaking as I fumbled to open the email message, "Hi Yoram. Just a quick note to let you know that I decided to commit and go ahead with your proposal. Please call me Monday for payment. Thank you."

Wait, what ??? The message was simple but I had to read it again. Then a third time, just to make sure. The proposal which Glenn had just accepted was a $10,000 coaching package. I sat there watching the screen, waiting for a pop-up message to say, "Nah, just kidding"…but it didn't happen.

I just made $10,000! It took a moment for my feelings to catch up with what I had read. It was still day number 90 – this money counts! I actually made it – $103,000 in 90 days! A part of me wanted to jump out of my chair and break into my happy dance. I was feeling pride, joy, and a sense of accomplishment all in the same moment. It was the first time ever I felt confused by success.

Then the other penny dropped and my heart stopped, again. *(Note to self: I must quit these heart stoppages. I doubt if it's very healthy.)*

I remembered the pact I made. Um, holy smokes… I must now donate $10,000. That was the deal I forged…The sale that gets me across the goal line becomes a charitable donation. And tonight is fundraiser night.

Ten. Thousand. Dollars. Donation. Tonight.

The largest donation Shifra and I had ever given before amounted to $360. That was a lot for us and we made that decision together, during a financially great year. I can never make this donation without talking to Shifra first. Oh… did I mention that I had not shared with Shifra this little deal I made with myself and with God? Nope, I did not mention that. Shifra didn't know I was willing to give away such an enormous amount to charity. I was in trouble, oh, so much trouble.

My friend Emma must have noticed something was wrong. Settling into a chair beside me, she watched my face for a moment before speaking. "What's up, Yoram?" she asked, "Is everything ok?"

It took me a long while and a lot of breaths before I could utter a word. I told her what happened. I was ashamed of my situation. Embarrassed for even having such conflicting feelings when I just made so much money. I felt frustrated and unsure what to do next. Emma took it in. She was present, silent, holding space, offering no advice, or pretending to know what I should do. Instead, she took my hand, "Let's pray. Dear God. We ask that you send Yoram comfort and that you guide his heart, in your infinite wisdom, to make the best decision. We trust in your counsel for it is all-knowing." That prayer felt surprisingly comforting. For a moment, I felt grateful even without the answers.

Sometimes you pray just to be reminded of the obvious. It was obvious I had to call Shifra. It wasn't going to be an easy conversation, but it had to be done right now. Imagine your life partner calls you out of the blue on a weekend in the midst of picking out apples at the grocery store. "Hey, guess what? I just made $10,000 and I'm going to give it away because of a promise I made and never told you about…" Think about how you would reply. It did not go very well for me either. Not at all. It was a long, tense call.

We finally reached an agreement we would decide how to donate $5,000 each and that we do it only after the money had been received. I felt conflicted. I wanted to donate that night during the fundraiser but we could not agree. I wanted to trust in Glenn's email commitment, but I couldn't transfer that trust to Shifra, she didn't buy it.

With this conflict, I headed back into the room, a bit hungry, and much confused. I didn't want to miss the next session, although had I known the topic, I might have skipped it and hid. The topic was 'Integrity at the Soul Level'.

Integrity is a popular conference topic. Most say integrity occurs when one's actions align with one's word and then one does what one has said. This was integrity at a higher level. To my surprise, it turns out my soul has integrity and I had not even known. "Integrity at your soul level," Marcia explained, "It means showing up in congruence with who you are at your core." To be at this level of integrity, you must not only *know who you are*, but also honor, articulate, and express it. I heard the message loud and clear. It meant that making a promise like the one I had made about my challenge, must have come from deep inside my soul and had to be kept.

Marcia made her point crystal clear. How I show up in life must be a congruent reflection of the qualities and core values my soul carries. Integrity at the soul level is both a question about who I am, plus a decision about how I want to show up in life. "Are you the kind of man who, in your heart of hearts, you know you want to be?" she asked. Thanks Marcia, I felt like crying, way to rub it in! She wasn't done, though. With every word I was gently, yet firmly, being pushed towards a decision I was afraid to make.

I knew what I had to do, but doing it was a totally different matter. Shifra and I just made an agreement and here I was about to break it, not even an hour later. It sucked, but either I kept my pact – or I didn't. It was time to decide... I felt very lonely. How was I to choose between an agreement with my wife and the one my soul made with God? The questions from the session rang in my head. A part of me wanted to hide and wait for this to be over; another part was yelling at me to step up! So I did. I filled out the donation form and handed it in. Done. I was relieved. I knew in that moment, I was a bigger man than I had ever been. The storm inside me was over.

The next morning and last day of the conference was a bit anticlimactic. In the aftermath of my breakthrough I didn't expect things to surpass the growth of the day before. The first order of business was announcing the results of the fundraiser. A big drum roll ushered the next slide onto the screen. $161,500!! The room roared. Many were in tears, impressed at making what seemed like an impossible goal. It was a wake-up moment to what is possible.

Seeing the number on the big screen, I realized how important my donation was. My $5,000 donation got us across the fundraiser finish-line. I was proud! This must be how Michael Jordan feels when he scores the winning basket, I thought. How fitting for the deal that got me across the finish line of my 90-day goal to also bring the group across the finish-line of our fundraiser goal. In my pride, I almost missed the real message.

Then the truth hit me! Success is only success when we all succeed. When I showed up, I did my part, helping the group make our goal. Had I held back, I would have single handedly brought everyone down. All of us would have collectively failed, had I succumbed to my own fears. Our job is not to single-handedly save the day. Our job is to do our part. If we fail to do our part, small and insignificant as it seems, failure ensues.

Growing up, my male role models were James Bond and John Wayne. They taught me that being a man meant emotional control, invulnerability and above all being the hero that saves the day on his own. But in this fundraiser, I could not save the day all by myself. To do that I would have had to take on the entire group goal alone, a task both impossible and unnecessary for me.

Instead, I realized the era of the lone rider saving the day is over. I felt for a brief moment that I single-handedly made the difference, only to recognize we all did it together. It wasn't just me. Welcome to the century of doing your part. When you do your part, you fill in a spot in the great puzzle of Life. You complete the picture. When you do not do your part, you leave a hole.

Do! Your! Part!

PS. In the aftermath of growth, one thing was left to be mended: my broken agreement with Shifra. That storm wasn't going away silently! It did however open the door to a healthy conversation about money, agreements, and integrity, a conversation that left us stronger as a couple. And with a newfound integrity at one's soul level, that's priceless!

IGNITE ACTION STEPS

*Do not tell inspiration to shut-up. Through decades of coaching I often see people abdicating their dreams, their life purpose. "It's too big for me," they say, "I cannot get involved with this right now." This is an excuse, a story we use to avoid stepping up. Yet, what is too big for the one may not be too big for the many. If the idea feels meaningful it is yours to act on. Find your part… then do your part.

*Your part is a *part*, not the whole thing! You can't fix it all by yourself. Do not fall into the trap of wanting to do it all on your own. Don't tell yourself, "If I can't fix it all the way, why get involved at all?" Instead, ask yourself what you *can* do. The part which you can do, is your part. Do that part.

*Step up. Commit. Take action. Do something. Anything! However small and unimportant it seems, take action. Your action causes a ripple effect and changes everything. The quarter you give to the beggar may complete the dollar they need for today's meal. Do your part.

*Learn from success. This step is an outlier, but it's the best one. Above all, *learn from success*. People know mistakes are learning experiences. Yet, most of us tend to ignore success as a source of deeper wisdom. Your success may be a veil that hides an unexpected lesson just as mine did.

*Life is not here to stroke our egos. Our egos do that on their own. Left to our devices we would bask in that glory all day long. Life grants us success because Life trusts us, on probation, to learn from it. Personally, I rest assured, if I didn't learn from my success, a failure would have ensued to teach me the same lesson.

When you have done well, when you succeeded, prevailed, when you've won the day, ask yourself, "What is the lesson that Life crafted especially for me in this success?"

Yoram Baltinester - USA
Founder: Decisive Action Workshops
https://HeyYoram.com
www.facebook.com/yoram.baltinester
www.linkedin.com/in/yorambaltinester/

ZENAS CHIN

"The true fulfilment you seek in life resides within your courage
to be vulnerable and awesomely human."

**It is my hope that my story will encourage and empower you to embrace
the reality that we get to choose and show up with vulnerability and
humanity at any point in life. When we do, we give ourselves the space
to accept new opportunities and possibilities. Ultimately, it is not about
how people react to you, but rather about showing up for yourself and
knowing that you can be courageously vulnerable. Nobody needs you to
be perfect, but everybody needs you to be perfectly you.**

COURAGEOUS VULNERABILITY IS YOUR SUPERPOWER

A photo of a handsome young Caucasian man laying naked on a bed
with pearl white sheets. That was the final text message I ever received in
my last long-distance relationship. I recognized that bed – the one with pearl
white sheets – it was hers.

I couldn't comprehend... My body was frozen. My heart was heavy.
Then thoughts started rushing into my head, "What's going on? Who is that?
Is she trying to send me a message? Is she playing games with me? Is she
breaking up with me?"

I felt like my entire chest had tightened up. I struggled to breathe.
Everything around me no longer mattered as I fixated my eyes on the screen
of my phone, hoping that I had misinterpreted something or that it was a bad

joke.

I called, but there was no answer.

Time passed. I do not know how long, but eventually, reality caught up to my mind. My chapter with her had come to an abrupt end. I felt like my world was falling apart. It was painful... confusing... humiliating... "Is it something I did? Maybe it is something I didn't do? Why isn't she talking to me about this?"

Then the blame kicked in. Not her. I was blaming 'me' for not being enough for her.

That day I began wearing a mask of self-sufficiency and independence to hide the hurt because I did not want to risk opening myself up to such pain again.

I could feel my confidence leaving my body.

I did my best to be authentic but, I held back from every opportunity for an intimate, loving, interdependent relationship. The moment anyone showed signs of romantic interest towards me, I'd be triggered and act in a self-sabotaging way to push them away – even if we were both drawn to each other.

For half a decade, I consistently turned away opportunities because deep down I was afraid of going through that pain again. It is not something I'm proud of being consistent at. I thought I was taking charge of my life by protecting myself. It took me three years to realize that it was an illusion of control simply because I couldn't put myself in any position to be rejected.

My mentor once told me, "How you do anything is how you do everything." Without knowing it, my fear of rejection had spread and affected other areas of my life beyond love and relationships. In retrospect, I had to acknowledge I had been shying away from opportunities at work when I could have shined. I gave up my own boundaries and did not speak up with my thoughts, ideas and visions simply out of fear of being rejected. I swallowed my own voice.

Even though I was given the space to innovate and experiment at work, I played it safe. I stuck by the book and didn't dare to do anything against the status quo. My mindset was terrible and I placed way too much importance and power on the opinions and words of others. I was painfully dependent on external validation out of fear of rejection.

Then the summer came and I met her.

I flew to Barcelona, Spain for a one-month immersive event (yes, a whole month!) so that I could take my personal growth to a deeper level. I couldn't make it to the beginning of the event though, due to work, so I arrived in the second week. By then, it was obvious that people had already started to form closer friend groups.

It was obvious what I had to do if I wanted to make friends: I had to put myself out there and introduce myself to people. Despite the little train of thought visiting my mind saying, "They might not like you, you know? You are weird and different and not quite on the same level," I took action and did it anyway. I am grateful for the decision, intention and commitment I made that month because I met some of the best friends in my life.

One of them was Sidney. We clicked promptly after we met. Although, she confessed later that she first found me ever-so-slightly annoying because of how ridiculously enthusiastic I was when I showed up. Well, I guess that was ONE way to make a lasting impression.

She was gorgeous but our relationship was platonic. We would talk about everything – our paradigms, our curiosities and interests, even other dating opportunities. We dove into the deep sh*t & the bullsh*t. I was beyond ecstatic to be able to share my world with my new friend and to explore hers without holding back. Before long, she had become one of my best friends. It is incredible how close and raw you can feel with someone in just a month. My mentor once told me, "A friendship is not based on the length of time you spent together. It's based on the depth and foundation you built together."

With Sidney, our shared experiences, raw conversations and fun adventures together led to an unexpected evolution in our relationship. One day, something shifted. I felt my heart beating faster when I was around her. That was odd, but I didn't put much thought into it. Then, I realized I had become incredibly sensitive to her energy. When she walked into a room or was close by, I would instantly know. It was like a sixth sense.

To my surprise, I became smitten with her. Sometimes my mind would even go blank. Oh yes - I was now romantically drawn to her. I did not see that coming, at all. The escalation was so gradual from our intimate friendship, "Like a frog in boiling water." The perfect setup for the "Friend Zone".

After a month together, my friends from Barcelona felt like family to me. Both Sidney and I were a part of an intimate friend group even after the event. I didn't want to risk changing what we had. I mean, there was so much at stake, right? "What if asking her out made things awkward for our closely knit group? What if she was not interested in me? What if…?" Many negative excuses jumped to mind for not taking action. Surely if I didn't do anything about it; if I chose not to be vulnerable, I would be "safe". I won't be euphoric, but I'd stay "safe".

But then, a thought lit up... "What if she says 'Yes'?"

Bronnie Ware, in her world-renowned book, *Top 5 Regrets of The Dying*, shares one of the top regrets people have: *"I wish I'd had the courage to express my feelings."*

So I finally picked a day while we were having our daily calls and I queried, "You know, I like you, Sidney. Beyond that of a friend. Do you feel the same way about me?"

Raw. Bare. Vulnerable... Unnerving.

I'm sure it was just a few seconds before she replied, but I swear it felt like a century. Then I heard the words spoken in her sweet voice, "Yes, I do."

Cue the music! It felt like my world lit up. My heart sang. I could not contain the big smile on my face.

For five years, I had kept myself 'safe' by talking myself out of opportunities in fear of rejection. But right then and there, I had broken the cycle by taking a huge risk with a magical reward. The risk was worth it.

But here is the catch, Sidney and I lived in different countries. The thought of another long-distance relationship frightened me. I could not get into a new romantic relationship with this gigantic cloud hovering above me. So I had to take another risk: I sat her down, took a deep breath and communicated with full transparency and candor about my past – my traumas, my pains and my fears.

Like any moment of vulnerability, there were trains of thoughts visiting me. Unfortunately, they were not the most encouraging ones, "Am I going to ruin what we have? Will she judge me for my past? Will she reject me for my feelings and more importantly, my fears?"

She listened with compassion and what happened next was unexpected. She loved everything I said and shared with me her past, feelings and thoughts. I listened; and I accepted it all. I fell in love with her for that.

We looked into each other's eyes, held each other's hands and made a commitment to be on the same team and to do our best to co-create an interdependent relationship together. Our story as a conscious couple began that day.

As our relationship progressed, I unlocked new opportunities for vulnerability. The fateful day came when I realized I could not hide from her anymore.

After we decided to take the leap of faith to elevate our relationship to the next level, we moved in together into a two-level studio apartment. When I was first inspecting the studio, it seemed perfect. It had a high ceiling with floor-to-ceiling windows for the sunlight. I walked onto the balcony and was welcomed by beautiful greenery and the pool. It seemed to me there was more than enough space to fit all of our belongings. Throw in a new couch and some vibrant plants as our companions.

Or so I thought. What I did not fully prepare myself for, was for the two of us to energetically be in each other's space constantly. I felt like I was a specimen in a jar with all my character traits and quirks readily and immediately observed. Growing up, I was always told by my community that a man needs to be a number of things in order to be successful and attractive: Strong. Wealthy. Wise, etc.

'Being vulnerable' did not make that list.

As a kid, it didn't feel safe to be vulnerable with my peers at all. I was an immigrant and was different. I was bullied for showing up uniquely. Imagine every day going to school and being called names or boycotted whenever you mustered up the courage to reach out and be friendly. Imagine being picked on and laughed at every time you expressed your unique sense of humor. Imagine consistently getting a message from your peers that being who you are is not good enough for them.

Back then, I chose to always show up with a smile on my face, hiding the emotions that I thought were frowned upon. Feelings I kept inside an imaginary room deep inside my heart.

What I learned in school from the traditional men was...Sadness showed weakness and people would reject you for that. Never be sad in front of others. Feeling stressed? That meant you were incompetent; you would lose your friends and loved ones if you showed signs of that. Don't ever share that you are experiencing stress. Angry? That only causes pain to people and yourself. Disregard that the moment it appears! I became more and more afraid of peering into that 'closet' to see what was inside. I felt that if I did, I would be flooded by all the emotions I had crammed into it.

We all have a desire to fit in and be accepted. There is nothing inherently wrong with that. However, we sacrifice our identities and lose our self-worth if we compromise our values and principles, just so we can hear the words, "You are one of us now."

Fast forward to moving in with my partner. It did not hit me until the first time I was under stress and working hard on solving a challenge, that I realized that there were no isolated spaces in our new home. No place to hide. As I looked around the two-level studio, I couldn't find a place private enough or one that was out of sight. Sure, there was the bathroom. Trust me, I tried to stay there as long as I could so that I wouldn't appear stressed out in front of her.

We made a commitment when we started the relationship that we would be transparent and vulnerable with one another. But that only added more anxiety to my situation. I could feel the pressure building. My heart rate was racing. And I became quieter.

Trains of insecure thoughts visited me, "I am not certain where my career path is heading to. Would she judge me for that?" "I have debt I am paying off. What if I cannot provide her the lifestyle that she deserves?" I felt tense around her. Finally, she asked the golden question, "What is wrong?"

We had a pact that we'd always be honest - especially when asked. I took a deep breath, poured my heart out and told her everything. My challenges, my worries, my fear of showing her my "weak" side. She accepted all of me. Then, she told me she loved me even more.

I learned a valuable lesson. People cannot love us for who we are unless we choose to show up fully as ourselves. I had chosen to reveal who I was - beautiful with all my scars. And with that, I felt that I truly belonged.

Embracing my authenticity and showing up with vulnerability has served me by attracting the people that genuinely lift me up and appreciate me for who I was, who I am and who I can become. Find your courage to embrace who you are. Don't be afraid to share your mistakes or failures. It is when you share these things that people can truly relate to you. Just act in accordance with your values and what is important to you. Take that step even if you might be rejected because the rewards are worth it. Nobody needs you to be perfect, but everybody needs you to be perfectly you.

Mark Twain said, "Twenty years from now you will be more disappointed by the things that you didn't do than by the ones you did do."

Every second of every day, we get to choose whether to act in alignment with our values, our principles, our truth. We gain greater confidence and self-love when we show up fully with our humanity and vulnerability. We catapult towards fulfillment when we honor our feelings and act with integrity.

Ignite Action Steps

* **Identify your Top Six Values.** To truly belong to a tribe or community, you need to first feel belonging within yourself. Live in alignment with your values.

* **Courage and confidence are like muscles. Train them!** Do one thing that truly aligns with your values every week – even if it's unconven-

tional. You'll be surprised by your results.

* Immerse yourself in one event every quarter with people whom you'd like to have in your network. Set an intention to show up fully as the best version of yourself and watch the magic happen.

* Celebrate your successes and lessons every week. Too often we forget to acknowledge the little wins we have in life that build up to the big wins. Each and every one of them is important to set you up for success!

* BREATHE. Whenever you feel overwhelming emotions or you are about to take massive action... Did you hear me?.. BREATHE.

* Know that everything is okay. Feel love for yourself. Acknowledge yourself and do that thing that you've been compelled to do. Take one massive action today to fulfill your greatness.

Zenas Chin - Canada
"Chief Empowerment Officer" at Champions of IMPACT, Speaker
@zenaschin

DAMIAN CULHANE

"Suffering can be transformed into healing.
It starts with learning to love yourself first."

I share from my heart hoping my story will inspire you to transform your emotional pain. To help you navigate the map of chaos that unconscious sabotage causes and free you from your psychological wounds – reconnecting you with your soul. You will learn how to light that spark in your life, inspiring you to embrace your truth and liberate your soul.

LOVE IS AN INSIDE JOB

Imagine waking up on Christmas Day as a seven-year-old boy, full of excitement, joy and wonder of how the day would unfold. The pleasure of sitting down to watch a favorite movie or a family show; the magic of unwrapping gifts and sharing a festive meal. But something didn't feel right for me. I wasn't certain why I felt uneasy, but I sensed the atmosphere and sadness creep over me like an overbearing shadow. What was missing?

In the kitchen, my Mum was busy preparing Christmas lunch. Our festive meal would consist of a roasted turkey with all the trimmings! This meant I would have to eat my annual Brussels sprout – a crowd pleaser at our table. I noticed Mum was unusually quiet. She was always soft with her affection, but hard to read. She didn't really enjoy cooking any meal, but I sensed the simmering stress gently bubbling under the surface. Maybe this year I would eat two sprouts, to try and cheer her up. We gathered round the tree to exchange gifts. Dad was not there. I had been wondering where he was going to be for Christmas? He had moved out a few months earlier and I saw him on weekends, but this was the first time we gathered as a family since he had left. Nobody was talking about him and the heavy silence was interrupted with the next present that was passed for me to unwrap. It felt strange not having Dad with us.

After our ritual present unwrapping, I retreated to my room with my stash of seasonal treasure, placing the gifts on the bed next to my Christmas stocking. An orange and a red shiny apple rolled out from the stocking and I caught a glimpse of the multipack of six full size chocolate bars. I admired the colorful writing, removed a wrapper and without thinking, took the first bite. It felt good as my teeth broke through the layer of milky sweetness. I savored the moment, sitting for a while to enjoy the sensation. There was still a long wait until lunch and my stomach felt empty. I spied the red velvet stocking, the discarded fruit and chocolate bars in their shiny wrapping. Maybe one more bar would satisfy my emptiness. With the experience of youth on my side, I merrily munched through all six of them, drifting away in a sweet dream.

The muffled voice of my Mum downstairs brought me back to reality, calling us for lunch. We took our seats, laid with special plates. When lunch was served, I sat looking down at my plate brimful of turkey, sausages wrapped in bacon, vegetables, potatoes, gravy, cranberry sauce and my favorite – bread sauce. Mum, liberated from her cooking duties, was in a happier mood enjoying her annual glass of Vueve du Vernay. Relieved, the bubbles had lifted her spirit, "I'll only have to eat one sprout," the last item on my plate. With my stomach swelling, I just managed to squeeze in some Christmas pudding coated in brandy sauce – the final spoon stretching my elastic stomach to its limit.

This was my first experience of comfort eating. I didn't really know why I had indulged in the chocolate bars, then stuffed myself with food... it was like an unconscious trance. *The emptiness I felt inside had not gone away.* That day's tension, led to the pattern of eating to fill a void. It took time to cement into a coping strategy! But the foundation was laid for binging and addiction to junk food. Throughout my adult life, I often, to cope, would conceal or hide my overeating, secretly indulging on my own.

Over the next three decades, I tried to shift focus and change my behavior. Multiple short-lived attempts to quit old habits resulted in many years of yo-yo dieting. Struggling with the highs and lows of emotional eating never addressed the underlying issues. A roller-coaster of negative beliefs dominated my thoughts. I believed I could not trust others with what I was feeling. I felt alone with my thoughts, weak and disempowered. I wrestled with those feelings for years silently suffering with the sadness inside. Then in my late thirties, my life changed forever. My youngest son was diagnosed with a life-limiting, muscle-wasting disease. My mental well-being took a significant downturn. It was as if my heart had been wrenched out and stomped on. I was numb.

The oppressive path I had to travel was not one I had chosen, but nevertheless I had to make the painful drawn-out journey accepting the loss. The unbearable frustration of being absolutely powerless and the sadness of not being able to take the burden away from my child. I was submerged in an inescapable conflict, determined to focus on being positive, whilst battling with long periods of sadness and depression. I was positive and strong on the outside for everyone else and never spoke about my true feelings. I was suppressing my emotions and concealing my fear living with the gluttonous empty feeling that would never be satiated. The grief was insurmountable and would darken my thoughts and fill me with foreboding trepidation. To protect me from enduring sufferance, a new mask was formed – carved by a devious and unconscious ego for me to hide behind. An unfamiliar persona I barely knew or recognized.

My unconscious addiction shifted a gear. I rewarded my unexpressed suffering with more over-eating of junk food, and also becoming secretly addicted to pornography and sex, which led to making some very poor choices. I was becoming more aloof to my thoughts and feelings, hardened by the unwanted burden of mental wretchedness. I was distancing myself from my true identity. A pattern developed: I regularly drank excessive volumes of alcohol, passed out, then experienced fleeting periods of amnesia. For nearly ten years, I wallowed in self-pity, self-medicated and obstructed emotional pain, keeping my suppressed feelings numbed and myself in denial.

Silently battling to overcome the demons, the struggle felt like an eternal loop that I was stuck with. I'd make a little progress, then relapse, the inner conflict and mindset going right back to the beliefs of *not being good enough* or *not being capable of change*. I'd come back more determined, 'try' even harder, only to fail again just as spectacularly. It was as if I had no control over the stubbornness of my untethered ego, no choice in my destiny. I would blame external factors or seek answers outside of myself, citing the circumstances or the conditions to justify my lack of success. Anyone who has yo-yo dieted or struggled with addictions may understand the mindset. I was trying to slay a dragon that was getting stronger and more resistant with each new battle.

I had spent years sabotaging my life; my career (multiple times in a loop, believing I'm not capable); my relationships (believing I was not worthy of love); my success (believing I was not good enough). I was completely unaware of why or how that had all happened. In my darkest thoughts, I had considered the ultimate sabotage of my own life, morbid contemplation that would keep me awake at night. Eventually my unconscious ego became the master of my destiny, destroying my marriage of 24 years.

As a result of the marriage breakdown I sabotaged my cherished relationship with my two sons, Conor and Ben. By separating from their mother, I became persona non grata for a while. The decision to dissolve the marriage was painful for everyone. The brokenness of two people in their own worlds growing further apart over the years. Despite concerted mutual effort, my unconscious ego convinced me I would be happier on my own. It had become obvious that the separation was inevitable, and I decided for us. Of course, the outcome caused sadness, confusion, uncertainty and I was in no frame of mind to cope with the fallout for my family. I punished myself with more self-loathing, more guilt, shame and a depth of sadness I had never felt before.

For long periods, I would not see my sons. Communication was sporadic and transactional, more business-like than father and sons. I saw them infrequently and the tension was unbearable. I would be sad and unhappy, haunted by the awkwardness of distancing myself from them. I knew I couldn't go back into the marriage for my own self-respect, but I missed daily contact with them. I hadn't been an ideal father-figure, but I had been around and always had time for my sons.

The worst moment was on Christmas Day that year. For the first time ever, I was not with my sons on that day. It took me back to my childhood and the impact my father's absence had on my life. How could I be such a fool and inflict the same experience on both of them? I imagined how my father must have felt being absent from us on just such occasions. The sadness was overwhelming, and I felt the tears welling up inside. I was unable to suppress the years of tension and resistance that had been hiding behind my veil of deception; the invisible mask was now engulfed by a flood of tears – a tidal wave washing away my pride. My heart and soul shrinking as I wept.

For several months I went on wallowing in self-pity and sadness, all self-inflicted. I became addicted to my negative emotions, finally reaching an emotional dead end. The void I had created was too big to ignore. And yes, *I had created it*. I had no one else to blame, it was my actions, my responsibility and only I could be held to account. I was sabotaging my relationship with my sons and denying what my heart most desired: love and connection with Conor and Ben. It seemed I was hypnotized by my unconscious that was insistent on manifesting my ego's dysfunctional purpose to avoid receiving their love. That was a crazy mixed-up mindset. Driven by my pattern of sabotage to the extent I was impairing my relationship with my sons, driven by thoughts of not being capable as a father and avoiding responsibility for my behavior.

At that point in my life, I just knew I had to do something to transform my thinking. I had to explore the ways to resolve the situation and overcome my weakness in character, to find the mental resilience to overpower my demons. I took a deep dive emotionally, exploring what had led me to that profound regret. I had to face my own journey of discovery from a place of solitude, to transmute my sorrow and rise up from a place of suffering. My mindset had to shift dramatically and swiftly.

Little by little I began to rebuild my true identity. Step by step I unraveled how I had unconsciously masked the pain and concealed my emotions, a false and empty existence. I had hidden behind the brave face for decades. I had been reckless and out of control, inauthentic with my relationships; thoughtless in my consideration for others. I had sabotaged my career, avoided receiving love and lost connection with my values. My heart's desires had been neglected in a pattern of unconscious choices, pursuing a set of bullshit beliefs and I had become too arrogant to admit my failings.

I had already read countless books on personal development, attended numerous workshops and dozens of training courses. Including those run by the best speakers, the most reputable organizations and the most inspirational coaches in the world. Yet I still did not have the answer and did not know how to change my mindset. It was during this time, when I had reached the lowest point emotionally, I discovered how to navigate a pathway back to my soul. How to continue my journey and how to shift my mindset.

Over time I gradually rediscovered who I really am. I reconnected with my soul and embraced my true purpose. I studied the art of consciousness, learned how to transform my thinking and explored ways to transmute my mindset. Understanding oneself at the deepest level leads to a degree of self awareness most people would fear. There is no hiding. There is no one else to blame. No one else to be taking ownership. No one else to be held accountable. To move forward, the only obstacle at that point was myself. The only person that remained to take responsibility – was me.

Eventually I figured out how to heal my suffering and my recovery swiftly accelerated when I put effort and momentum into a structure and ritual of taming my dragon, embracing my truth and liberating my soul. Day by day I work on rebuilding my relationship with my sons; I show up differently now, grateful for the opportunity to be a parent again. I shift my vibration and energy to love them with an open heart, embracing vulnerability as a threshold to accessing deeper connection with them. I am connected to my purpose to heal suffering through teaching transformational thinking. In the last few years I have worked with parents of children with muscle wasting conditions; sharing ways to overcome their sadness and how to cope with fear, supporting them through their feelings of anger. I also work with others to neutralize their ego and rise above their suffering so they can create a life they love. I am passionate about that the most, because I have learned it is better to live in the present moment rather than letting your past define you. My desire in sharing my story is that you will know how to reconnect with your soul and create a life you love. I hope you will find your path to connect with your heart and honor your true self.

IGNITE ACTION STEPS

How many times have you set out to pursue a specific end result and failed to achieve it? Maybe you resolved the tension by playing small, getting distracted or felt the energy fizzling away as your desires wane and you lose momentum. This causes conflict internally, which can eat away in your mindset. Your unconscious reminds you that you are 'not good enough', 'not worthy' or 'don't belong'. These beliefs can lead to low self-worth and leave you feeling sad.

The conflict arises when you know you are capable of more and want to transform your life, but you are totally unconscious to how the ego shows up to cause havoc. This can create chaos, confusion or even anger, leaving you with a feeling that you are out of control. You may feel disconnected or even depressed at not being able to achieve more, putting others needs ahead of your own or simply withdrawing and separating. By following the steps below, you will learn how to use your special gifts and talents to serve the Universe, how to embody the emotions you desire at your highest level of self and manifest a life worth living.

*Self love and compassion: learn to feel love for yourself in every cell of your body. Treat yourself with respect and kindness. Be gentle on yourself. What would you do if you were dating yourself? How can you nurture your inner child with compassion?

*Gratitude: acknowledging the things to be grateful for, to develop a habit of showing genuine appreciation. Choose two or three experiences, people, situations or whatever is obvious for you. As you build awareness, be truly and genuinely thankful.

Forgiveness: start with forgiving yourself. You are on a journey, a path of learning. Everything you experience is happening for a reason. What growth opens up for you when you accept your journey? Who do you need to forgive to release the emotional pain and heal your past? Holding on to past anger and suffering is futile.

*Humility: tread softly and treat others with an open mind. Suspend judgement and accept your place in the Universe. You are special and so is everyone else. We are all on a journey, so be humble and suspend your ego to truly connect.

*Vulnerability: your ancestors survived for thousands of years and your soul is here for a reason. Surrender to what the Universe is bringing you; be open to receive the support of others and share yourself authentically to deepen your connections.

*Healing: Take time out for mindfulness; put yourself first. Start with breathing exercises and move on to meditation. Others will benefit from your *self*-ishness.

*Follow your bliss: connect with your passion and focus on what you love. Serve others through your special gifts and talents to contribute to a bigger cause in the Universe. Listen to the whispers of your soul. If they spark a light inside you, then follow through. The Universe needs you to align with your purpose to bring joy, happiness and love, which elevates the collective consciousness.

*Awaken The Divinity Within: each and every one of us possess a power, a resilience to overcome resistance and a light to shine for others. This is self-leadership, where you show up and make a stand for what is right. Where integrity and authenticity rise up to neutralize your fear and you get to play a bigger role in the Universe. Give yourself permission to unapologetically be you. Channel your guttural aggression into something pure. Be in harmony with your yin and yang to manifest the best inside of yourself, to awaken the best in others. Depending on your gender you either awaken the inner kingdom or awaken the powerful goddess within, maybe even both?!

Damian Culhane - United Kingdom
CMgr., FCMI., FISM., MIOD., MEMCC., Teacher, Coach, Speaker
www.damianculhane.co.uk

KETAN LADVA

"It's always about moving forward, never about standing still or going backwards, even if it is a micro step, things will always get better and progress."

Sometimes we get in so deep we don't know what to do. It is never as bad as it seems. I ask you to see how I let go of my emotions and started with something small. Taking action, no matter how minute, really works. If you derive anything from my story, it is this. Just keep pushing forward and never give up.

GETTING UNSTUCK

There I was lying in bed, wide awake at 3:00 AM, quietly sobbing. My wife, Kiran, next to me fast asleep. The waves of sadness and emotions started to pour over me. I remember hearing, "You're an idiot. Can't you take care of your own family? What kind of man are you? You're such a loser. You lost everything. What are you going to do?" That loud shouting voice was in my head. My fears and thoughts screamed inside of me. The final notice from the lawyer arrived only five days earlier. We had 90 days to hold off the mortgage company. It was February 2010, a full 18 months after the global downturn and my butt was still getting kicked.

Ever had amazingly bad timing? Well, we had that on September 15th, 2008. My team and I had just spent the past six months conducting due diligence, working to buy a prime office building in downtown Saskatoon,

Canada. The office building was ideally located just a block from the hustle and bustle of the main core. We had completed our feasibility study, lawyers were engaged, financing was approved, and we were flying into Saskatoon to sign the papers to transfer the title of the property. As I left the lawyers' office after completing all of the documents, I heard the news. Later, it would be known as the defining moment of the Global Financial Meltdown of 2008. Lehman Brothers had collapsed. Would you believe it? On the same day I was buying a $5 million-dollar property, one of the major investment banks of the world was collapsing and the financial markets dove into chaos.

Over the next 18 months, the world was in financial turmoil. The red-hot Saskatchewan economy came to a grinding halt. Financial lending stopped. The businesses my team and I were targeting for our commercial building ceased all expansion. Everyone was on standby mode. Within six months, the largest lease we had in the building did not renew and left. Our capital started to dry up. Soon, I could not make the mortgage payments and one thing after another compounded our problems. The foreclosure process on our new acquisition was in full force. Legal paperwork was flying back and forth faster than a tennis ball in the Finals of the Wimbledon Championships. Not only was our commercial property in foreclosure but since I was a personal guarantor, my own home and assets were being targeted by the lawyers and the lender.

My bank account was empty. I was an entrepreneur and sole earner in our family of four. My children were only six and three. My wife was not working at the time. To keep things afloat, I tapped into all of our savings. When that ran out, I was forced to swallow my pride and borrow from my family. My business was floundering. The economy was stuck; at least that's what I told myself. In reality, it was my mind which was stuck. It was stuck in the overwhelm of it all. When a person is continually being hit with negative or depressing news, over and over again, the strain begins to pile up. Imagine being in a boxing ring with another boxer. He's jabbing and throwing punches. You are on the ropes and doing everything you can to stay upright. Dodge. Duck. Parry. Hit back. Miss. Dodge again. Get hit. Get hit again. I was boxed in the corner and the opponent wasn't letting up until I was knocked out. Day after day, month after month, I kept experiencing roadblocks. The strain, stress and pressure kept mounting. Dealing with the barrage of legal emails, documents and the constant, long, tiresome calls sapped all of the energy out of me. Everything kept piling on top of the tremendous weight of the burden I was carrying.

The pressure kept building until that fateful early morning in February of 2010, when the weight of the mental burden I was carrying became just too much. Our desperate attempts to provide a very wide range of proposals to repay the mortgage had finally hit a wall. The Lenders had made their final application to the court. We were about to lose it all and even more. I lay in bed overcome with guilt and regret. My wild negative thoughts pounding. My breath began to falter and heave. Tears start to roll. I turned to my side away from my peacefully sleeping wife and held myself from crying but it's too late. The raw emotion and hurt came out. I got out of bed and sat in the basement sobbing away. I let it all out that night. I felt spent and emptied.

I cannot say how long I sat in the darkness. But something inside me stirred. Was it hope? Or, was I still mad at what had happened? I became aware it was not anger. Maybe I was feeling defeated. Was that it? Nope, wasn't that. There was a lightness I started to sense. The longer I sat in silence, the more peaceful I became. I realized I was experiencing something new which I had not felt in a long time: the calmness and relief of shedding all of the negative, pent up emotion which for months had been trapped inside. The weight of self-inflicted regret, guilt, anger, sadness, remorse and self-pity were being stripped away and exposing the raw essence of myself.

Sitting there in the dark, I realized the stress was not over, but it would not win. The sun would shine the next day. Feeling emotionally cleared, my thoughts drifted to what can I do next? I decided all I had to do was the best I could to keep things moving forward and go back to basics. Everything else will unfold as it does. It was a moment of surrendering to life. Exhausted physically, I got up off the couch and went back to bed. I slept the best sleep I had in a long time and awoke with a new sense of energy.

I have always been an action-oriented and motivated self-starter. It's in my nature to create things and take action. The progress of life and success occurs when there is motion. Even the slightest of action can lead to the biggest of impacts. Without motion, everything becomes stale. Sometimes moving forward can be emotionally difficult. The first emotionally hard action for me, was to share what I was going through with my wife Kiran. I was filled with regret and guilt. I had been purposely shielding her and the family from the pain of uncertainty and insecurity. I had been raised to believe that I was the head of the house, and the buck stopped with me. I, as the "man" of the household, should have all of the answers and my family was my complete responsibility. Now, I was having to share with my wife that I failed miserably. I had to confess there was tremendous uncertainty, insecurity and change coming, even if we didn't do anything.

A few days after that mental release, I plucked up the courage, fought off my self-doubt and sat with Kiran to explain everything. I disclosed the stress and our financial uncertainty. I revealed the emotional turmoil I was going through. We talked about how it all happened and why I had not shared with her earlier. Kiran was amazing and listened with compassion and understanding. She was kind and gave me encouragement that everything would be alright. Having Kiran's support and encouragement helped me reverse the negative cycle I was in. I felt comfortable I had someone to share my frustrations with. I wasn't hiding the struggle anymore and that alone allowed my energy and positivity to increase.

Kiran and I made some adjustments. The kids' new school required a cumbersome 45-minute commute. We agreed to sell our home and rent closer to the school until we were back on our feet.

Once, we decided to sell our home, I started to feel guilty and regretful. My negative thoughts started to flow back in. I heard myself saying, "How could you lose your home? What a complete failure you are!" But I swallowed my pride and called our local realtor and made an appointment. Within two months, the home was ready to be sold, listed and in the rising real estate market, our home sold within thirty days. Three months later we had completed the sale. The guilt and remorse came back as I handed the keys to the new owners. Kiran and I hugged and we moved into our new rental home hopeful.

Our legal and financial problems didn't magically disappear simply because I was feeling lighter or better. The serious problems and challenges were still there. The deadline was still looming over us. I had to go back to basics. But I felt freer. I sat one day and simply unloaded all of the thoughts, triggers, little nagging ideas and any other part of my mental psyche onto a single gigantic list. I learned this technique from the book, *Getting Things Done* by David Allen. Allen talks about freeing your psychic memory by writing everything down on paper. He explains that the process of physically writing down all of your to-do's, nagging bits and things occupying your mind allows your brain to relax.

I began to write and write. I spend over three hours detailing everything in my brain. I wrote about the chores around the house, the elements of my business, my corporate and personal taxes being due, the various family birthdays coming up, the selling of the house, the foreclosure pieces, the legal pieces, the fun places I have been thinking about. I wrote about the kids' education savings program, the financial open loops and anything else that was on my mind. At the end, I had a four-page typed list of open loops. When I unloaded everything like this, I immediately felt even lighter and freer. I didn't have to remember everything!

Next, I looked at the foreclosure and legal parts of my massive brain dump. I collected all those actions and open loops into one new consolidated list. At the top, I wrote the title "My Move Forward List." It looked daunting and scary. Taking a deep breath, I scanned the tasks, and realized there were items I was waiting on other people for. I remembered David Allen's suggestion of creating a "Waiting For List"; designed to capture all the things which other people were doing but you need to keep track of. So, I took another piece of paper and moved those "waiting for" items to the new page. I now had two lists. My Move Forward List and the Waiting For List.

I scanned my Move Forward List and began looking for one thing I could do that day to move myself forward. What would have the biggest impact? What would be do-able right now? Was there an action that required minimal effort so I could get a quick win? It was all about keeping the process moving forward. It did not matter how quickly or how big the movement was. What was supercritical to get out of the mess, was to take one action – just one. I selected a small little task, a short email to one of the realtors I knew. I quickly completed that little task and marked it done on the list. I taped both lists on my white board and ended my day feeling like I had a big win. I could feel a sense of momentum starting.

Every day after, I reviewed My Move Forward and Waiting For lists. I would first go through the Waiting For list and update it if anything had changed. If there was something on the list that was being stalled or delayed, I would prompt the person who was responsible with either a quick follow up email or a short phone call.

Then, I would review My Move Forward list. Once again, I scanned the list and chose one action from My Move Forward list to complete. I would finish that one right away. On some days, when I was feeling good, I would end up doing multiple actions. On those days, ideas started coming to me. New epiphanies, connections and options were coming together.

Not every day was one of bliss and happiness. The dreaded legal calls were still draining my energy. The conflict with the Lenders continued. The stress of the situation was still there. The sense of overwhelm still came at times. However, I was more prepared and aware of my emotional state. I purposely took time to step away from negative challenges. This could be as simple as having a cup of tea by myself. I would go for short walks to clear my mind. I talked to Kiran. I played with the kids. I learned self-care is not selfish. Taking the time to be aware of my emotional and physical states helped me manage those darker, negative periods.

One of the biggest self-care shifts which resulted from that fateful early morning breakdown was an acceptance that I was allowed to cry. I was brought up in a culture where I created the belief I had to portray a strong image of self-confidence and strength. Crying or emotion was seen as showing weakness. It was viewed as unacceptable and unmanly to cry. The age-old adage, "be a man" was what I believed to be true. That evening, I had let my emotions run wild. I cried and sobbed like never before as an adult. The release of the emotions cleanses your body, mind and soul. With the experience of having a good cry, I allowed myself moments to let my emotions out. I gave myself permission, where I felt safe and unjudged, to vent and express my frustrations, sadness, joy, anger, regret, guilt and any other emotion which came up.

As the daily practice of taking small, minor actions,(even if it was one email), the momentum began to build. My connections continued to grow. I knew the only way to get out of the mess was one of two options: either I find new money to pay off the Lender or I sell the property at a price satisfying the Lender. Daily, I worked and focused on both of those two options. Over time, I reconnected with my original mortgage broker. She was a seasoned veteran of the mortgage and real estate business. Through the course of unrelated events, she connected me to a potential Buyer for the distressed property. The Buyer, sensing an opportunity to capitalize on our misfortune, was in a position to make a strong, qualified proposal. Unfortunately, their proposal would leave me short in paying the Lenders off and my personal guarantees were still at risk. Continuing my daily action plan, I began to work between the lawyers, the Lender and the Buyer to negotiate a way out. During the process, I had to maneuver for extensions with the Lender to prevent legal troubles from escalating. Finally, after several months of daily actions and constant follow up, we had an agreement between everyone. The agreement required me to surrender significant assets to the Lender along with the title of the property, but it protected me from future liability. Most importantly, it cleared me of the huge cloud over my business and my head. I was free to start again and keep moving forward. At that point I felt rejuvenated and my optimism soared.

Today, I am a partner in a very successful property development company in Vancouver, Canada called Kingswood Real Estate. I continue to lead my team through daily 'action lists' and 'waiting for lists'. We work energetically to keep things moving forward with simple small daily actions. We never give up.

It is never as bad as it seems. You have it within yourself to push through your emotions, fears and overcome any obstacles you may perceive as too daunting. It just takes one step forward to start the process. Take that step now.

IGNITE ACTION STEPS

*Find a trusted person with whom to share your emotions, thoughts, feelings and frustrations. Someone who approaches you with kindness, sincerity and without shame. Use a counsellor, life coach, your doctor or professional if you are uncomfortable sharing with your family or friends. The relief and freedom to let go of some of your emotional pain is like a boulder being lifted off your shoulders.

*Complete a mind clearing brain dump. Get a pad of paper and a good pen. Start writing down everything on your mind. *Write without blame, judgement or fear. No one will see the list. Write every task, every reminder, any bills you have to pay, anyone you need to call, anything that needs fixing or you want or needs for your house, any trips you want to take, any thought that is nagging at you . . . write it all down.* Line by line. Once you've written your list, mark a "W" beside every item that someone else is doing; this represents your "Waiting For List." Move the "W" items to a new list and cross them off the first list. The simple act of emptying your mind will bring you freedom and mental relief.

*Identify your self-care habits. What re-energizes you when you're feeling low? Get a 3 x 5 index card. At the top, write "My Energy List". Next, write 10 things that energize you. For example, taking a walk, having a cup of tea, meditating, taking a nap, getting a hug, kissing your partner, doing 10 jumping jacks, etc. Once you've written your list, put the index card on your computer monitor or a prominent place you see all the time. Next time you are feeling low on energy or down, do one of the things on the card.

Taking action is the key to getting things done, Have fun with it.

Ketan Ladva - Canada
Entrepreneur
www.kingswood.ca

AJ MAXWELL

*"Defining your mantra is the key to becoming
and Being the CEO of Your Life."*

We all live the stories we tell ourselves. Often we settle for a story which isn't who we really are. May my story help you on your path to your greatest version of your story and becoming the CEO of your life, every day. The journey of a leader lies within.

THE FAMILY MANTRA WOKE ME UP

As I stood on the beach with my feet in the sand, I glanced out at the horizon where the sky meets the Pacific Ocean. The sun was dancing in my eyes and pressing warm on my skin. I pondered how this reality had come true. I felt a sense of freedom of location and time that felt surreal. My new friend, a highly successful executive stood by my side, and he was pondering, too. In his eyes I could see this restless hunger and yearning for something more. His questions reflected a deep dissatisfaction with his current highly successful life. He rattled off a stream of inquires like he was searching for the road map. "How did you manage to quit corporate life and end up living here in Paradise with your family in Nosara, Costa Rica?"

As he said those words, I reviewed the many steps on my journey that led me to this moment and my version of freedom. While we stood there, my thoughts wandered. The next great revolution is upon us...breaking free from the tyranny which society, government, community, family, and ancestral patterns imposes on us. Most humans blindly stay stuck in this paradigm. Ultimate freedom lies within. Through our imagination, we have the power to create new worlds of being. We are pioneers of the next generation of freedom.

In a flash, I instantly dropped into one of those defining moments remembering my path, and how I arrived here. It was years ago, I was gripping the wheel hard on my late-night commute home on the Washington, D.C. Beltway. Though that night was not different from any other, I felt a sense of defeat. I'd been in the boardroom. But deeper than that, I had crossed many hurdles in my career effortlessly. Always buoyed up with a seemingly endless fountain of confidence and positivity, yet perhaps, many times I was unaware of the shark-infested corporate waters that surrounded me. My mantra was: I always assume positive intent. This belief allowed me to show up with little judgement or bias when dealing with tough issues. Yet somehow, that night was different. I felt totally consumed by negativity. It was in my blood, pulsing through my veins. I felt it in my bones. The negativity had made its way deep into my consciousness. I was oblivious that I was enveloped in it, until that moment. I didn't realize it had taken hold of me like a dangerous virus. I was infected.

I grew up in a tough home where we made the bed we laid in. Words weren't minced, and every day was a learning day. Loyalty was your word, and above all family mattered. My father was both an executive and a John Wayne and Rambo figure rolled all into one. He once was chased on the Alaskan tundra by a grizzly bear that he stopped and faced down. One night, while holding a teddy bear, I witnessed my fearless protector single handedly prevent a biker gang from invading our home. My favorite memory, when I was eight years old, was when he drove me into the middle of the Mojave Desert in the midst of searing heat, blowing dust and tumbleweeds, and implanted in me the profound concept of vision-to-reality. We stepped into the future. With blueprints in hand, we looked across the desert as he took me on an imaginary tour of the location of one of his largest projects. A year later, I saw it come to fruition; that experience etched in me a new way of seeing the world, not as it was, but as whatever I wanted it to be.

Then there was the heart and soul of our family, my mother, a social change agent. She was once told she didn't understand how the school system worked, so she ran for a school board position and spent 30 years contributing to shaping the lives of our youth. So, from an early age, I excelled at getting things done and I was fortunate to receive a collegiate football scholarship. I always poured myself into a task and plowed ahead with my eyes on the end goal. I was blessed with intuitive patience and understanding. I have always had an uncanny sense of seeing patterns, connecting the seemingly abstract in useful ways and rallying people to create amazing results.

But that night, in the car, with no traffic around, I witnessed myself dying by a thousand cuts. Like a frog not realizing the water is getting hotter until it's too late, I heard myself saying things that didn't sound like me. I was in victim mode, blaming others for where I found myself. I had never crossed that threshold before and had always taken the higher road by re-framing everything around me: Things always work out for me. I saw what was great in situations, knowing I could learn from it to do better and be better.

Yet, I found myself listening to a man having a pity-party. As I gripped the wheel, my knuckles turning white, tension throughout my body, I sped through the darkness, feeling good about blaming others to vindicate my shortcomings. I had taught leaders about cognitive dissonance and the challenge most people have with fully taking ownership of a problem. But there I was crossing that negative threshold.

The corporate meeting we had earlier that afternoon was the culmination of many weeks of preparation. I had rallied a large team, prepared and gathered tons of information. I had taken the extra steps, prepared information packets and sat with each senior executive on several occasions in advance of the meeting to ensure buy in.

As you have probably guessed, the meeting didn't go well. I didn't get consensus to move forward to the next phase of the project. During the meeting, some of the executives even had the balls to leverage the data I provided to utilize it to make counter points and objections. But this really isn't the point. This sort of stuff happens in corporations everyday. Agendas, politics, and self-interest is commonplace. I thought I had conditioned myself to deal with it and take it all in stride. Maybe I had. Perhaps that was part of the problem.

After the meeting, on the journey home, I noticed everything felt incongruent. It was as if I was seeing someone else in this victim state. It was not me. My thoughts were like a foreign language. I said out loud in retaliation, "Wait!? What!? This doesn't happen to me!" As I spoke, I had a burst of divine clarity, and it hit me like a lightning bolt. Boom! The words came into my mind, clear as day, "I Am the CEO of My Life!"

I spoke those words out loud, "I Am the CEO of My Life!" I felt tremendous. I started laughing...at myself. Laughing because it felt so liberating. I then erupted at the top of my lungs, "I...AM...THE...CEO... OF...

MY...LIFE!" I did it again and again. Another 50 times. So empowering. So healing. So perfect to reclaim my life.

Try it: Speak these words out loud, "I...AM...THE...CEO... OF...MY... LIFE!

When I spoke those words for the first time it was a huge relief, a therapeutic remembrance of who I am. A soul remembrance. The words dropped out of my mouth like heavy stones. Such a release. As I repeated this mantra, I reclaimed my power each time, owning everything that showed up or had shown up in my life. Each relationship. Each situation. Reclamation. It was a complete reset. All the mental distractions and stories were evaporating before my eyes. I felt like I was literally healing those thousand cuts. Healing my soul. Each time I said my power mantra, I had flashes of memories, and it felt like an electrifying pulse reenergizing me to the core. I had glimpses of rewriting my stories and my experiences with full ownership. Our words are very powerful, lest we forget. Each of our voices holds a unique signature frequency. When our words are aligned with our soul, our words can be inspiration for ourselves and others. We see this in song and speech, and I learned this on the football field.

In college, I played in a football game where a mantra changed the energy and course of a game. My team was coming off the field and heading into the tunnel at halftime. It had been a long season, we'd taken an average skilled team all the way to the championship game. Yet as we entered the tunnel at half time, we were stunned with a pummeling, 14-28 down. Then it happened. We heard 20,000 crazed fans from the opposing team having fun at our expense yelling and screaming at us, which we usually took in stride. But several guys started throwing their drinks on us. Something hit me, it triggered the lion in me. I looked up and roared, **"We are not leaving until we win!"** My voice caught the tunnel and reverberated larger and louder than I had ever heard it!. I looked into the stands and yelled it again, **"We are not leaving until we win!"** It became electrifying and contagious; it took off like wildfire across our team. Everyone in unison roared. From the tunnel to the locker room, then back to the field. And win we did in a miraculous double overtime victory 35-28.

On that football field, my mantra changed our team's momentum, as we charged back on the field to win. That experience solidified in me the understanding that our emotional state, our positive energy and our beliefs have a great influence on our achievements. Whoever brings the most energy to the game, to work, to life, wins. My team learned that principle and went on to play in the largest comeback collegiate football game in history, down

35 points in the third quarter.

Years later, I was at a gathering, and a friend spoke these words, "We all live the stories we tell ourselves." It was like the world slowed down a bit, and her words wrapped around my head for a brief span of time – their hidden code landed on my soul. The goosebumps of intuition spoke to me: we are the true creators of our lives. Every choice. Every word. Every deed. Matters.

That night my 'CEO' mantra galvanized a reminder for me of the shared vision my beautiful wife, Tera, and I created years ago, "We Thrive As A Family To Serve And Inspire Others." It was time for me to honestly look at my corporate life and determine was it truly in alignment with our vision. Our family mantra has been our rally call, the bridge out of our most difficult trials and the gateway to our brightest moments along our sacred union path. We come back to it time and time again. That introspection of our sacred mantra provided a quantum shift leading to many other shifts that led to the life I enjoy today. I've blended my expertise in building leaders and organizations, helping startups and substantial businesses scale with their own version of freedom. I do so from my home in Costa Rica raising my three children in the most amazing natural environment. My CEO mantra is the foundation of my life. I continue to use it as the cornerstone of my daily routine. I call upon it anytime I need to remember and shift my energy, perspective, or focus.

In Costa Rica, I feel free to enjoy my life. One day as I entered the surf break, the words "Trust, Surrender, and Breathe" came into my mind. Tera and I were preparing for one of our unleashing human potential retreats where we invite a tribe of freedom-seekers to join us in Paradise. During our final preparation, we often set intentions and go to the water for inspiration. Surfing is a transformative experience. This day started rough, a big wave pulled me under. I use a longboard so when inertia from the wave takes my board, it's a wild underwater ride. This time though, as the physical fear started to set in, the words "Trust and Surrender" entered my mind and in that moment I had a completely peaceful and grounding reframe. I popped up and caught my breath and paddled out for the next set of waves. The mantra our clients have come to know is "Trust, Surrender, Breathe, & Love."

As this memory of that dark night and my miracle mantra flashed through my mind, I turned to my executive friend as we watched the surf break and said, "Use your heart as your filter and remember your mantra, and it'll be your guide on your path."

We often get swept up in chasing daily life where time spins away causing us to forget that the journey of a leader begins within. Remember, we have access to infinite wisdom and guidance as spiritual beings having a human experience. The paradox of this life is that we let our humanness override our true essence, and we don't shine our gifts as brightly as we are meant to and what our spirit desires.

Everything is perfect, even when we don't think or feel it is so. Remember, *You Are the CEO of Your Life.* You decide the mantras which keep you aligned with your soul!

Ignite Action Steps

Research tells us our brains run through thousands upon thousands of thoughts each day, most of these thoughts carrying over from yesterday. Our brains are divine supercomputers with supernatural capabilities, what we program into it grows. Most of our core programming happens during childhood. The stories we tell ourselves shape the way we see the world, become our paradigm. Studies also reveal our brains cannot distinguish between an experience and the perception of an experience. This is key, as we can reprogram our brains reframing our paradigms, deleting negative self-talk and replacing it with positive thoughts. A paradigm is a word which means "a pattern or general perspective," a mental map. Our paradigms represent our explanations for what we observe in the world around us and our view of ourselves.

Reframing our paradigm is the change in our perspective concerning the way we perceive things. Stephen Covey describes how once he was frustrated in the subway to see the very bad behavior of a man's children. He was completely triggered, but when he found out that they were coming from the hospital where the mother had just died an hour before, his perspective changed completely.

A mentor often says, "Our Roots Create Our Fruits." This fruit tree metaphor simply and elegantly illustrates how our paradigm impacts our results. He's mastered positive framing and the paradigm reframe where our beliefs, intentions, thoughts, words and actions shape our patterns, habits, and results. He's lived these principles going from rags to riches. It's basically a cause and effect relationship. If you are not happy with where you are at in life, your fruits (family, health, wealth or contribution) first look at your roots (beliefs, intentions, words). Reframing and reprogramming are powerful tools to create the results you seek.

Pursuing your purpose and building your dreams isn't easy and often an emotional roller coaster. And it's not in the doing, it's in the being. "If you can meet with Triumph and Disaster, and treat those two imposters just the same" [Rudyard Kipling] ... that is mastery.

*Define Your Power Mantra: When creating your mantra a great place to start is going to your favorite place in nature; your garden, park, ocean, jungle, forest, mountain top or a fancy spa. A place that positively elevates your emotional state of being your vibrational frequency. A place where you find your flowstate. In this place, create a sacred space and with sincere intention, close your eyes and tap into your heart, your soul's desires. A great way to raise your consciousness is by simply asking yourself a couple questions: "If I had all the money in the world, what would I do, who would I be?" "When I step into the future to the end of my life, what have I accomplished?" Let your souls intuition guide you. Let it flow. It's usually in a brief instance your guidance brings you clarity. Journal your experience and use it to shape your mantra.

*Create A Full Body Experience (Voice, Breath, Movement). When practicing your mantra, ancient wisdom has taught us how we move in the world is how the world moves around us. The more clarity, confidence and conviction we have with our beliefs, thoughts, intentions and words, the more connected we are to our soul and the souls around us. So stand up. Raise your hands. Jump up and down. Pound your chest. Find your rhythm. Smile. And speak your mantra to the world.

*Repeat Your Power Mantra Daily, Out Loud: High Performance follows a natural pattern, consistently following a proven process. It's a good practice to weave your mantras into your morning routines. Pay attention to your energy and use your mantra to raise your energy. Energy is the currency of high performance.

*Next Level Bonus, Set An Hourly Reminder: With many thoughts racing through our minds, it's important to consistently and continually create pattern interrupts and reprogram ourselves. Your power mantra can lift your spirits dramatically - the more you think it, read it and say it, you will be it.

AJ Maxwell - Costa Rica
High Performance Coach
www.scalingforgrowth.com

MARTIN STORK

"Discover your roots. Come home to yourself.
Live your purpose."

I am on a mission to inspire men to push past their emotions, push the limits of their comfort zones, and find out who they truly are. For those who persist, the unique experience of 'coming-back home' awaits. My story is meant to support men like you to reconnect with your father, ancestors and ultimately yourself. Discover your roots. Cut invisible anchor lines from emotions that are holding you back, and allow the man inside of you to propel forward into a life fueled by purpose.

COMING BACK HOME

I dial the number. My heart races. A man picks up, *"Hello."* Do I know this voice? I am not sure. I was hoping the man would say his name, but he didn't. I am starving for certainty, "Who is this?" I ask. A determined voice barks back at me, *"You're calling me, you better tell me who you are!"*

I don't know why this tone feels familiar, but it does. I go for it, words trembling out of my mouth, "Maybe it's your son." Silence. Decades of silence, decades during which I have been unknowingly disconnected from my source of masculine energy. A less determined voice tentatively utters my name, *"Martin?!"*. Now my heart does not know what to do: jump for joy or run away. My mouth responds unconsciously, "Yes!".

I arrived in Edmonton, Canada, the city of my birth. I was equipped with only his name, date of birth, and a deep desire to find my father. At two years old, I lost him when my parents split, destined to grow up in Germany without him. My mother feared my father would 'hijack' little Martin and take him back to Canada. Today I am conscious that my younger self made this fear his own. Hence, there was no intention from the little boy to reconnect with his father. Teenage and adult Martin did not have much of that desire either. I was unaware that my father tried for years to connect but gave up after his unsuccessful efforts rewarded him only with pain and he was unable to be the father he desired to be.

"Where are you?" his voice pulls me back. "In Edmonton."

"What are you doing here?"

"I am looking for you, Dad." Emotional silence. I can hear the man on the other side struggling for words.

The previous weeks had been an emotional roller coaster ride. I had contacted all possible governmental institutions to find my father: car registry, property records, and pension institutions. No luck. The only information I was allowed to receive was the fact that no death record existed. Great news, I thought. If he is not dead, I will find him. A missing person report was my final resort. One final check with the google oracle yielded a number. *"So where are you? Don't you have my address?"* he asked.

"No Dad, I only have the old address where we used to live together when I was still a baby. I went to the house which I recognized from old pictures, but none of the neighbors could point me in your direction." Feelings of fear overwhelmed me as he tells me to come to his new address.

I recognize the anxiety in me, creeping up my chest. I felt it as a little boy in Germany, while my father was talking to me on the phone. "Sorry Dad, I can't make it today. Let's meet in a couple of days."

His voice flips back to barking mode. *"In a couple of days?"*

"Yes, I need to arrange some things first." His barking continues. I simply hang up. The little boy in the body of the 38-year-old man is about to book a ticket back to Europe, to run away from his father, giving in to 36 years of fear which is not even his own.

No way! I have come so far and you are planning to run away? adult Martin silently argues with young Martin. I have to go beyond my fear to find inner peace and freedom. Otherwise, the hurt little boy will continue to rule my life. I put on my running shoes and head to my father's house. I need to see what feelings arise when I am near. I won't knock on his door yet. After jogging a couple of miles, I turn onto his street. I spot his new house. Closer. A man appears. My heart jumps out of my chest. It is him. Old fear floods my veins.

I want to turn and run away, but that is not going to happen! The man with the white hair walks towards me, stops, talks to his neighbor. I am about to pass them. My father is standing with his back towards me. Our auras intersect. He turns. He looks at me. I can feel his mind trying to connect the dots but it is not able to do it. I am looking different than what his mind remembers. I continue to run. He turns back to his neighbor. I can feel my joy from seeing him, overruling my little boy fear and hesitation. I'll come back tomorrow, I tell myself. For good.

The next day I ring the bell. The white eagle appears. He opens the door and looks at me. I look at him. Our eyes meet. Silence. The connection is present. We embrace each other. Minutes pass. I hear the words I will never forget, *"I'm glad you have made your way son, I have been waiting for 36 years."* I am at a loss for words.

"I have something for you Dad," handing him the letter I wrote to speak my truth regardless of what might happen.

Letter to my father

More than 38 years ago, I was born in this city. I have been roaming the streets these days and I felt no connection. I was visiting the old house in which I spent the first two years of my life. All of a sudden, old memories started to appear. My subconscious mind started to share some of its wisdom with me. It was a beautiful feeling, a feeling of connection to the place I was born, grounding me. Thirty-eight years is a long time. Becoming older opens up new perspectives. One starts reflecting on one's life in different ways. I always wondered who my father was, what it is that I carry within me from him. The man who got out of Hungary to live in freedom, away from communism. The man who smuggled my mother across the iron curtain into a free world. Over the last few years, I have spent a lot of time on personal development, reflecting on myself. To grow as a human being. To serve my purpose. On this challenging journey, I came across my limitations; I wanted to know why I acted or behaved in specific ways. Throughout the process, questions came up which only one man could answer: my father. Over the years, the only feelings I had for my father were rejection, anger, and disgust for what he allegedly did to my mother...to me. I could feel anger, even rage, coming up. At the same time, whilst looking at old baby pictures where he is playing with me, I could feel tears coming to my eyes. Feeling the love for him that is inside me. Experiencing these completely opposite emotions made me curious—aware that each story has at least two sides. I sought information to better understand my father. Then I saw different angles, acts of love and desperation. A father denied. A man, not able to accompany his son on the journey to manhood. A man also with pain and anger. A man waiting for his son to reach out, to reconnect. Everything in life happens when it is meant to happen. I always thought if I want to break free, I have to forgive my father for everything he did. Today I know that forgiveness is not the right word. Instead, understanding replaces forgiveness. To understand why my father did the things he did. To acknowledge his pain and hardship unfolding along with our joint story in life. To recognize why he lived his life the way he did. Understanding is way more insightful than simply forgiving, as the latter does not entail learning. Forgiving can be a one-way street. Understanding goes both ways. Today, I know you cannot solve a problem with the same energy that created it. Anger will not dissolve anger. Instead of becoming unconscious when old 'wounds' are getting triggered within me, I have chosen to drop into love and understanding. I am curious to hear first hand how my father experienced his life. What made him the man he is today. All these years, I lived with my mother's fears and have made them my own... the fear that my father could take me away from her. Only very recently I fully comprehended that fear. When I let go of it, I felt tremendous relief. I felt freedom in its purest form. Pure Energy. It was like cutting the anchor line, propelling myself forward. Before this "freedom" moment, I had the underlying feeling that I have to return to the place where I was born, like a salmon making its way up the river, to start looking for my father, whose contact details I had lost because I thought I was done with him, once and for all. I have come a long way on my own. Growing up without a father is an experience I do not wish others to have. Looking for a father figure in difficult times meant I had to find other ways, and I did. Today, I have achieved a lot. The key is in the inner work one does, the journey within ourselves. I am where I am today because of the qualities I inherited from my father; his leadership skills, his persistence, his love of freedom, being able to spend time alone, not depending on anybody, enjoying the simple things in life, watching the sunrise and savoring ultimate silence while being alone in the wild, beautiful nature. I am grateful for all of the adventure. These qualities allow me to push my limits in business and in life, like running ultra marathons for days or spending time in the mountains, an experience I genuinely love. In these moments, on my own, my heart is wide open, experiencing pure love and freedom. I am curious to find out if my father had to give up any of his dreams, his visions, or career for the choices he made. I wonder, if what he has experienced as a child, teenager or young man still plays a role today in how he acts, makes choices, or behaves? We are all run by our own "autopilots". The moment we start questioning and looking underneath these programs, we can break free. Today, my father and I do not owe each other anything. At the same time, we both are holding the keys to release each other from the pain of the past. The question is, are we ready to see beyond all these emotions and experiences, and look further than where our autopilots have misled us, pouring concrete in the locks guarding our hearts. Instead of failing to fulfill the expectations of each other, isn't it time to reach an agreement, an agreement that prevents further disappointments and allows us to use the keys to our hearts to allow each of us to be who we are. It is time to break free, once and for all. In love, Your son, Martin

My father takes the letter and smiles, *"Oh, thank you. I hope you don't mind that I won't read it now. I don't want you to think I am behaving differently because I read it."* Wow, I didn't expect that kind of self-reflection from the man my mother had painted in my mind. I was glad he made this effort to be himself. He wanted me to experience him the way he was without being influenced by any remnants of the past.

"I have something for you too son." My father disappears, coming back with a large box. "All the letters between your mother and myself since 1982. Ink does not lie. It is all yours. I have kept them for you, should you return one day. You can burn them, read them, or keep them. The choice is yours."

Sitting in my father's house for a week, I was reading and gaining insight. My suspicion was right. Here is a man, prevented from fatherhood, who fought a battle he was meant to lose. He knew it, yet kept going. A man true to himself and his values, he had tackled the demons of loss, only to be surprised by life, with the opportunity to be the father he always wanted to be, sharing his skills and wisdom with the next generation, his son.

Reading all the letters, my anger shifted from my father towards my mother. My father answered my questions. He noticed my anger towards my mother building up. *"Son, there are some things you probably do not know about your mother. After the end of the Second World War, during her younger years, she went through a tough experience with a man. That was before my time. With all I know today, I can understand why things turned out between us the way they did. I realized that we were not meant to be together for the long run. I do not take that personally anymore. Your mother acted with best intentions, controlled by her own beliefs and experiences. For both of us, all we did, together and individually, were acts out of love for you, our son. I can only invite you to see your mother in the same light of understanding."*

My father's words sent a chill down my spine. A deep feeling of inner peace expanded in my body. I will never forget when my father provided me with this final piece of the puzzle, called my life.

Since arriving at my father's house, it has not been all sugar and honey. We have had plenty of fights. Then it clicks! I realize I have found a man, on the other side of the world from where I grew up, who is exactly like me! When my mother was mad at me in my younger years, she used to shout my last name, "You are such a STORK! Exactly like your father!" 'Being a Stork' became a bad thing and a part of me I rejected to make my mother happy. Now, here with my father, two Storks, I begin to see how like my father I am – the reason why we are fighting. The same magnetic poles are pushing each other apart. I share my insight with him. We laugh and embrace.

"Are you curious what your roots are? Where your name 'Stork' comes from?" My father offers, *"What If I told you that our male ancestors were German and left in the 18th century to create a new life in Hungary?"* I am stunned. I grew up in a small town, north of Frankfurt am Main. There were many Storcks around, only their last name was misspelled, as the real "STORK" is without a "c". That was my line of thought at the time. Our lineage of male ancestors reached back to 1610, to a small village south of Frankfurt, called Groß-Bieberau. So I grew up near where my ancestors came from over 400 years ago. Their last name was spelled with "c", Storck. So my last name was the one misspelled. I am still at a loss for words.

"You are the last man standing from our lineage." my father states. Thoughts are rushing through my mind. I am the last one? I cannot be the last one! I decided to go back to Germany and start searching.

I step onto the land my ancestors owned 400 years ago. I found traces of them in old archives. It took me nine months to get here, to find out if I am the only one left from my ancient tribe of Stor(c)ks. I am filling in the gaps. The sun is shining on my face and I can feel the grass under my feet. The old mill shines in its full beauty. I can feel my ancestors waiting here for me. I am the first one to close the circle, being the first Hungarian Stork to "return home". I have learned that my family was one of only four in the village that survived the "Thirty Years' War" (1618-1648). I am proud. I have the same blood running through my veins. Not only have I found my ancestors′ land, but I also found traces of descendants in Germany. I managed to connect with them. I am not the last one.

Being called a "Stork" by my mother used to be a cuss word for me. Today it fills me with pride and energy. Having found not only my father and my ancestors, but I have also found myself, my mission, and my purpose.

My father and I plan to follow our ancestor's′ path. From Groß-Bieberau, heading to the city of Ulm, we will take a boat along the Danube to Hungary where my father was born. From there, we will head to Canada where I was born. Connecting. Bonding. Making up time. My meditations have shown me the place—a log house at the beach on a lake, surrounded by mountains. We will travel around and let this place find us. Then we will build a house together, father and son. We will create a place for men to reconnect with themselves, their fore-fathers, and ancestors. It will activate a never-ending source of energy to fuel their journey and live a life of purpose. These men will be supported by two Storks to reconnect...we welcome you. Come home.

IGNITE ACTION STEPS

Get ready: mentally and physically – Strengthen your body and mind to sustain your emotional journey. Fuel your body through endurance and strength exercises. Find an exercise you love and stick with it. Feeling at your best improves and prepares you.

Discover your roots – How well do you know your father? What do you know or remember about him—the beautiful, and the not so beautiful experiences? What about your grandfather, or your great-grandfather? Do you know your 'tribe' origins? Can you trace your family history back 50 years, 100 years, 200 years? What themes reflect your family history? Which qualities did you inherit from your forefathers? What conscious, or unconscious, roles have they played in your life so far?

Discover your purpose – What is your mission, bringing light into your life? What is your shadow mission, making your life a mess? Which one of these has been the driving force in you so far? What's next to direct you into the light?

Find your source of energy – Who do you serve and why? Have you drafted the manifesto for your life? Connect its intention with powerful emotions that allow you to push past all obstacles. Visualize how it feels to live your mission relentlessly, connecting with your true self. To live a life of purpose. To come back home to yourself.

Decide – To live your purpose is only one conscious decision away. It is a "Hell, yes!" decision, not a "maybe". Bliss, inner peace and freedom await those who are ready to conquer their shadows. Are you ready? Hell, yes! Well done! I salute you!

Martin Stork - Austria
Coach (ICF ACC) mencoho.com, martinstork.com
Mencoho - Men Coming Home

§

Please know that every word written in this book, and every letter on the pages has been meticulously crafted with fondness, encouragement and a clarity to not just inspire you but to transform you. Many men in this book stepped up to share their stories for the very first time. They courageously revealed the many layers of themselves and exposed their weaknesses like few men do. Additionally, they spoke authentically from the heart and wrote what was true for them. We could have taken their stories and made them perfect, following every editing rule, but instead we chose to leave their unique and honest voice intact. We overlooked exactness to foster individual expression. We left in nuances and unique cadence. We even forsake some literally rules to be true to their voice. These are their words, their sentiments and experiences. We let their personalities shine in their writing so you would get the true sense of who each one of them is completely. That is what makes IGNITE so unique. Authors serving others, stories igniting humanity. No filters.

A tremendous thank you goes to those who are working in the background, editing, supporting, and encouraging the authors. They are some of most genuine and heart-centered people I know. Their devotion to the vision of IGNITE, their integrity and the message they aspire to convey, is at the highest caliber possible. They too want you to find your ignite moment and flourish. They each believe in you and that's what makes them so outstanding. Their dream is for your dreams to come true.

§

BOOKS AND RESOURCES MEANINGFUL TO
THE IGNITE YOUR LIFE FOR MEN AUTHORS

Eric Edmeades ~ Founder, WildFit, www.EricEdmeades.com

Mark Eggiman ~ For detailed recommendations on how to transform towards self love, visit www.mindkatana.com

Santiago Rafael Pascual ~ *A New Earth* by Eckhart Tolle, *The Four Agreements* by Don Miguel Ruiz and find free resources LAFAM.org Try the *Six Phase Meditation* from Vishen Lakhiani.

Zenas Chin ~ *Top 5 Regrets of The Dying* by Bronnie Ware

***

Menspective (Noun)
(The extra emphasis on pride and ego)
1. The state of one's ideas biased to the male perspective , the facts known to one, etc., in having a meaningful interrelationship:
You have to be married for a few years to see conditions in menspective.
2. A perspective exclusively weighted towards the male gender.

***

Ignitified (Adjective)
1. Ignitified is the state of being infused with additional purpose, power, passion and positivity to expose its concealed energy.
2. These would be ordinary, everyday moments with just about anyone. A dinner with friends, a meeting at the office. Once ignitified, the scene gets energized with a new idea, added momentum or more interest and emotional involvement from anyone participating.
3. An ignitified moment is more fun than it was before.
4. An ignitified discussion is more meaningful than it was before.
5. An ignitified project carries more passion that is put in by the people involved.
6. What will you ignitify today?

Upcoming Books in THE IGNITE SERIES

If you feel you have had an IGNITE moment and a story you would like to share, please apply at www.igniteyou.life/apply. We look forward to all the applications.

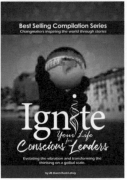

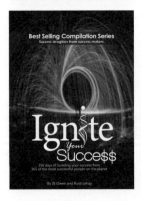

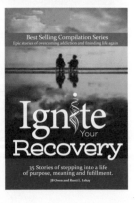